WATERLOO

A New History of the Battle and its Armies

GORDON CORRIGAN

Atlantic Books
London

First published in hardback in Great Britain in 2014 by Atlantic Books,
an imprint of Atlantic Books Ltd.

This paperback edition published in Great Britain in 2015 by Atlantic Books.

10 9 8 7 6 5 4 3 2 1

A CIP catalogue record for this book is available from the British Library.
E-book ISBN: 978-1-78239-392-4
Paperback ISBN: 978-1-84887-929-4

Printed and bound by CPI Group (UK) Ltd, Croydon, CR0 4YY

Atlantic Books
An Imprint of Atlantic Books Ltd
Ormond House
26–27 Boswell Street
London
WC1N 3JZ

www.atlantic-books.co.uk

CONTENTS

ILLUSTRATIONS

SECTION TWO

Le Caillou (© *Imogen Corrigan*)

Wellington's Headquarters (© *Imogen Corrigan*)

Battle of Waterloo, June 18th, 1815. The Life Guards charging the Imperial Guards by Franz Josef Manskirch, 1815 (*Courtesy of the Anne S. K. Brown Military Archive, Brown University Library*)

The Farm of Mont-Saint-Jean (© *Imogen Corrigan*)

The Battle of Waterloo by Aleksander Sauerveid, 1819 (*Courtesy of the Anne S. K. Brown Military Archive, Brown University Library*)

La Vielle Garde à Waterloo. 8 Juin 1815 by Hippolyte Bellangé, 1869 (*Courtesy of the Anne S. K. Brown Military Archive, Brown University Library*)

Ende der glorreichen Schlacht von la Belle Alliance den 18 Juny 1815 by Fredrich Campe, 1821 (*Courtesy of the Anne S. K. Brown Military Archive, Brown University Library*)

Meeting of the Duke of Wellington and Prince Blücher at La Belle Alliance after the Battle of Waterloo by Charles Turner Warren, 1818 (*Courtesy of the Anne S. K. Brown Military Archive, Brown University Library*)

Buonapartes feige Flucht nach der Schlacht von la Belle Alliance by Fredrich Campe, 1821 (*Courtesy of the Anne S. K. Brown Military Archive, Brown University Library*)

Pursuit of the Prussians by moonlight by Charles Turner Warren, 1818 (*Courtesy of the Anne S. K. Brown Military Archive*)

The field of Waterloo, as it appeared the morning after the memorable battle of the 18th June 1815 by John Heaviside Clark, 1817 (*Courtesy of the Anne S. K. Brown Military Archive, Brown University Library*)

Château de Hougoumont. Field of Waterloo, 1815 by Denis Dighton (*Royal Collection Trust © Her Majesty Queen Elizabeth II, 2014*)

The execution of the sentence on Marshal Ney, in the garden of the Luxemburgh at Paris, December 8th 1815 by Innocent-Louis Goubaud, 1816 (*Courtesy of the Anne S. K. Brown Military Archive, Brown University Library*)

MAPS

INTRODUCTION

On 18 June 1965 the British army held a spectacular parade in the grounds of Hougoumont farm, south of Brussels in Belgium, to commemorate the 150th anniversary of the Battle of Waterloo. In those days the British army was twice the size that it is now and all the regiments that had fought there sent their regimental colour party, a guard of honour and their band. This author, then the tallest subaltern serving with the Gloucestershire Regiment, attended as the bearer of the regimental colour.

The 1965 influx of the largest number of British troops seen in Brussels since the liberation in September 1944 was not lost on the population. Contingents were billeted in Belgian army barracks, last refurbished in about 1880, and as the Belgians, with the possible exception of the Norwegians, are the only Europeans who actually like the British, any British soldier in uniform entering licensed premises in Brussels found he could quaff to his bladder's content without having to pay. Inevitably cells in guardrooms were rapidly filled up with Scottish soldiers returning to barracks bare-bottomed, having sold their kilts to a local. On the battlefield, preserved in the main by the Belgian equivalent of green-belting, there was little, if any, sign that the British had ever been there. Memorials to French grenadiers, statues of Napoleon, plaques bearing eulogies penned by Victor Hugo and taverns with names reminiscent of the Armée du Nord there were aplenty, but not so much as a modest mention of the Great Duke. The Belgians have long lived through an identity crisis. In the past 300 years they have been subjects of Spain, of Austria, of France, of Holland, and only since 1831 have they lived in their own independent state, albeit one that is still riven by racial and linguistic tensions. In the eastern part of the country, regardless of who actually ruled them, the inhabitants have generally considered themselves to be French, or at least francophone. In 1815 they were pro-French, if only as a better alternative to being part of the Dutch Netherlands, and while today they have no quarrel with the British, who did, after all, create their nation, they still lean towards France. Now, largely thanks to comments arising from the 1965 affair and the efforts of the British Waterloo Committee, there are British memorials on the battlefield, but the shop in the (post-1965) visitor centre sells mainly Napoleonia and re-enactors prefer dressing as *chasseurs à pied* rather than as privates of the 33rd Foot. Even the premier British scholar of the French Revolutionary and Napoleonic Wars, the late Dr David Chandler, regularly appeared in the uniform of a colonel of the Imperial Guard.[*]

Whether the 200th anniversary of the great battle in 2015 will be commemorated with quite the flair, panache and effort that went into the 1965 event is a moot question: will political

---

[*] It has, of course, to be admitted that the French uniforms of the period were rather more glamorous than their British equivalents, lending weight to this author's theory that the best-dressed army always loses.

correctness disapprove of the glorification of blood and slaughter? Will the British government want to avoid offending the French? Can Britain afford it? What is certain is that, with the exception of the Guards and the Household Cavalry, there is not a single British regiment that retains the name it had in 1815, or in 1965, such has been the pace of run-down and amalgamations of the British infantry.

In 1965 the Allies of 1815 were invited and contingents from Austria, West Germany, Holland, Belgium, Spain and Portugal were on parade, as were the Russians, despite this being the height of the Cold War. As the occasion was officially, if not in reality, a commemoration rather than a celebration, the French too were invited. Not unnaturally they declined to attend, and the story doing the rounds was that their president, the Anglophobic General de Gaulle, had refused on the grounds that he was too busy preparing for the 900th anniversary of the Battle of Hastings the following year.* As de Gaulle was not known for his sense of humour, the tale is almost certainly apocryphal, but it combines the two occurrences in British history that are indelibly engraved on the minds of every schoolboy: 1066 and the Battle of Waterloo. They all know the date 1066 but are unsure of what happened then, and they all know there was a battle at Waterloo but don't know the date.

In the long history of the British army there have been many battles that involved more men, lasted longer and had more casualties than the Battle of Waterloo, fought on one day in about two miles square of cramped farmland fifteen miles south of Brussels. Yet Waterloo creates more interest, claims more attention

---

* Although, perhaps surprisingly, a French naval contingent did turn up for the 200th anniversary of Trafalgar.

and has more words written about it than the Somme, Alamein and Normandy put together. It is not even that it was a purely British victory: the British were a minority of the Anglo-Dutch army, which was in turn smaller than the army of its ally, Prussia, and while the overall commander, the Duke of Wellington, was British, in truth it was not a battle in which great tactical acuity was a requirement. Rather, what was needed was the perceived British virtue of sticking it out until help arrived, a task that any number of available British generals would have been perfectly capable of overseeing.

Today Waterloo is seen as a stunning British victory against almost overwhelming odds. Perhaps in reality it was an Allied victory against odds that weren't all that bad. True, Napoleon's forces outnumbered those of Wellington, but not by anything like the three-to-one ratio generally considered necessary for a successful offensive. While much of Wellington's army was indeed 'infamous' (by which he meant 'not famous'), many of the British units had served in the Peninsula; and while he did not have the staff that he might have wanted to serve him, all of his divisional commanders and many of the brigade commanders had served under him at some stage in Portugal or Spain. They were well known to him and they knew and understood his methods.

When the contemporary accounts of the battle were written, most gave full credit to the Allied contribution – that of the Dutch-Belgians, the minor German states and of course Prussia – but very quickly fact began to be obscured by myth. In the case of the French, the result of the battle was supposedly decided not by Napoleon's failures, but by incompetence and betrayal by others; in the case of the British, the contribution of other Allied nations was progressively belittled or ignored altogether. It took Colonel

Charles Cornwallis Chesney, Royal Engineers, professor of military history at the Royal Military College Sandhurst, and later at the Staff College, Camberley, to restore the balance. On taking up his appointment in 1858, Chesney found the study of the history of their profession by army officers to be at best scanty and at worst seriously twisted. Most of the few recommended works for students were written by French authors in French, many had little basis in historical fact, and there was no attempt to encourage students to engage in a critical analysis of wars and campaigns. Chesney determined to change all that, and his examination of the American Civil War while it was still in progress stands out even today. He insisted on objective and unbiased examination of the history of warfare, and his essays on the Waterloo campaign, published in 1868, gave full credit to the Prussians (hitherto lacking in most accounts in English) and were the standard work on the subject for many years, having been translated into French and German.

Then, after the Franco-Prussian War of 1870–71, in which the French suffered humiliating defeat, British perception began to shift back to an Anglocentric view of Waterloo. While perhaps not becoming pro-French, opinion gradually became less pro-German: Napoleon III and his ex-empress were given sanctuary in England, their son was killed in the Zulu War serving with the British army, and the Kaiser's vocal support for the Boers in the South African War all roused suspicion of German intentions in British minds. Later, the naval arms race and then the First World War squashed any concept of Germany having a share of the victory of Waterloo. Indeed, British soldiers on the Western Front were astonished to find themselves opposed by German infantrymen wearing the battle honour 'Waterloo' on their sleeves: what on earth, they asked, had Waterloo got to do with the Boche?

Between the world wars and both during and after the second, there was little incentive to credit the Germans with anything, and, although one or two books in the 1960s did try to depict the battle as having been won by a multinational coalition, most pandered to the heroic myth of the gallant British, outnumbered and outgunned, holding off the foe until at last defeating the mighty emperor and saving the world by their efforts. That perception has changed, at least among historians, but it is a pity that the leading proponent of putting the Prussian contribution in its proper perspective, who has delved into various German archives and produced a number of well-researched books as a result of his findings, has made himself a figure of fun by proposing all sorts of unlikely conspiracy theories and threatening to sue anyone who disagrees with him.

That Waterloo looms so large in British historiography cannot be due to its military value alone; rather, it is seen as the beginning of the 'British Century' and the last throw of a French imperial era – the last chance that the Bonapartists had of creating a unified Europe under French hegemony after twenty-two years of almost continual warfare. In the long years of the French Revolutionary and Napoleonic Wars the one unchanging factor was British resistance to French ambitions. All the other powers, and many states that were not powers in the contemporary sense, were at one time or another conquered by France, occupied by France or temporarily allied to France. Only England, protected by the Channel and her navy, stood in constant opposition, supporting the seven Allied coalitions that were formed between 1793 and 1815 with her money, her navy, her industrial capacity and, where she could, her troops. Had Napoleon won the Battle of Waterloo he would still have lost the war: the difference is that England would not then have had the influence that she did have in drawing up the

post-war boundaries in Europe and in forming a system of checks
and balances that kept the peace, more or less, for a century.

Waterloo does not stand in isolation but must be considered
in the context of an age that began with the first attacks on what the
revolutionaries later named *l'ancien régime* in 1770 and ended with
Napoleon's landing on the lonely Atlantic outpost of St Helena in
1815. The declaration of war by France on England in 1793 (and had
she not done so England would eventually have declared war on her)
began the most prolonged period of hostilities in modern British
history, and until the events of 1914–18 when men talked about the
'Great War' they meant the war against France. In an age when, in
the West at least, military operations that last for more than a year
or so are increasingly subject to public suspicion, if not downright
opposition, it is noteworthy that the great majority of the British
public supported the French war for twenty-two long years. While
Britain was not then a democracy in the modern sense – in that the
idea of universal suffrage would have been regarded by most as an
extraordinary aberration – she did have freedom of speech and the
press, the rule of law, the absence of conscription and no restrictions
on the free movement of labour, and she was probably nearer to the
ideal of a free country than any other, with the possible exception of
the fledgling United States of America – although, unlike in America,
slavery in the home country was forbidden. British governments were
unquestionably the king's governments, but they had to take account
of public opinion, with a plethora of highly critical newspapers, tracts
and orators to ensure that they did. In no other European country
could a member of parliament constantly and very publicly oppose
the war, deride the government's war aims, continually call for a
negotiated peace, demand the exoneration of Napoleon and accuse
the Secretary of the Navy of corruption, as Samuel Whitbread of the

brewing family did.* It is inconceivable that in the midst of a war a Prussian, Spanish, Portuguese, Swedish or even Dutch prince of the blood could be put on trial accused of financial peculation in the sale of army commissions as the Duke of York, second son of King George III, was in 1809, albeit that he was acquitted (and probably rightly). It is perhaps because of these very freedoms to criticize that the British government could pursue a war that often looked like becoming a disaster, and had the broad backing of the people in so doing.

Most wars encourage technical progress – better weapons and medical advances being the obvious examples – but by 1815 there was very little in the hands of the army or the navy of any of the players that was not available in 1793, albeit that artillery had vastly improved, much other equipment had been refined and experience had produced more skilled usage of nearly everything. As far as the British were concerned, the war undoubtedly encouraged true professionalism in the pursuit of a military career, and while the British army of 1793 was not quite a mob of flogged criminals led by coffee-house fops, as its detractors alleged, it was certainly not the finely honed killing machine that it had become by the end of the war. By the first French surrender in 1814, British officers knew their business, all-arms coordination, with the infantry, the artillery and the cavalry all working together, was commonplace, and the army could rely on a logistic system that was the envy of the world.

That the British army was a victor on land was not necessarily to its advantage in the long term, however. Armies that are beaten ask why, as did the Prussians after Jena in 1806, reform themselves

---

* When he committed suicide in July 1815, it was said, rather unkindly, that his heart had been broken by the victory at Waterloo.

and produce something better. Armies on the winning side see no need to change the ways that brought them victory, and thus are in danger of stagnation. The initial British administrative disasters in the Crimea forty years after Waterloo must be laid at the door of complacent soldiers and uncaring politicians secure in the view that all was well and nothing needed altering. As for the French, who undoubtedly were beaten, the leadership of the army after 1815 remained in the hands of the same men who had led it for Napoleon, then briefly for the restored Louis XVIII, and then for Napoleon again until the final defeat of the Hundred Days. It is true that one marshal – Ney – was shot and a few others were exiled, but most simply turned their coats yet again and carried on as normal. There was thus little incentive to examine the reasons for defeat, or even to accept that military defeat, as opposed to political betrayal, had actually happened, and the French army of the Second Empire, organized, equipped and led in ways very similar to that of the First, went down to defeat yet again to the old enemy, the Prussians, in 1871.

Napoleon died on St Helena in 1821. His body was returned to France in 1840 and placed with great pomp and pageantry in the Chapelle Saint-Jérôme in Paris, and then reinterred in a magnificent specially built mausoleum in Les Invalides, where it still is. His tomb remains a place of pilgrimage for French army officers to this day, and it has to be asked whether the French army's craven performance in 1870, its insistence on constant frontal attacks in the First World War and its lamentable performance in the Second are somehow related to its clinging to an outdated ideal of military élan – and Napoleon certainly gave them much glory – while at the same time ignoring the lessons of ignominious defeat.

The sources, meanwhile, for the examination of the Battle

of Waterloo and what led up to it are many and varied. From the historian's point of view these wars were fought – for the first time – by a literate soldiery. From previous wars we have the accounts of senior officers but little from the ranks. Now we have a multitude of letters and accounts penned by junior officers and Other Ranks, giving us a more complete picture of what life was like in the early nineteenth-century armies, on both sides. Secondary sources are almost inexhaustible and the National Archives at Kew, the British Library at St Pancras and the newspaper library at Colindale are invaluable research assets, with their ever helpful and long-suffering staffs. The French military archives at Vincennes and the national archives in Paris (currently on the move to a purpose-built building) are essential – if one can access them. An English historian wishing to research in the French archives is met by the presumption that the point of the search is to find something that will make the French look silly. There is thus a lack of cooperation other than that required by job description. I have tried claiming to be Canadian (not entirely a lie, as my mother was Canadian) but was then faced with a French-Canadian speaker, and while my modern French is reasonable, the Canadians speak a form of French little changed from the time of the Seven Years War. Currently, I claim to be Irish (again not entirely a lie: I was born there) and, as the assumption is that the Irish hate the English, willing assistance is instantly forthcoming.

It might be asked why there should be room on the bookshelves for yet another book on Waterloo. The answer is simple: the battle and those who took part in it continue to fascinate and the interpretations of it vary widely. Personally I do not subscribe to the oft-touted criticisms of British army officers of the time being a bunch of chinless wonders. In fact, apart from the Guards and some of the smarter cavalry regiments, most army officers came from stout middle-class backgrounds. The knighthoods held by so many colonels during the period were nearly always rewards for military service, rather than inherited, and the majority of ennobled generals were peers of first creation. Nor do I accept that the purchase of commissions and promotion was necessarily the iniquitous system that it would seem to modern eyes, for in fact it worked and it worked well once the abuses were removed by reformers like the Duke of York.

In the past some of my readers have questioned my use of the term 'England' when discussing the politics of the time – surely I should refer to Britain, or the United Kingdom? I make no apology for using England. The facts are that it was England where the government was, England where the industry was, and England where the money was. Napoleon did not order Marshal Masséna to 'drive the mangy British leopards back into the sea'; rather, he referred to mangy English leopards. England, not Britain, was a nation of shopkeepers, and it was the English whom Napoleon said had been the most gallant of his enemies, not the citizens of Great Britain and Ireland. In global influence it was England that mattered, and while the Welsh, Scots and Irish unquestionably played a part, in politics and international relations it was England that directed. The army, however, was a different matter: it undoubtedly was British, with a large proportion of its soldiers of Irish extraction and around a quarter of its officers Scottish. Why this was so will be discussed later in this book.

I also make no apology for my frequent use of 'may', 'seems', 'perhaps', 'around', 'probably' and similar words in my account of the battles of 1815. Contemporary sources are legion and most disagree. This is hardly surprising: most people who were there knew what was happening to them and to those around them, but did not necessarily comprehend the bigger picture. Memoirs penned long after the event can be distorted, not necessarily deliberately, and in the case of at least some accounts what was published depended on cash on the table. In attempting to make sense of widely varying versions of events I have tried to describe what seems to me to be the most likely, although I accept that I may not always have got it right.

As ever, I have a great number of people to thank for their help in getting this book onto the shelves. Angus MacKinnon and Ben Dupré, who have once again been my editors and have saved me from prolonged litigation in the libel courts, and Lauren Finger, James Nightingale and Margaret Stead at Atlantic are all deserving of huge thanks, as are the staffs of the National Archives, the British Library and the Prince Consort's Library. As always my wife has done her best to prevent me from getting too pompous, not always successfully.

Publishing is going through a revolution unimagined since the monkish calligrapher was replaced by Mr Caxton's printing press. The power of Amazon, with its ability to massively undercut the traditional publisher, and the advent of the electronic reader, which eliminates the need for paper, are seen as a massive threat to the traditional printed book. We may browse in Waterstones, but we buy from Amazon; we no longer need an extra suitcase to carry our reading material on the move, but can take a whole library on our Kindle. But, I hear you cry, we like the feel of a book, the smell of a book, the thrill of opening a new book. Quite. So do I, but the digital generation is untrammelled by the conventions of the past, and no doubt there were many in ancient Rome who averred that the manipulation of a papyrus roll would never be overtaken by the new-fangled book. The digital book, the e-book, is here to stay. At present, however, while it is fine for fiction, it does not cope well with non-fiction. Footnotes and source notes are clumsy, plates and maps do not reproduce well, but this will improve and in a very short space of time the quality and ease of reading will surely bear favourable comparison with the conventional printed book. Will there still be a place for the book as we know it? Probably yes, but in libraries and places of reference rather than on the bookshelf at home. What of publishers? They will survive, but only if they come to terms with the digital revolution and embrace it. As for printers, they may, sooner rather than later, go the way of the typesetter and the printer's devil, joining the crossing sweeper and the lamplighter in the list of professions that no longer exist. In practice, they will reduce their staff, move to smaller premises and concentrate on printing newspapers and magazines, visiting cards and wedding invitations, all of which are unlikely to be superseded, at least not just yet. Suffice it to say that I am grateful for the faith that my editors and my publisher have shown in me by their willingness to publish another book of mine in the traditional format – although doubtless as an e-book too.

As for Waterloo, it does not stand alone. Rather, it was the culmination of a long period of military development and political manoeuvring that made Britain a world power – indeed the only world power for a century to come – and while the war-making aspects of Waterloo are of interest, they cannot stand alone, but should be explained as part of a great global sweep of linked military, economic and political development that culminated in a muddy field in Belgium on a Sunday afternoon 200 years ago. That I have attempted to do.

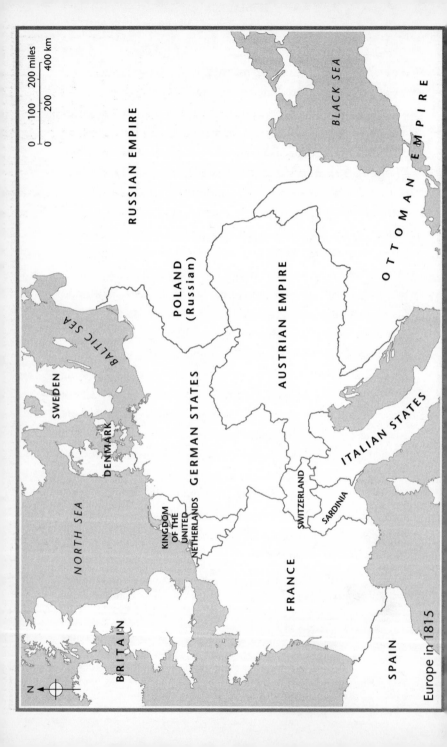

Europe in 1815

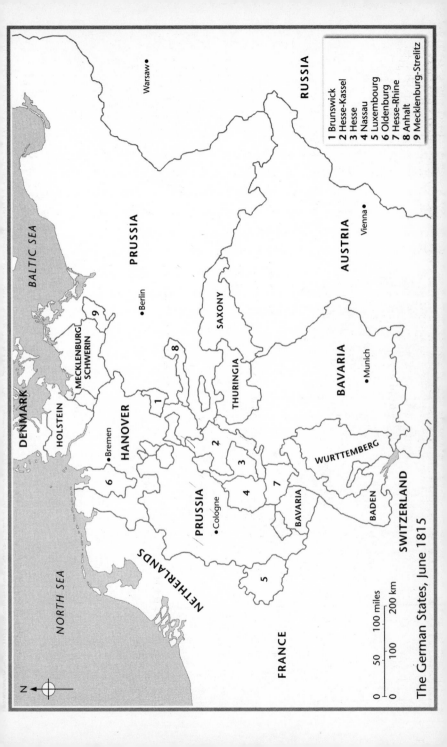

The German States, June 1815

Legend:
1 Brunswick
2 Hesse-Kassel
3 Hesse
4 Nassau
5 Luxembourg
6 Oldenburg
7 Hesse-Rhine
8 Anhalt
9 Mecklenburg-Strelitz

RUSSIA
AUSTRIA
PRUSSIA
BALTIC SEA
NORTH SEA
DENMARK
HOLSTEIN
MECKLENBURG SCHWERIN
HANOVER
NETHERLANDS
FRANCE
SAXONY
THURINGIA
BAVARIA
WURTTEMBERG
BADEN
SWITZERLAND

Warsaw
Vienna
Berlin
Munich
Bremen
Cologne

0   50   100 miles
0   100   200 km

N

France in 1815

WATERLOO

1

HOW IT ALL BEGAN

At nine o'clock precisely, on the morning of Sunday, 2 December 1804, the great wrought-iron gates of the Tuileries in Paris were flung open. From them emerged into the gardens the papal cross-bearer, one Signor Speroni, riding on a mule, which had been hired for sixty-seven francs and holding aloft a great silver cross with a curved crossbar on which hung an image of the crucified Christ. It was the Papal Crucifix, signifying the presence of no less a holy personage than Pope Pius VII himself, and, escorted by a squadron of dragoons, it led the papal procession to the cathedral of Notre Dame for the coronation of an emperor. It was to be a unique occasion. The French had been ruled by many kings, but never before by an emperor, and previous monarchs had undergone consecration, not coronation.

With the pope seated on a throne by the altar and with the ministers, the generals and the clergy, the diplomatic corps and representatives of the royalty of those states allied to or occupied by France seated in accordance of rank, the procession of the main actor in the drama left the Tuileries at eleven o'clock. Accompanied by massed military bands, squadrons of cavalry and a choir, a carriage drawn by eight bay horses took the soon-to-be emperor and empress to Notre Dame, where, ceremonially robed and wearing laurel wreathes, they entered and approached the altar. The ceremony was an amalgam of Roman imperial pageantry and ancient French practice with a sprinkling of Merovingian legend. A mixture of the sublime and the ridiculous – the latter confirmed by the launching from the door of the cathedral of an unmanned hot-air balloon festooned with lights in the shape of a crown – it was conducted in tandem at both ends of the cathedral, to emphasize the division of church and state established by the Revolution. It had been planned since the previous May, when the republican Senate voted for an emperor, a decision ratified by an overwhelming majority in a national referendum.[*]

Pope Pius VII, sixty-two years old and an Italian Benedictine monk who had progressed through the ranks of abbot, bishop and cardinal before being elected to the papacy in 1800, had initially decided that if you cannot beat something then you might as well support it, and he had welcomed the forcible establishment of the Cis-Alpine Republic by the invading French army in 1797. 'Catholicism,' he said, 'makes men good democrats.' Pius would eventually repent of his approval of revolution and regicide, and the latter part of his reign would find him in perpetual opposition to French ambitions, but for the moment he favoured and was in favour. Somewhat to the holy father's surprise, however, when, at the high point of the coronation mass, he lifted the imperial crown from the altar, it was plucked from his hands by the emperor, who placed it upon his own head, and then placed the smaller, female

---

[*] 3.6 million for, 2,500 against.

crown on the head of his empress.* Not one to be discommoded, the pope loudly proclaimed in Latin, 'May the emperor live forever', at which point the emperor left the cathedral to present imperial standards to his regiments.[1]

It was the culmination of a twenty-year journey which had taken a fifteen-year-old younger son with little money and fewer prospects from a cadetship at the École Militaire in Paris to the throne of the emperor of the French, idolized by his people and in control of much of Europe.

Napoleone di Buonaparte was born in Corsica in 1769, the son of Carlo, an impoverished lawyer. While the description 'impoverished lawyer' may seem an oxymoron today, the di Buonaparte fortunes, such as they were, had been largely exhausted in supporting the struggle for Corsican independence from the Republic of Genoa, to which the island had been subject for five centuries.† Carlo di Buonaparte had little financial aptitude, was a dreamer who loved music and poetry, and died young. In contrast, Napoleone's mother Létiza was a renowned beauty and a formidable woman of strong character and firm opinions who outlived her most famous son by fifteen years. She was married when she was fourteen and Carlo eighteen, and the di Buonapartes had thirteen children, of whom eight, five sons and three daughters, survived infancy – a mortality rate that was statistically normal for the times. Napoleone was the second son, and while he was the first to wear a crown, he was not the only one: his brother Joseph became king of Naples and then

---

* The original French crown had been destroyed during the Revolution and this one had been specially made and named, with an attempt to claim legitimacy, the Crown of Charlemagne.
† Genoa sold a rebellious Corsica to (Bourbon) France in 1764.

of Spain, Louis king of Holland,* and Jérôme, the youngest, king of Westphalia. The other brother, Lucien, would also have been found a kingdom, had he been interested in elevation to the purple. The sisters, too, were well looked after: Caroline became queen of Naples, Elisa grand duchess of Tuscany and Pauline duchess of Guastalla. But in 1769 all that was in the future.

While the family had little money, they were well respected in Corsica and had influential friends. Napoleone's godfather was the royal state prosecutor, and it was the patronage of the French governor, General Charles Louis René, comte de Marboeuf, who found the nine-year-old Napoleone a place at the Royal School at Brienne, 125 miles south-east of Paris – but only after the boy had taken a crash course in the French language at Autun. As entrance to the Royal School was restricted to those who could show four generations of nobility, a certain amount of fudging was necessary, but the future emperor studied there for six years before progressing to the military academy in Paris, where after a year of study he was commissioned into the artillery of Louis XVI in August 1785. Napoleone had always excelled at mathematics, so the artillery was a sensible choice, but it was also, with the engineers, the one branch of the army where an officer could advance by ability alone, rather than by birth and influence. In November of the same year he joined his regiment at Valence, sixty miles south of Lyon.

And then, four years later, came the Revolution. It was caused by a complex amalgam of an incompetent king, an unpopular queen, a sybaritic court, a wasteful treasury, an irresponsible

---

* And eventually father of Napoleon III, French emperor from 1851 to 1870.

nobility and popular unrest ranging from anger at an increase in the price of bread to the frustration of a rising bourgeoisie given little say in how it was governed. Although French kings were absolute rulers appointed by God and responsible only to God, a body of doctrine had grown up that French kings were expected to follow, and this included adherence to the Catholic religion and respect for the lives, liberties and properties of their subjects. By the eighteenth century, however, the system had become an unstable compromise between aristocratic society and the requirements of a modern state. The king, Louis XVI, grandson of his predecessor Louis XV, came to the throne in 1774 at the age of twenty and had known he would be king since the age of eleven and the death of his elder brother in 1761.* He was not a despot, nor was he opposed to some liberalization, and initially he appointed competent and reform-minded ministers, but he was gauche, withdrawn, solitary, graceless and unable to stand up to those who saw any attempt to put the administration of government on a modern footing as a threat to their privileges. At the age of sixteen Louis had been married to the fifteen-year-old Marie-Antoinette, daughter of the empress Maria Theresa of Austria. This was an attempt by Louis XV to reconcile the two nations but was hugely unpopular with all strands of French society, who saw Habsburg Austria, along with England, as a traditional enemy against whom they had fought long and costly wars.

The regard in which the royal marriage was held, or not held, was further reduced by the king's inability to consummate the marriage, which quickly became known to all and was the subject of much sniggering in the back streets of Paris, and indeed of the

---

* His father, the Dauphin, died in 1765.

kingdom as a whole. There are various theories about the reason for this, ranging from prudishness on the part of both partners to genital abnormality or a low sex drive, but given the importance of continuing a royal dynasty, the most likely explanation is that the king suffered from phimosis, where the foreskin is so tight that it will not retract, thus making intercourse severely painful or impossible. There is evidence that the king underwent circumcision at some point, but in any event the condition was eventually mastered, for between 1778 and 1786 the queen produced four children, two sons and two daughters. That it took so long for the queen to become pregnant only fuelled the animosity towards her and led to scurrilous rumours and posters that even in today's liberal climate would be the subject of prosecutions under the Obscene Publications Act. She was accused of rampant sexuality and of having affairs with both men and women, including relatives and several at once. There is no evidence whatsoever that she was anything but a chaste and faithful wife, but as has so often been the case, it was perception, and what the mob wanted to believe, rather than the truth, that mattered.

All French governments were short of money. An extravagant court combined with the tax exemption enjoyed by much of the landowning class and the nobility meant that taxation inevitably fell on those unable to influence policy, and as the poor had nothing to tax, the burden fell disproportionately on the craftsmen, artisans, merchants and intelligentsia. Support to the rebellious American colonists, given from 1773 to 1783 as a means to discommode the British rather than from any belief in democracy, was ruinously expensive to no French advantage, and there were many who, having helped give the Americans a constitution, rather wondered whether they might not have one themselves.

With the king's initial attempts at modernization nipped in the bud by vested interests, the one reform that did happen was that of the army. The comte de Saint-Germain, minister of war from 1775 to 1779, reduced much wasteful military expenditure, cut the number of household troops who looked pretty but cost a lot,* and reduced the number of military command appointments reserved for the holders of specific noble titles. He was unable to abolish the practice of buying and selling military ranks and appointments, but he did rule that on each sale the value would be reduced by 25 per cent, thus eventually eliminating the practice altogether. Saint-Germain was forced to withdraw this latter regulation as a result of lobbying by those who would lose money by it, but he was able to bring in General Jean-Baptiste Vaquette de Gribeauval to redesign the French artillery, who introduced lighter guns with interchangeable parts and better production methods that ensured that each gun of a particular type would have exactly the same characteristics. He thereby produced a family of French field artillery of twelve-pounder, eight-pounder and four-pounder guns that gave the French the best artillery in Europe and was to be the pattern for French artillery throughout the French Revolutionary and Napoleonic Wars.†

By 1789 street riots and general defiance of authority had moved to open rebellion with the storming by the mob of the Bastille Saint-Antoine, the Parisian state prison, and the release of a handful of prisoners and the murder of the commandant.

---

* Unlike British household troops, who had and have a combatant role in addition to their ceremonial duties, the French equivalent existed only to guard the king and look good on parade.
† The French pound was slightly heavier than the English pound, so a French eight-pounder was the equivalent of a British nine-pounder.

By this time Napoleone had completed the specialist training undergone by all newly joined officers, by spending some weeks first as a gunner and then as a non-commissioned officer (NCO), in order to learn thoroughly the gun drills. He had also participated in crowd control in Lyon, accompanied his regiment on its posting to Douai, commanded the demonstration company at the school of artillery responsible for carrying out various experiments (including the very hairy one of trying to find a way to fire shells from cannon),* and enjoyed what seems by today's standards to be an inordinate amount of leave. Along the way he had acquired a growing admiration for France, if not for her system of government.

Napoleone was a child of the Revolution; it was the Revolution that made him and, although some claimed and claim that he betrayed it, there can be little doubt that had it not been for the climactic events of the 1790s, the world would long ago have forgotten that he ever existed. On leave in Corsica Napoleone swiftly found himself caught up in revolutionary fervour. Unsure of the loyalty of the standing army, the National Assembly in Paris authorized the raising of volunteer battalions, its officers to be elected, and by 1792, as an officer of the regular army, albeit only a very junior one, Napoleone found himself as both a regular captain and a volunteer lieutenant colonel and second-in-command of a Corsican volunteer battalion. His tenure in Corsica was not a success – or perhaps it was too much of a success, for his adherence to the Revolution came into conflict with his Corsican nationalism

---

* The problem, never solved, was that if the cannon was loaded with sufficient powder to project the shell (a hollow iron ball filled with a bursting charge) to the range required, the shell was liable to burst in the breech, risking blowing open the gun and killing the crew.

and he chose the Revolution and France, leaving Corsica with his family altogether when the great Corsican patriot Pasquale Paoli shifted from espousing integration with France to demanding outright independence.*

Meanwhile, in 1791 Louis, still technically the head of state but increasingly under threat and in practice powerless, attempted to flee France secretly for Austria. He was spotted and stopped at Varennes, only a few miles from an Austrian military detachment sent to escort him to his wife's homeland. After this it could only be a matter of time before the king himself came under attack, and in 1792 the National Assembly declared the monarchy abolished, and the Terror, administered by the Committee of Public Safety from April 1793, began. From now on anyone of noble birth, or with money, or owning land or property, or associated in any way with the royal government was liable to be hauled before a revolutionary tribunal and condemned to death after a hasty trial – which often needed no more evidence than a statement that the accused was an aristocrat – before summary execution on the recently invented guillotine.† Many old scores were settled, and in 1793 the king went to his death, bravely by all accounts, and was followed nine months later by the unfortunate Marie-Antoinette. Even the di Buonapartes were not immune. Having been forced

---

* In 1794 Paoli offered the crown of Corsica to George III and a British governor and garrison arrived and stayed until 1796, when Britain withdrew.

† First used in April 1792, the guillotine was intended as a humane method of capital punishment, which would be applicable to all classes. It was designed by a committee, of which Dr Guillotin was only one member. It meted out instant death by decapitation and was a lot less cruel than the previous methods of hanging or beheading by axe or sword. It continued in use in France until the abolition of capital punishment in 1981.

to leave Corsica, they came under suspicion as possible nobility, despite pleading poverty and mother and daughters claiming to be dressmakers. What saved them was Lucien's membership of the Jacobin party in Toulon and his impeccable republican credentials and political contacts.

For those army officers who survived the Revolution and the Terror – and most did not, being imprisoned, executed or forced into exile – it was a good time to be serving, for with the departure of so many officers there was ample room for promotion. In the pre-revolutionary army Napoleone could have expected to serve for fifteen years as a lieutenant and, if he was really lucky and very able, to reach the rank of major before retirement on half-pay after thirty years. As it was, he became a captain after only seven years and would shortly be promoted further. It was the siege of Toulon that first brought Napoleone's abilities to the attention of the revolutionary high command. In 1793, with Austrian and Prussian counter-revolutionary armies closing in, France declared war on Great Britain (and on just about everyone else). Coincidentally there were royalist risings in Marseille, Lyon and the Vendée on the west coast and, in August 1793, in the port of Toulon, on the Mediterranean. The British were swift to capitalize on this and a fleet of the Royal Navy, commanded by Admiral Hood, duly entered Toulon and landed troops.

The newly instituted Committee of Public Safety was in panic mode: unless this vital naval base was recaptured, and that soon, the risings could spread and the Revolution would be strangled in its infancy. Battalions of soldiery, regular and volunteer, were cobbled together and sent south. The British were occupying the landward defences, and if there was to be any chance of a quick result, siege artillery would be needed, but there was little to be had.

The shortage was not because the guns did not exist – they did, in quantity and, thanks to Gribeauval, in excellent condition – but the chaos consequent upon the continuing attempts to amalgamate the revolutionary volunteers, the various militias and the remnants of the regular army into one cohesive body, coupled with the lack of trained officers and logisticians (most of whom were dead or in exile), had produced administrative constipation. So when Captain Buonaparte (he had dropped the 'di' indicative of genteel birth) was sent off to join the siege, he was provided only with a mixed handful of guns, siege and field.

On reporting to the siege lines outside Toulon, the young captain soon found himself commanding the artillery with a promotion to major when the previous commander was wounded. By harrying and hustling, prodding and persuading, threatening and cajoling, Napoleone managed to extract guns from arsenals all over the south of France, and by conscripting retired artillery officers living in the area and putting somewhat unwilling infantrymen through conversion courses to turn them into gunners, he made a major contribution to the recapture of Toulon when the British fleet re-embarked the troops and sailed away in December 1793. Napoleone had demonstrated his military competence – he had already shown his political reliability by the publication of a pamphlet opposing the rising in Marseille, which had been seen and noted by the brother of Robespierre, effectively the leader of the Committee of Public Safety – and he soon found himself promoted to brigadier (*général de brigade*) at the age of twenty-four. For the early part of 1794 he commanded the artillery of the Army of Italy campaigning against the Austrians in that peninsula of Austrian client states.

Then politics intervened. In what became known as the coup d'état of Thermidor (July/August of the revolutionary calendar, abolished by Napoleon in 1806), Robespierre, who had sent so many to the scaffold, followed them, along with many of his adherents. A purge of those connected with the Committee began and Brigadier Buonaparte, on account of his association with Robespierre's brother, spent two weeks in prison before the Convention, which had replaced the Committee, admitted its error and released him. Now his political reliability was tested once more, when in October 1795 a crowd of several thousand – composed of royalists, disgruntled national guardsmen, political agitators and the usual members of the Parisian unwashed, who went along for the fun and the possibility of plunder – began to march on the Tuileries, where the Convention was in session. Paul Barras, a member of the Convention and entrusted with its defence, sent for Brigadier Buonaparte, who had no compunction in lining up his guns to cover the approaches to the Tuileries. The baying mob approached, and when the guns opened fire with several volleys of canister at a range of a hundred yards or so, 200 were killed and probably three times as many wounded.* The survivors dispersed in haste and the power of the mob to influence the progress of the Revolution was broken for good.

The year 1796 was the beginning of Napoleone's rise to real power, when he was appointed to command of the Army of Italy. In that year he also dropped the Italian spelling of his name – henceforth he would use the French rendering and be Napoleon Bonaparte – and married Joséphine de Beauharnais, a widow

---

* History tells of the 'whiff of grapeshot', but it was more likely canister. Grapeshot was primarily a naval weapon, consisting of eight or nine golf ball-sized balls fired from one gun intended to smash rigging and spars. The canister round was a tin canister filled with hundreds of musket balls that split open when fired, showering the target with very large-grain buckshot. At short ranges it was deadly.

whose husband had gone to the guillotine for failing to defend Mainz with sufficient vigour against the Austrians and Prussians in 1793. Only the fall of the Committee and the end of the Terror saved her from the same fate.

Napoleon spent 1796 and most of 1797 in Italy. In many ways this was the most skilful campaign of his entire career. Without the huge numbers of men and materiel, which he could dispose of later, with few officers he could trust and with an army that was little more than an outnumbered, barely trained and undisciplined militia, in a daring and brilliantly conducted series of manoeuvre battles making particular use of the new Gribeauval guns, he forced the Austrians to the negotiating table. Now he was the talk of Paris and the darling of the newspapers. Refusing command of an army raised for the invasion of England, on the very sound grounds that the strength of the Royal Navy made such a proposition impossible, he took command of the Army of Egypt instead, with the aim of occupying the overland route to India and threatening British power there and in the Mediterranean. Initially he was successful – the Battle of the Pyramids saw Napoleon crush an Ottoman army and take Cairo. But the sinking of the French fleet in Aboukir Bay by Nelson in August 1798 cut him off from France, and when a miserable retreat from Syria back to Cairo across the desert began to take its toll on a now plague-ridden army, Napoleon, still well informed on matters political in Paris, left his army to eventual defeat (by a British army in 1801), disease and imprisonment, and hurried back to France, narrowly avoiding being intercepted by the Royal Navy on the way. Never called to account for his desertion and arriving in Paris at the same time as news of his earlier Egyptian victories – and before news of his defeats – he was greeted by cheering crowds, albeit by a distinctly cool Directorate.

Now another coup, that of Brumaire (November 1799), removed the Directorate and replaced it with the Consulate, of three consuls: Napoleon, ever the opportunist, Jean-Jacques Régis de Cambacérès and Charles-François Lebrun. Most people in France had never heard of the other two, and very soon Napoleon would be First Consul, then First Consul for life. In the meantime, he conducted another campaign in Italy, negotiated the short-lived Peace of Amiens,* and was finally crowned, or crowned himself, as the hereditary Emperor of the French.

Napoleon was now supreme ruler of France and head of its armed forces. What he had to do now was end the war, preferably by winning it. France had been at war since 1793, and from initially being a war of defence, in which other European powers, themselves monarchies, had attempted to crush the Revolution, it had now mutated into a war of aggrandizement with *la mission civilisatrice* being exported by force of arms. Throughout all this the one consistent factor had been England. It was England's implacable opposition to French ambitions, England's money and the Royal Navy that had provided the impetus and the finance behind the three anti-French coalitions that had so far been created (there would be four more). If only England could be removed from the list of his enemies, then the others could be persuaded or forced to make peace. But how could it be done? England could not be invaded, and if that was not sufficiently clear before the Battle of Trafalgar in 1805, it most certainly was after it. England

---

* Really only a breathing space for all parties, it did, however, see the dropping of the long-standing English claim to the French throne, which dated from 1337. Attempts by this author to persuade every politician he meets to revive it have (so far) fallen on deaf ears.

was, however, a trading nation that made its money – and newly industrialized England was the richest country in the world – by importing raw materials and exporting manufactured goods. Additionally, she imported much of the food that she ate, perhaps as much as 20 per cent. If no one would trade with England, ran the Napoleonic logic, then she would run out of money and starve. Hence the Continental System, in which, by the Decree of Berlin of 1806, all those countries allied to, occupied by or under the influence of France would refuse to sell England anything or buy anything from her.

Compliance with the decree was generally good. Of the three countries that objected, Sweden was defeated by France in the campaign of 1805–7 and Spain, a member of the First Coalition but since 1795 a reluctant ally of France, voiced half-hearted objections and then gave way; only Portugal refused to comply. But it did not work. Some British manufacturing industries did suffer a slowdown and unemployment rose, but while the governments of most countries under French influence agreed, or affected to agree, to implement the system, trade with Europe diminished only slightly, smuggling received an enormous boost, and the Royal Navy ensured that raw materials and food could still be obtained from the Caribbean sugar islands, North America and India.

Portugal had long been an ally of England. Indeed, by the Treaty of Windsor signed in 1386, she was England's oldest ally, and she had always seen England as her protector against Spanish designs.* Her refusal to cease trading with England or to expel British envoys precipitated a Franco-Spanish invasion in 1807,

---

* The treaty is still in force and was invoked in both world wars and in the recovery of the Falkland Islands in 1982.

thus beginning what later became known to the British and the Portuguese as the Peninsular War. As the armies commanded by the French Marshal Junot moved south from Spain, the Royal Navy removed the Portuguese royal family, the treasury and some of the army and conveyed them to the Portuguese colony of Brazil. The last instructions of the regent, John, to his people before his departure were an exhortation not to resist the invasion, at least for the moment, for there was nothing to resist with and to do so would only invite severe retaliation.* Although Portuguese and Spanish armies would fight as allies from 1808, the Portuguese never forgot that Spain was a partner to the 1807 invasion.

In Spain momentous events were in the offing. The king, Carlos IV of the house of Bourbon, had come to the throne in 1788, the son of the reformist Carlos III, and as his first act had undone most of his father's attempts to liberalize the constitution and root out corruption and incompetence in the administration. He became increasingly unpopular, partly because he was thought to be too friendly with the French, and partly because of the very public adulterous affair indulged in by the queen with the prime minister, Manuel de Godoy.† There were those in Spain who favoured closer ties with France and who felt that the Spanish administration was in need of reform (as indeed it was) and that some of the less violent French revolutionary ideas might be the necessary catalyst. But old, noble and Catholic Spain – and those who mattered in Spain were old, noble and Catholic – saw any

---

* John, or Joäo, was the regent because his mother, Maria I, the queen regnant, was mad, or in the twee way they had of expressing it at the time, 'suffered from melancholia'. He became King Joäo VI in 1816.
† One presumes that Godoy's liaison was a means to gain power and influence, for while Maria Luisa may not have been the ugliest woman ever to sit upon a throne, she would certainly be in the frame.

move towards liberty, fraternity and equality, coupled with the Revolution's anti-clericalism, as nothing short of heresy, which threatened their own positions.

In the year 1807 Napoleon reached the zenith of his power. He had knocked Austria out of the war at Austerlitz in 1805, Prussia at Jena in 1806 and Russia at Friedland in 1807, and when signing the Treaty of Tilsit with Russia, he agreed with the Tsar that the one thing they had in common was a hatred of the English. Now there was only England, which was not only surviving perfectly well despite the Continental System, but also blockading France, snapping up her colonies, encouraging resistance everywhere and, as the height of impertinence, removing the very fine Danish navy to England before the French could snaffle it for themselves – and doing so under the noses of France's allies.

Napoleon was suspicious of Spanish intentions, well aware that there was increasing opposition to the French alliance and knowing perfectly well that, despite Spanish protestations to the contrary, British merchantmen were sailing in and out of many of the Spanish ports, delivering English exports and taking on those of Spain. King Carlos was persuaded, by a certain amount of arm-twisting, to transfer some of his best regiments to the Baltic, about as far away from Spain as Napoleon could send them, on a pretext of their acting as a bulwark against Swedish irredentism (Sweden had lost Pomerania in 1807) but in reality as a guarantor of Spanish good faith. At the same time increasing numbers of French troops were being sent into Spain under the pretext of protecting that country from an invasion by the British – who at that stage had neither the intention nor the means of doing any such thing. The presence of French troops only intensified the hostility of the population towards the king, and with increased lawlessness manifesting itself in riots, on 19 March 1808 Carlos abdicated in favour of his son, Fernando VII, who was considered to be less pro-French and was known to harbour an intense dislike for Godoy. Then, when law and order had been restored, Carlos withdrew his abdication, although this was not accepted by Fernando or by his supporters. Carlos appealed to Napoleon to mediate and the Spanish royal family was invited to Bayonne, on the Franco-Spanish border.

Now began an almost farcical hotchpotch of Napoleonic intrigue and Spanish irresolution. Carlos was persuaded to confirm his original abdication. Fernando, after a series of threats and bribes, then abdicated in favour of his father, who abdicated again and placed the Spanish throne in the hands of Napoleon, who placed the Spanish royals under what was effectively arrest – albeit very comfortable arrest in France – and appointed his brother Joseph Bonaparte as king of Spain. Joseph had been king of Naples and was replaced there by Marshal Murat, husband of Napoleon's sister Caroline and hitherto commander of French forces in Madrid. Napoleon could, of course, simply have deposed Carlos and Fernando by force and imposed Joseph on the Spanish, but by going through the charade of a series of abdications and the gifting of the disposal of the crown to him, he hoped to establish a legal justification for the change of regime.

The Spaniards were unimpressed. Those who met Joseph rather liked him. His affectionate nickname was 'Tio Pepe', or 'Uncle Joe', although he was also, perhaps less affectionately, known as 'Pepe Botella' in recognition of his liking for strong drink. He was an intelligent man of liberal disposition who, had he been allowed to, would have been a far better king of Spain than any of the hopelessly inbred, dribbling, corrupt and incompetent

Bourbons. But that was not the point. The Bourbons were Spain's, whatever the opinion of them internally might be, and Joseph was neither Spanish nor of royal blood, and to have him imposed upon them was an outrage to most Spaniards, regardless of social class or political leanings.*

In the months before the regime change, French troops had been quietly taking over Spanish fortresses and citadels, usually in the guise of reinforcing the existing garrisons, or sometimes simply waiting until siesta, the hallowed Spanish practice of going to sleep for most of the afternoon, and then walking in. So when the announcement of Joseph's accession to the throne caused a rising in Madrid on 2 May 1808 – a date still celebrated in Spain as a public holiday† – it was put down speedily and brutally in one of Murat's last acts before leaving for Naples. Contrary to French expectations, the suppression of the Madrid rising was not the end of Spanish resistance. For now revolt flared all across the country: a provisional government – the supreme junta ruling in the name of Fernando VII – was formed, initially based in Seville and then in Cadiz (a city the French never did manage to take), and lesser juntas sprang into being in the various provinces, commanded by bishops, noblemen, army officers or even by men – and they were all men – who were neither clerical nor noble but hated the idea of foreign domination. So began what the Spanish call the War of Independence.

If the Spanish were to have any hope at all of getting rid of the French, then they could not do it by themselves – they

---

* The Bourbons were not really Spanish either, being descended from a cadet branch of the Capetian kings of France, but they had been in Spain long enough to have become Spanish.
† Although distinguishing a Spanish national holiday from any other Spanish day is not easy in a country with more bank holidays than any other in Europe.

did not have the men, the equipment or the finance to take on the French superpower. There was only one country that they could turn to, and that was England. It was not easy for the Spanish to ask for British help as – despite a few very brief periods of alliance – for centuries the two nations had been at odds: either at war with each other or in competition for trade, for markets, for colonies and for control of the seas. Spain was old, Catholic, agrarian, broke and on the way down; England was brash, industrialized, enormously rich and on the way up. Nevertheless, swallowing her pride, Spain did ask for help – although that help was not, it was emphasized, to include British troops (a stricture that would not last long) – and that help was speedily forthcoming. Amongst the huge quantities of weapons and equipment supplied by the British to the Spanish in the first year of the uprising were: 155 artillery pieces, 200,000 muskets, 40,000 tents (the British army had no tents), half a million yards of cloth and £1.5 million in cash. As a comparator, that cash sum was just over 2 per cent of total British government spending for 1808; in 2014 the same percentage would be £13.5 billion.[2]

The happenings in Spain encouraged the so far quiescent Portuguese, and there too the populace rose under the directions of a junta headed by the Bishop of Oporto. Unlike the Spanish, the Portuguese had no qualms whatsoever about calling on their old friends the English, and the British government despatched an expeditionary force of 10,000 men, mainly infantry, under the command of the then Lieutenant General Sir Arthur Wellesley (about whom more, much more, later), with orders to expel the French from Portugal. The force landed in Portugal in August 1808 and marched south towards Lisbon, which was held by the French under Major General (*général de division*) Jean-Andoche

Junot. In the same month Wellesley fought two battles, at Roliça and Vimeiro. As the British government had now decided, after Wellesley's departure from England, to expand their efforts in the Iberian Peninsula, he was nominally superseded by two generals senior to him during the Vimeiro battle, but both had the good sense not to interfere and to let him get on with it. The French had had enough and asked for terms. The result was the Convention of Cintra, signed at the British headquarters at Cintra on 30 August 1808, by which the French agreed to evacuate Portugal, their troops to be returned to France on British ships, taking their military and personal bags and baggage with them.

The convention caused great outrage in London, and some grumblings in Oporto. Why, demanded the contemporary equivalent of the English chattering classes, well removed from the war, had the French been allowed to return home? Why had they not been taken as prisoners of war to the soon-to-be-commissioned facility at Dartmoor specially built to house prisoners of war? Why, wondered the Portuguese junta, had baggage been interpreted as including quantities of church plate, paintings, furniture and other valuable items acquired by a year's looting? All three generals were recalled to England to answer for their conduct. Many historians today regard the convention as a mistake and wonder why Generals Dalrymple, Burrard and Wellesley signed it. The reality is that the terms were the best that could be got: the French would not have accepted internment nor the searching of their baggage on embarking; the aim of expelling the French from Portugal had been achieved, and the alternative was a prolonged campaign with more battles. The convention was a perfectly sensible agreement and the generals should not have been tarnished by it. As it was, Dalrymple and

Burrard disappeared into unemployed obscurity and Wellesley, as the junior, escaped censure.

With the departure of the three generals involved in Cintra, command of the British troops in Portugal fell to the recently arrived Lieutenant General Sir John Moore, son of a Scottish doctor and a man of great humanity and considerable tactical acumen. By now the initial Spanish reluctance to having the uniformed heretics of England on their soil had evaporated and Moore came under considerable pressure to move into Spain and support the Spanish armies in their attempts to stem the French takeover. Moore knew that as long as he stayed in Portugal he was safe – he could be supplied by the Royal Navy through Lisbon and could defend the Lisbon peninsula against another French invasion – whereas were he to venture into Spain, his lines of communication would become longer and longer and he would risk being cut off by one or more French armies. Political pressure built up, however, piled on by John Hookham Frere, the British minister to the Spanish supreme junta, and in November Moore moved from Portugal to Salamanca, with the intention of retiring back to Portugal through Ciudad Rodrigo if necessary.

Frere, born in the same year as Napoleon, was educated at Eton and Cambridge and was a professional diplomat. He had been British envoy to Spain before, from 1802 to 1804, but was recalled after falling out with Godoy. Reappointed in 1808, after the fall of Godoy, he was anxious to promote Spanish resistance to France and determined to use British troops to that end. He constantly urged Moore to take the offensive, assuring him that Spanish armies would support him and that baggage wagons, medical support and rations would be provided. All this was nonsense: Spanish armies were being beaten and dispersed all over Spain; more and more French troops were pouring in over the Pyrenees; there were no wagons to be had; Spanish armies were themselves starving and there were no rations for the British. Winter was rapidly approaching and it was no time to be going on the offensive, even if Spanish support had been forthcoming. Frere was adamant, however, and Moore had no choice but to march north from Salamanca with the aim of joining with troops under Sir David Baird, who were on their way from Corunna, and operating against the French army of Marshal Soult, which was known to be somewhere in northern Spain.

It all went wrong. Moore fought and won a skirmish at Sahagun on 21 December 1808, and then heard that Napoleon himself, who had taken command of the armies in Spain on 5 November (his only visit to the peninsula) and had taken Madrid on 4 December, was marching north at the head of an army and was now only four days' march from Moore. With Soult ahead of him and Napoleon behind, Moore had no option but to retreat north-west to Corunna. The retreat, which lasted from Christmas Eve 1808 until 17 January 1809, was marked by appalling weather conditions, terrible terrain, near starvation, a breakdown in discipline in some units and great gallantry by the light brigades, which, with some of the light cavalry and horse artillery, formed a rearguard and managed to hand off the French for long enough to allow the Royal Navy to fulfil one of its traditional tasks of removing a defeated British army to be used elsewhere. Napoleon himself, convinced that the British were beaten and that only mopping up remained, had left Spain on 12 January to return to Paris.

Moore was killed during the last battles around Corunna, and his death gave rise to the 1816 poem by Charles Wolfe that all

British schoolboys used to have to learn.* Had Moore survived, he would have commanded the British army in the Peninsular War, rather than Wellesley, to whom he was senior. Tactically he was probably every bit as competent as Wellesley, but he was incapable of cooperating with difficult allies (he was once placed under arrest by the king of Sweden), and since he was a Whig under a Tory government, his relations with politicians were uncomfortable. On being sent to Portugal in 1808, he was told by Castlereagh, Secretary for War and the Colonies, that, had any other officer been available, he would not have got the job. If he had not been killed and had acceded to the command in 1809, it is unlikely that he could have managed the complexities of operating in a difficult coalition, and the result of the war might well have been very different. Perhaps it was as well, as Wolfe suggested, that he was left alone with his glory.

Despite the disaster suffered by Moore, the British government had not given up hopes of achieving something in the Iberian Peninsula. If the flame of resistance could be kept alight there, then other Europeans might be encouraged to take up arms again, and so once more Sir Arthur Wellesley was despatched to Portugal to take command of the reinforced British troops there. After arriving in Lisbon in March 1809, he marched north, and at the Battle of Oporto on 12 May he defeated the second French invasion of Portugal, sending Marshal Soult's army reeling back over the mountain passes into Spain. Wellesley followed and

---

* Perhaps they still do? Moore was not buried on the ramparts but behind them, nor at the dead of night but at around 8.30 p.m. Described by Byron as 'the most perfect ode in the English language', 'The Burial of Sir John Moore after Corunna' is hardly that, but a jolly good poem all the same.

secured another victory at the Battle of Talavera on 28 July, but – let down by Spanish promises of administrative support, which failed to materialize – he moved back to the Portuguese frontier for the winter of 1809 and spring of 1810, before retiring in the face of the third French invasion of Portugal. This was a deliberate manoeuvre by Viscount Wellington, as he became after Talavera, designed to draw the French on to the defences known as the Lines of Torres Vedras, perhaps one of the greatest feats of military engineering in the history of warfare. These three lines of trenches, gun positions, forts and redoubts were constructed to the north of Lisbon under the supervision of the Royal Engineers during the winter of 1809/10; they stretched for thirty miles or so from the River Tagus in the east to the Atlantic in the west, with a ten-mile belt of scorched earth in front of them. By fighting a delaying battle at Busaco in September 1810, Wellington ensured that the pursuing French followed the route he wanted them to follow, and when the British moved in behind the Lines, the French, who had known nothing of their existence, found that they were impenetrable. The French commander, Marshal André Masséna, could either starve or retreat, and he wisely chose the latter. By the end of 1811, Wellington's combined Anglo-Portuguese army had made Portugal secure.

Portuguese cooperation in the war was wholehearted. New battalions were raised and old ones reconstituted. The Portuguese asked for, and got, a British commander-in-chief, and while they would have liked Wellesley/Wellington, they settled for William Carr Beresford. A major general since April 1808, Beresford had served with Wellesley in India, had been at the siege of Toulon, led the storming party at Martella Point in Corsica (the fort there was the inspiration for the Martello towers),* was briefly the governor of Portuguese Madeira, where he learned Portuguese,† and was with Moore on the retreat to Corunna. With Beresford came a cadre of British officers; the inducement to transferring to the Portuguese army was an immediate promotion of one rank, and some of these men were ex-sergeants whose inducement had been a commission. Initially, one Portuguese battalion would serve in every British brigade; then, when enough experience had been gained, Portuguese brigades would serve in British divisions; and eventually the Portuguese would have their own divisions. The procedure was a resounding success, and by the end of the war Portuguese units were every bit as good as their British counterparts. Particularly good were the Portuguese Cacadore ('hunter') units – light infantry and rifle battalions trained to skirmish and to snipe, whose brown-coloured uniforms made them very difficult for an enemy to pick out at any distance.‡

By 1812 Wellington knew he was ready to go into Spain, but if he were to do so and maintain an army there, he would need to control the only two passes that would support large numbers of

---

* With a garrison of only thirty men and three guns, the original tower resisted the bombardment of two British warships for two days in February 1794, until eventually it was captured from the land. The British noted the efficacy of such fortifications and copied the design, erecting them along the English coastline as anti-invasion defences. Many remain today.

† Imperfectly by all accounts, but a lot better than any other British officer at the time.

‡ For long this author assumed that the brown was a deliberate attempt at a camouflaged uniform, pre-dating khaki by nearly a century, until meeting the direct descendant of the officer who raised the first battalion of Cacadores, who explained that the only way his ancestor could obtain enough cloth to make identical uniforms for 600 men was to go into a monastery and requisition the monks' habits.

wheeled vehicles and guns: the pass in the north running from Almeida in Portugal to Ciudad Rodrigo in Spain and the one in the south from Portuguese Elvas to Spanish Badajoz. On a cold, foggy morning in January 1812 the Light Division erupted out of the mist and surrounded Ciudad Rodrigo, and after a siege of eleven days it was taken by storm. On 6 April Badajoz fell and now Wellington struck for Salamanca. The Battle of Salamanca on 22 July was the tipping point of the Peninsular War. After it, although there would be British setbacks, the French would always be on the back foot. They had lost their balance and they would never regain it. The Battle of Vitoria in June of the following year was the last French attempt to retain a meaningful presence in Spain, and when King Joseph's last stand ended in defeat and the loss of millions of pounds of accumulated loot, the French could do little but retreat back into France, fighting rearguard actions in the Pyrenees as they did so.

While the cooperation of the Portuguese was wholehearted, the same was not true of Spain. The Spanish knew that they could not drive out the French without British help, but that did not mean that they had to like it. The Spanish army was underfunded, badly paid, ill rationed and poorly equipped. Its soldiers were tough Spanish peasants, well able to cope with the vagaries of weather and terrain, but the junior officers were commissioned from the ranks and lacked education, while the field officers (company and battalion commanders) held their commissions by virtue of being from the nobility and saw themselves as Castilian gentlemen whose role lay well above the grubbier aspects of campaigning.* When faced by a

---

* The requirement of noble birth was dropped in 1812, too late to make very much difference.

French army, Spanish armies nearly always lost, usually disastrously, but having been scattered far and wide, they proved capable of reuniting in a remarkably short period of time, all ready to receive yet another severe kicking. Spanish generals made extravagant promises, which were rarely kept, and while Wellington urged them not to attempt open battle, he did say that, placed in defensive positions from which they could not run, they would fight well (as at both sieges of Saragossa they assuredly did). To avoid tying down British or Portuguese troops, Wellington would ask the Spanish to garrison captured cities and forts, but only his understanding of the political imperative and his ability to cajole prickly allies persuaded the Spanish to adhere, at least in outline, to a war-winning strategy.

Spanish guerrillas were a different matter altogether. Untrammelled by the requirements of noble birth or the demands of machismo, the guerrilla bands were led by men who rose by sheer bloodthirsty ability, unimpressed by any code of conduct or moral constraints. They sniped, ambushed and assassinated, providing instant intelligence of French movements and strengths. Any French soldier who left the line of march or was foolish enough to go wandering off was liable to be kidnapped and tortured, with his headless body hung upside down on a tree for the edification of his fellows.* The guerrillas were of enormous help to the British during the war and ensured that British officers could move almost anywhere outside the cities, whereas French generals and despatch riders could only move with a large escort.

---

* Goya's sketches, some possibly drawn from life (or, in the case of mutilated French bodies, from death) are particularly informative. When the Taliban behead people, we complain that it is disgraceful behaviour, bad form and not cricket. When the Spanish guerrillas did it, we said bravo and more of the same, please. One man's terrorist is indeed another man's freedom fighter.

It would be foolish to pretend that it was the Anglo-Portuguese army, supported by Spanish guerrillas – and without the guerrillas the British could never have kept an army in being in Spain – that brought Napoleon down. The re-entry to the war of Prussia and Austria and the disastrous invasion of Russia in 1812 did that. Napoleon took an army of half a million, half of them French, the others Poles, Hungarians, Italians and conscripts from various German states, to Moscow and then, having failed to bring the Tsar to the negotiating table, had to withdraw back to French territory in the depths of winter. In one of the most horrific retreats in military history, 300,000 of Napoleon's soldiers were killed or died of starvation or the cold, 100,000 became prisoners of war, 50,000 were wounded and survived, and only 50,000 effectives returned to France. The British contribution in Portugal and Spain was peripheral, but it did cause a haemorrhage of men, money and assets that would have been better used elsewhere. It was Napoleon who called it the 'Spanish Ulcer', tying down up to 230,000 French troops against an Anglo-Portuguese army that rarely exceeded 100,000 and usually numbered only around 80,000, backed by a scattering of Spanish armies that were useful enough in static garrisons but rarely a match for the French in the field.

Although Napoleon fought a skilful campaign in northern Europe in 1814, the Prussian, Austrian and Russian steamroller was closing in. Wellington, meanwhile, now a field marshal and a duke as a result of Vitoria, was battling his way over a series of river lines in southern France, fighting the last battle of the war at Toulouse on 10 April 1814 – four days after Napoleon's abdication, although news of this was unknown to anyone that far south at the time.

Napoleon abdicated on 6 April because he had no option. His position was hopeless. France was war-weary. Her enemies were closing in, she had lost all those territories held in 1807, and neither the marshals nor the deputies would stand for war any longer. On 31 March Allied cavalry entered Paris and the game was up. The Treaty of Fontainebleau was signed by the Allies and the French plenipotentiaries (two marshals and a general) on 11 April 1814 and ratified by Napoleon on 14 April after a failed, and for many years concealed, suicide attempt. According to this agreement, Napoleon surrendered his hereditary right to the French throne and was granted the right to the title of emperor and the sovereignty of Elba, one small island and a scattering of even smaller ones, in total around eighty-five square miles, off the Italian coast of Tuscany and about thirty miles east of Corsica. He was to be paid a pension by the French government and was permitted to take with him an escort of 600 men, a troop of lancers, four guns and the band of the Imperial Guard. After an emotional farewell to the Old Guard, he left Paris on 20 April, embarked on a brig of the Royal Navy on 28 April and arrived on Elba on 3 May. He would not be there for long.

2

THE SHEEP WORRIER OF
EUROPE IS ON THE LOOSE

Napoleon's nine months on Elba, where he mused on what had been and on what might yet be, were not unproductive and he made genuine attempts to better the lot of his few thousand subjects. He initiated an ambitious scheme of road-building, ordered the construction of a hospital, issued decrees for the planting of vineyards, introduced a variant of the civil legal code that he had already established in France, and paraded his little army. But if one has had the whole of Europe at one's feet, being the mayor of, say, Grimsby is not quite the same thing, and as the Bourbon government failed to pay the promised subvention of two million francs, most of his plans came to nothing. Elba is only seven miles off the coast of Italy, and, although the Royal Navy patrolled the waters of his tiny kingdom, Napoleon was not a prisoner and it was impossible for him not to be kept informed of what was going on in the rest of the world. While his wife, Marie Louise of Austria, who had replaced Joséphine in 1810, and his only son were confined to the empress's homeland, Napoleon's old confidants came and went, his sister Pauline visited him (the only one who did) and the marshals, most of whom had happily turned their coats and were serving the restored regime, ensured that they kept open a channel of communication with their old master, just in case the wind changed. The same applied to the two most influential civilian functionaries: Joseph Fouché, the minister of police, who had served the Revolution, Napoleon and now the Bourbons, and Charles Maurice de Talleyrand-Périgord, the foreign minister, an excommunicated bishop who had enjoyed an even more varied career as a servant of Louis XVI, the Revolution, Napoleon and the restored monarchy. Both kept in touch with Napoleon and both would serve him again.

In 1814 the population of France had had enough of war, its bloodshed and its taxation. The marshals, too, had had enough, and when Louis XVIII,* nephew of the executed Louis XVI, arrived in Paris from exile in Buckinghamshire a few days after Napoleon's departure,† he was greeted by cheering crowds and rapturous relief as the victorious powers, which now included representatives of newly reinstated Bourbon France, settled down in Vienna to decide the future shape of Europe. Had the Bourbons accepted that France had changed and that many aspects of the Revolution were right and necessary, then all might have been well, but while Louis himself – timid, fifty-nine years old and grossly overweight – was relatively harmless, those who accompanied him were not. A whole rag, tag and bobtail of former generals, clergy, émigrés, nobles and dispossessed landowners came flooding back, all expecting to be restored to their pre-revolutionary positions and

---

* Louis XVIII because the son of Louis XVI was considered to be Louis XVII, although he never ruled and died in prison.
† And a pretty miserable exile it must have been, with only one hundred servants to look after him.

to be compensated for their losses. The Allies had insisted that the restored monarchy should be constitutional, as opposed to absolute, so there were limits to Louis' ability to revert to the status quo ante, but he did his best. That he signed the constitution forced upon him by the Allies 'in the nineteenth year of our reign' was a pointer of what was to come. Much of the army was demobilized – an economic as much as a political necessity – with eighty-eight regiments of infantry being disbanded and the remainder reduced to two battalions per regiment instead of three, while the cavalry lost ninety-one regiments of various types. The Imperial Guard became just another regiment of the line, Swiss mercenary regiments were raised to replace French ones, the Légion d'honneur, instituted by Napoleon, became a civil as well as a military distinction, and Louis particularly upset the Paris mob by ordering that bars should close on Sundays.

In a remarkably short space of time the popularity of the returned monarchy evaporated. The civil rights won by the Revolution may have been eroded during the long years of war, but Napoleon had given France firm government while the Bourbons had spent their time drinking tea in England – as the king was forcefully reminded by Marshal Ney – and had been restored as the puppets of foreign powers. French frontiers had shrunk back to those of 1792 and Belgium had been ceded to the Netherlands, a crippling blow to French pride. France was still an agrarian society, and one sector that had done well out of the Revolution was the peasantry. Released from indentured labour and all sorts of restrictions that had existed under the *ancien régime*, many had become established as independent small farmers in their own right following the redistribution of land confiscated from executed or absent magnates. The threat of losing that land to the returned original owners alarmed them. Although the king issued a decree promising that, while the original owners would be compensated, there was no intention of restoring their lands, the peasantry did not believe it, or if they did, they thought that the king's brother and heir, the comte d'Artois, would revoke any promises made. The army, too – its veterans and its demobilized soldiery – missed the prestige that they had enjoyed under the emperor, and more and more the cafés would fill with gatherings of ex-officers on half-pay or pensions that were paid late or not at all, who would hark back to the glory that had been theirs. Prisoners of war returned to find that there were no jobs for them. Veterans defiantly wore their medals, won at a hundred battles, and sentries of the new royal army saluted them, whatever the regulations might say.

While the regimental officers, the ex-officers and the rank and file grumbled and grew ever more bitter, most of the marshals and generals soldiered on. Of the twenty-six marshals created by Napoleon, three were dead by April 1814, two were kings or crown princes, one was retired and one remained strictly neutral. Of the remaining nineteen, no fewer than eighteen declared their loyalty to Louis XVIII and kept their titles and lands and lucrative appointments – something that did not go unnoticed by their juniors.

Napoleon had never accepted that his empire was at an end – he was sure that sentiment in France would turn towards him once more, as indeed it was doing. In final exile on St Helena, he remarked in hindsight that he should have waited until the Bourbon regime collapsed, when he could have returned by popular demand. But in truth, by early 1815 he had to make his move swiftly. He knew that there was disagreement among the Allies at Vienna, that the Austrians and the Russians wanted him removed to somewhere much farther away than Elba, and that at any moment he could well be the target of an assassination attempt. In any case, he was running out of money to pay his soldiers. So, on 26 February 1815, Napoleon left Elba, with those soldiers, his horses and his guns aboard the brig *Inconstant* and a tiny fleet of smaller vessels, and on 28 February, having narrowly evaded patrolling warships, he landed at Golfe Juan, west of Cannes, and began to march north. The region of Provence was unrepentantly royalist, so his best route lay through the mountainous passes along the Italian border. At first nobody noticed his arrival: the news that he had absented himself from Elba took several days to reach Paris, and even longer to reach London and the Congress in Vienna. The population of the areas through which the little expedition passed stayed quiet, waiting to see what would happen. When the news that the 'hound had slipped the leash' did reach Paris, the army under Soult, a former marshal of Napoleon's, was instructed to arrest him. Soult deployed far more troops than would have been necessary for that task – 60,000 regulars and 120,000 reservists – and presumably did so with a view to jumping ship when the time was ripe, while Marshal Ney, now commanding the Bourbon cavalry, assured King Louis that he would bring Napoleon back to Paris 'in an iron cage'.

Napoleon and his party had travelled twenty-five miles a day since landing, an extraordinary achievement given the roads and the weather. The first confrontation took place at Laffrey, south of Grenoble, on 7 March, when he was faced by a detachment of the 5th Regiment of the Line, drawn up across the road under the command of a captain. Now occurred one of the underpinnings of the Napoleonic legend. Ordering his own men to stand still with shouldered arms, he walked alone towards the serried ranks of the men sent to arrest him. He opened his greatcoat and spread his arms wide, saying, 'If you want to shoot your emperor, then here I am.' It would have taken only one shot, or even an accidental discharge, to end the whole adventure, but instead cries of '*Vive l'empereur!*' went up and the entire detachment returned to its old allegiance. The following day Napoleon entered Grenoble, having covered another twenty-five miles, to find cheering crowds, the artillery refusing to fire on him and the infantry pulling out of hiding the imperial colours and eagles. As he continued to move north, his army grew larger and larger as troops sent to stop him instead joined him. In Paris wags put up tracts that declared: 'Dear Louis, please do not send me any more troops – I have enough. Signed, Bonaparte'.

At Lyon, which he reached on 10 March, his army swollen by the defection of yet another garrison, Napoleon issued the first decree of his new reign: Bourbon placeholders were dismissed; commissions and appointments granted or made by Louis XVIII were cancelled; Swiss regiments were disbanded; Bourbon insignia were to be replaced by those of the Revolution; land taken back by émigrés was to be restored to the peasants; changes in the legal code were nullified; and a provisional government was formed. On 14 March, Ney, for all his bombast about iron cages, found he could not resist the charisma of his old commander and also joined him, taking his troops with him. By now, Napoleon had eleven regiments of infantry, each of two battalions, two regiments of cavalry, nine batteries (fifty-four guns) of artillery and a host of ex-officers and soldiers – perhaps 25,000 men in all.*

---

* A French infantry battalion was around 600 men and a cavalry regiment 400, but as all were under-strength, the total was probably around 12,000 infantry and cavalry regulars. The exact numbers of former soldiers and/or hangers-on is not precisely known but was perhaps around 10,000 to 12,000. These were equipped with a variety of weapons or, in some cases, none at all.

The momentum behind Napoleon was such that nothing could stop him. Diplomats began to leave Paris and royalists to liquidate their assets. On Sunday, 19 March, the day Napoleon reached Fontainebleau, Fat Louis and his court left Paris for Ghent in Holland. By nine o'clock that evening, Napoleon was in Paris, once more Emperor of the French. He had achieved the restoration of his regime in a mere three weeks and without firing a shot. Now he had to consolidate his position. He could no longer rule as an absolute autocrat, and by forming a broadly based government and summoning an electoral college, he tried to appease those who wanted to return neither to the *ancien régime* nor to the imperium. Decrees flew from his pen: the abolition of slavery, the abolition of feudal (royalist) titles, guarantees of press freedom and civil liberties, and universal suffrage. But more than anything else, if he was to have any chance whatsoever of remaining in power, he had to have peace.

From Napoleon's point of view, it was unfortunate that, when he absented himself from Elba, the Congress was still in being. The representatives of the European powers were still all together in Vienna and able to consult and take decisions swiftly, which might not have been the case had they dispersed to their home countries. Napoleon sent letters to all the heads of state and governments: he would accept the 1792 frontiers, he had no intention of territorial aggrandizement, and he hoped that peace and tranquillity could prevail. But the Allies had heard all this before: there had been occasions during the long years of war when Napoleon had first appeared to accept reasonable proposals and then reneged. Whatever they may have thought of the Bourbons (not much, in most cases), they were not prepared to trust Napoleon under any circumstances and letters were returned unopened and representatives spurned. In Vienna, the Tsar turned to the

Duke of Wellington, there to represent the British government, and said dramatically: 'Now it is for you to save the world again.' Napoleon was declared an outlaw and yet another coalition – the seventh – was formed to depose him. The coalition armies would be composed of a great many German, Austrian, Russian and Dutch troops, with the addition of such British troops as might be available (not many) and a great deal of British money.

The declaration of outlawry was unusual but supported the legal fiction that it was not France that was the enemy but the usurper Napoleon personally. Britain had refused to sign the Treaty of Fontainebleau, which brought the war to an end in 1814 and consigned Napoleon to Elba, and had done so on the grounds that the treaty recognized that Napoleon had been a legitimate ruler. However, since outlawry technically allowed anyone to kill the outlaw without fear of sanction, Samuel Whitbread's castigation of the British government in the House of Commons, as he accused it of being a party to the encouragement of murder, gave rise to much ministerial feet-shuffling and weasel-wording.

At first it was thought that Napoleon's return would lead to civil war in France, King Louis' army set against the Bonapartist adventurers, and that Allied troops would merely stand by to reinforce the royalists if necessary. When it became apparent – as it did rather quickly – that there was no royalist army and that most of the population welcomed the return of the emperor, there was no option for the Allies but to remove Napoleon themselves. It was agreed at Vienna that the Austrians would provide two armies of 210,000 and 75,000 men, the Prussians 117,000, the Russians 150,000, and the British and the Dutch 110,000 between them. As Britain was unlikely to be able to produce anything like the number of men agreed, she would contribute £5 million in sterling, money that would not only finance the coalition as a whole but also pay for soldiers provided by the minor German states. The Austrians would approach from the upper Rhine and from northern Italy through the Riviera; the Russians would mass on the central Rhine; the Prussians would approach through Liège, on the left of the Anglo-Dutch, who would move from the area of Brussels. Then, all armies would strike for Paris, forcing Napoleon to split his armies, never certain from where the main thrust was coming. It would, of course, take time for all the Allied armies to position themselves on the French frontiers, and while the Anglo-Dutch and the Prussians were in Flanders by May, it would be some time before the others were ready. This gave Napoleon time that he sorely needed.

The French army that was left once the restored Bourbons had finished reducing it numbered only about 200,000, nothing like the size that would be needed if Napoleon was to have any chance at all of dealing with the five armies of the coalition. An instant reinforcement came in the form of 75,000 veterans, unemployed since Napoleon's abdication, while about 15,000 as yet untrained volunteers enlisted. Border guards, policemen and redundant sailors could also be drafted in, and units of the National Guard – a revolutionary militia or home guard, disarmed by Napoleon (and generally useless) but recalled in 1814 as part of a last-ditch attempt to defend the French frontiers – could be used to garrison towns and static fortifications to release soldiers of the army proper. All over France, drapers were making uniforms and powder mills cartridges, gunsmiths were turning out muskets and horses were being requisitioned for the artillery. More cavalry was needed too, and in citadels across the nation grizzled sergeants attempted to contain their exasperation as recruits fell off their mounts and horses galloped riderless over the horizon.

Despite the problems of finding the necessary manpower, training it and equipping it, the army grew steadily in numbers and competence. The old numbers and names were restored, imperial standards and flags reissued, and once again regiments had their eagles, although this time only one per regiment, held by the first battalion. Despite all this, it would not be anything like large enough to deal with all the Allied armies at once. Napoleon therefore had two options. He could station his field army in a defensive posture in the vicinity of Paris and rely on the Allies' need to capture and then man all the frontier garrisons. This would reduce his enemies to a manageable size and might allow him to win a victory outside Paris, but it could only postpone the inevitable: the Allies would simply pour more and more troops in until he was overwhelmed. Alternatively, he could take the initiative before the Allies were in position and try to defeat them one by one.

As in the earlier wars, Napoleon's most dangerous enemy was England, not because of her relatively tiny army but because of her deep pockets and the Royal Navy's blockade. If England could be knocked out of the war, then without its paymaster the coalition would fall apart. A crushing military defeat of the British army in Flanders, sending the remnants reeling back across the Channel, would cause the Tory government to fall and to be replaced by a Whig administration that would make peace. So ran Napoleon's logic, although as a keen student of history he should perhaps have noticed that being booted out of Europe in the past had generally served to make the British more grumpy rather than less. As it was, both the Prussian and the Anglo-Dutch armies were stationed where they could watch the French frontiers. But although they were deployed in positions from which they could invade France, they were not disposed to defend against an attack coming out of France. Furthermore, while the armies kept in contact with each other, physically they were many miles apart. If they were to combine, they would outnumber anything that Napoleon might be able to muster, but if they could be attacked separately, before they had a chance to join, then they could be defeated separately. It was a huge gamble – but then Napoleon had always been a gambler: it would either re-establish Napoleonic France as the dominant power in Europe, or it would bring everything crashing down around him. Napoleon had a very great deal to gain, and nothing to lose.

The armies that would fight the campaign of June and July 1815 were very similar in some respects, and very different in others. By the time the Austrians and the Russians were close enough to take part, the fighting was all but over, so the armies that actually fought the campaign were those of the French, the Prussians and their associated German states, the Dutch and the British with their own Germans. As the British army was the only one that had been neither taken over nor utterly defeated by revolutionary or Napoleonic France at some stage in the wars, it is apposite to consider it first.

Unlike the armies of any of the other players, the British had no conscripts. In many European countries a period of military service was (and until very recently still was) part of the process of becoming a citizen, but in modern times conscription had never been levied for the regular army in the United Kingdom. It had, briefly, been tried by both sides in the English Civil War, found not to work and swiftly abandoned. Conscription would have been regarded as an unacceptable imposition on the liberties of a freeborn Briton, and British soldiers were volunteers who signed on 'for life' (in reality twenty-one years). Because it was a wholly professional army, it was highly skilled at what it did. British soldiers spent hour after mind-numbingly boring hour, day after day, week after week, loading and firing their weapons, moving from column into line into square, back into column, route marching and drilling. Unlike European armies, who restricted firing practice in peacetime because of the expense, the British soldier was required to fire thirty live and sixty blank rounds in training every year, as well as to carry out daily dry practice. By the end of the Peninsular War in 1814, the British army was probably professionally the most capable army in the world, but as a professional army it was inevitably an expensive, and therefore a small, army, accustomed to cooperating with allies and using technology as a force multiplier – that is to say, as a means of compensating for lack of manpower.

All armies of the time relied on the smooth-bore musket as the personal weapon of the infantry, the men who fought on foot and were the backbone of all armies of the period. The British musket, known familiarly as the 'Brown Bess', had been in service in various models since standardization in 1716 and would remain in service until superseded by the rifled musket with a percussion lock in the 1840s. In 1815 there were two types of musket in use in the British army: the 'Short Land Service', first issued in 1768, which weighed 10½ pounds and was 4 feet 10½ inches long with a 42-inch barrel; and the India Pattern, 1½ pounds lighter, 3 inches shorter and with a 39-inch barrel. These latter were originally manufactured for the armies of the East India Company, but on the outbreak of war in 1793 the batch was taken over by the British government before it could be shipped to India. Both weapons were of the same calibre, 0.76 inches, and fired the same ammunition, and both could be fitted with a 17-inch bayonet.* Both had the same flintlock firing mechanism, such that, when the trigger was pulled, a piece of flint or iron pyrites held in the 'cock' was released and sprang forward, striking the frizzen, a serrated piece of metal hinged to the pan cover. The frizzen was pushed forward, opening the pan and at the same time drawing sparks from the flint. The sparks ignited a small amount of powder in the pan and the flame ran through the touch-hole into the bottom of the barrel, igniting the main charge and firing the musket.

Loading the musket was a complicated business. The soldier had to cant (tilt) the musket forward, holding it at the point of balance in his left hand. With his right hand he pulled the cock back to 'half cock' so that the pan was open. He then took a cartridge from a box-like pouch on his belt, also with his right hand. The cartridge consisted of a lead ball, weighing just over an ounce with a diameter of 0.71 inches, and black powder, the whole wrapped in paper – 'cartridge paper' – and sewn closed with thread. The soldier opened the paper end of the cartridge with his teeth and poured a tiny amount of powder into the pan, and closed the pan cover. He then brought the butt of the musket to the ground with the barrel vertical and poured the rest of the powder down the barrel. Next he dropped the ball down the barrel and pushed the screwed-up cartridge paper into the muzzle.† He now withdrew the ramrod, secured under the barrel, and rammed the whole lot down

---

* The logo of today's British infantry is the bayonet. Some years ago it was proposed to remove it as not being representative of what the infantry did. There were heart attacks in the shires and the suggestion was dropped.
† Despite the excellent *Sharpe* series, nowhere in any drill book is there mention of the soldier retaining the ball in his mouth and spitting it into the barrel.

the barrel, before returning the ramrod to its keepers. The point of including the paper – the wad – was that it prevented the ball from rolling out of the barrel if the musket was pointed downwards. To fire the weapon, the soldier first pulled the cock back to 'full cock', placed the butt against his shoulder, aimed along the barrel (there were no sights) and squeezed the trigger. The whole process of loading was then repeated.

As the diameter of the barrel was 0.76 inches and that of the ball 0.71 inches, the difference of 0.05 inches – called the 'windage' – made for easier loading, but also made the weapon inherently inaccurate. As the ball did not fit tight to the barrel, it rattled up it when fired and – depending on which part of the barrel it rattled against before exiting the muzzle – went above, below, right or left of the aiming line. One authority said that a soldier would probably be hit by a musket aimed at him from 80 yards away, but be very unfortunate indeed to be hit by a musket at 150 yards, provided his antagonist aimed at him, and that 'as to firing at a man at 200 yards with a common musket, you may as well fire at the moon'.[3] The way to make use of the musket in war was to line men up shoulder to shoulder and fire in volleys, as close to the enemy as possible, for only in that way could effective fire be brought down, and provided the men aimed low (as the musket tended to kick high, they were told to aim for the waist belt), great holes would be torn in the opposing ranks.

Unlike the infantry of every other European power, the British regiment was a purely administrative unit, not a tactical one. A regiment might have two, three or even four battalions, but they did not necessarily fight together and, while wearing the same cap badge and facings of the same colour, might be stationed at opposite ends of the world. The fighting unit was the battalion, commanded by a lieutenant colonel, which had ten companies, each commanded by a captain with two subalterns, two sergeants and eighty junior NCOs and privates. Two of the companies were 'flank' companies. One, which always took post at the right of the line, was the 'grenadier company', which was originally intended to be made up of grenade throwers, and thus the tallest and strongest men in the battalion. That tactical role had long disappeared, however, and by 1815 the grenadier company performed exactly the same tasks as any other company, although it was occasionally extracted for what might now be termed special operations. The other flank company, with a very definite tactical role, was the 'light company', which consisted of men who had been specially trained to act as skirmishers. Skirmishers, who could form as much as a quarter or even a third of a British army in defence, were deployed in loose order in front of the main defence line, in order to persuade the enemy to deploy early and fire its first volley (which, loaded when not under fire, would be the most accurate). The skirmishers would aim to cause as much mayhem as possible before the advancing enemy closed with the British main body. Having fulfilled their task, the light company, armed and equipped as any other company, would then retire and fall in on the left of the battalion line. By 1815, in addition to the light companies, there were whole battalions of light infantry, who could be used either to skirmish or to stand in the line, or both.

At full strength, therefore, a battalion of line infantry would be over 800 strong, although in practice most were well below that. Operationally, two, three or four battalions were combined into a brigade, commanded by a colonel (with the appointment, but not the rank, of brigadier general) or a major general. Two or more brigades formed a division, commanded by a major general or lieutenant general. The British army was never large enough to form corps, each of two or more divisions, except at Waterloo when, as we shall see, the Anglo-Dutch army was divided into three corps.

The small British army, while perfectly capable of fighting an attacking battle, preferred to find a piece of ground that suited it and take up a position where the enemy would have to attack it, and then make use of superior British musketry to blow approaching French (and it was nearly always French) infantry away. British musketry was superior not because of the musket, which fired only a marginally heavier bullet than its French equivalent, but because British soldiers' training was better. Although most armies in line stood in three ranks, the British stood in two, and thus were able to bring every musket to bear. Statistically about one shot in every seven was a misfire, whether because the flint broke or the powder was damp or in the heat of battle the soldier had failed to load properly. Given that the British preferred to stand in defence and allow an enemy to attack them, and then to be destroyed by British musketry, it was vital that fire was continuous. As the rate of fire of the Brown Bess was two rounds a minute (claims of three or even four rounds a minute are nonsense), if the men of a battalion in line all fired at once, there would be a delay of thirty seconds while they reloaded – ample time for an advancing enemy to close with the bayonet. The answer was 'platoon firing', where smaller bodies fired in sequence, so that a proportion of the battalion always had its weapons loaded and ready to fire. In a ten-company battalion the fire unit – the 'platoon' – was the half-company of forty men. The company commander – a captain –

would command one half and his senior subaltern or a sergeant the other half. There were thus twenty fire units, and while there were various sequences of firing, the simplest method, and that used most often, was for the two outside fire units, those on the extreme right and left of the battalion, to fire, followed by the next two in, and so on until the two fire units in the centre fired, by which time the extreme outside half-companies had reloaded. The procedure could then be repeated until the enemy were all dead or gave up and ran away, or had taken so many casualties that they were unable to continue.

This system of platoon firing at a rate of two rounds a minute for each firer depended upon there being a pause of three seconds between each firing. Stop watches had not been invented, so half-company commanders had various ways of calculating three seconds: 'One thousand and one, one thousand and two, one thousand and three – Fire'; 'Officers' wives get pudding and pies, sergeants' wives get skilly – Fire', and the like.

If we assume that a British battalion in line, with 800 men in two ranks, is being attacked by a French regiment of 1,800 men in three battalions in column, then the column frontage is forty men across. Most exchanges of fire did not take place at a range of more than 150 yards, so if the advancing French are to close with the British line, then – marching at the standard pace of seventy-five 28-inch paces to the minute – they will take just over two-and-a-half minutes to cover the distance, during which time they will have 4,800 rounds (six shots from each defender) fired at them, or 120 rounds per yard of front. In reply only the front two French ranks can deliver fire, and they cannot reload on the move, so they return but one round per ten yards of front. Even allowing for misfires and faulty loading, it is small wonder that attackers never got anywhere near a British line that was prepared to receive them. Even where the French did manage to deploy into line when advancing, they still invariably failed, simply because the professional British soldier knew that if he stood in line and carried out the drills he had practised over and over again, then – short of running out of ammunition – nothing could withstand him.*

Contrary to popular belief, the British army was not (and is not) opposed to technology, for if you have a small army that regularly takes on far larger ones, you need to make use of every possible development to substitute for flesh and blood. The British experimented with rockets (and used them, briefly, at Waterloo), tried out various patterns of cavalry sword and, most effective of all, made much use of the rifle.

As we have seen, the smooth-bore musket is, by its very design, inaccurate because the bullet is unstable. If the bullet could be stabilized, then it could travel farther and more accurately than one fired from the Brown Bess, and the way to stabilize it is, first, to ensure that it fits tightly in the barrel and, second, to impart spin to it. This is done by a rifle, a weapon that has spiral grooves inside the barrel that grip the bullet and make it spin. The British had used rifles in the American wars, against the French and the rebellious American colonists, but it was thought that they were not suitable for European warfare, being either not soldier-proof or taking too long to load, until there was a change of mind in the 1790s. Gunsmiths all over the United Kingdom were invited to

---

* The British soldier carried sixty rounds of ammunition and it would be rare indeed for him to fire that many rounds in one battle. Only once – in the case of Abercrombie's brigade at Albuhera in 1811 – is there a record of men running out of ammunition.

tender to supply the British army with a rifle, and after extensive testing by the Board of Ordnance in early 1800, the rifle chosen was that submitted by Ezekial Baker, a gunsmith of Whitechapel, London.[4] His rifle was a flintlock weighing nine pounds; it had a calibre of 0.61 inches and fired a lead ball weighing 0.8 ounces. The barrel had seven grooves, giving the ball a quarter-turn, and being only 45¾ inches long with a 20-inch barrel, the weapon could be loaded lying down. The loading procedure was similar to that of the musket, except that the ball was wrapped in a greased leather clover-shaped patch before being rammed down the barrel, the patch being gripped by the grooves. Owing to the need to wrap the ball and to the tight fit that meant that ramming took longer, the loading procedure was slower than that of the musket, and the rate of fire was probably no more than three shots every two minutes. The rifle was sighted up to 200 yards, but it was accurate to a much greater distance in skilled hands,* and its possession meant that riflemen could kill soldiers armed with the musket long before the latter could get close enough to reply.

The regiments selected to use the rifle had their origins in the Experimental Corps of Riflemen, set up at Shorncliffe in 1800. Under Colonel Coote Manningham, a 35-year-old enthusiast, it was to be manned by infantry regiments in the UK sending one officer and fourteen soldiers to be trained as riflemen. Commanding officers rubbed their hands and off went the drunks, the welfare cases,

---

* The classic example, often quoted, is that of Rifleman Thomas Plunket, of Dublin and the 95th Rifles, who shot and killed Brigadier General Colbert at Cacabelos in Spain during the retreat to Corunna in January 1809. Most modern histories give the range as 800 yards. This author has paced it out and it is nearer 400 yards, but this was an example of excellent marksmanship against a moving target nevertheless – and still would be with a modern rifle.

the debtors, the useless and the ill-disciplined. By complaining to the commander-in-chief, the Duke of York, Manningham had the unpromising material removed and replaced by men with good records. It was harder to get rid of fat and idle officers, with some of whom he had also been burdened, but a regime of daily runs from the beach to the officers' mess before breakfast soon persuaded them to transfer to posts where soldiering was taken with less seriousness.* The Experimental Corps eventually became the 95th (Rifle) Regiment (later the Rifle Brigade), of five battalions each of eight companies; the existing 60th Foot was converted to a rifle regiment; and various Allied units such as the Brunswick-Oels Regiment, the King's German Legion light companies and the Portuguese Cacadores were issued with the Baker, of which around 30,000 were manufactured during the wars. Dressed in a camouflage uniform of black and dark green, riflemen would skirmish, ambush and snipe. Their particular targets would be officers, *fanniers* – bearers of small flags who were stationed on the extreme left and right of a French formation and were responsible for keeping direction – and drummer boys, these last because on the battlefield, where shouted orders would be drowned out by the ambient noise, signals were given by beat of drum. That many of the drummers were boys of twelve or thirteen was a pity, but if they did not have a sense of humour, they should not have joined. The intention of all this was to disrupt the enemy chain of command and control, and when their task was done, the riflemen would retire behind the main body, as their rate of fire was too slow for them to stand in the line.

---

* The barracks at Shorncliffe is still there, it still houses a (Gurkha) rifle regiment, and the run from the beach to the mess is just as exhausting as it was in 1800.

British cavalry were probably the best mounted of all the armies in 1815, mostly on hardy cob types of between fourteen and fifteen hands for the soldiers, and light or medium hunters for the officers, who, having to range farther and wider around the battlefield, needed a faster horse. British cavalrymen were more caring of their horses than most, getting off and leading their mounts with girths slackened where possible – something that a French cavalryman would have considered beneath him. Despite the wide variety of titles – horse guards, life guards, dragoons, light dragoons, hussars – the British mounted arm was divided into heavy and light cavalry. The Royal Horse Guards (the Blues) and the Life Guards – generically the Household Cavalry because of their traditional role as the king's personal troops and guardians of his person – and the dragoon regiments were heavy cavalry, on generally heavier horses, intended for shock action – that is, charging as a formed body against enemy cavalry or infantry – and equipped with a straight heavy sword (but not, like their French equivalents, partially armoured with metal cuirasses and back-plates). Light cavalry – light dragoons and hussars – were intended for outpost duty, reconnaissance, piquets, escorts and pursuit of a beaten enemy. The men were unarmoured and equipped with a curved sabre. The titles bore no resemblance to their 1815 roles – dragoons were originally mounted infantry who rode to the battlefield and then dismounted and fought on foot, while hussars were Hungarian light cavalry, noted for the splendour (and impracticality) of their uniforms – and many British light dragoon regiments had changed their titles to hussars, for reasons of fashion alone. Both types of cavalrymen were equipped with a carbine, a cut-down version of the infantry's musket, for use when on dismounted sentry duty, and some heavy cavalry also carried flintlock pistols ('horse pistols').

Despite being better mounted than their enemies, British cavalry did have a reputation, sometimes deserved, for delivering a magnificent charge and then disappearing over the horizon in search of loot and not reappearing until tea-time. Partly this was because the cavalry did have a better chance of acquiring such loot as there might be, but it was also because of the problems of finding training areas in England. The battles of Hyde Park and Hounslow Heath had been fought many times over, but most English farmers were not keen to see the cavalry gallop over their land, and in any case the fields, much smaller than today's and enclosed with thick hedges, did not lend themselves to the rehearsal of wide-ranging cavalry actions. The result was often that, when the cavalry found themselves on wide open spaces, control was lost.*

British artillery was divided into horse and foot artillery, the former to support the cavalry, the latter the infantry. Horse artillery troops (modern batteries) were established for five six-pounder guns (although at Waterloo some had nine-pounders) and one 5½-inch howitzer. The maximum effective range of the nine-pounder gun was 520 yards, and of the howitzer around the same, or slightly less.† Each weapon was pulled by eight horses, and as the guns had to move at the same speed as the cavalry it was supporting, all the gun crew members were mounted, as were the farrier, the surgeon,

---

* The problem remained until at the behest of Prince Albert the army bought a large chunk of Salisbury Plain. Thought at the time to be far larger than would ever be required, it is now far too small for anything other than short and small-scale exercises, and major British army formation training now takes place in Canada, Poland and Kenya.
† Maximum effective range was the range at which 100 per cent of shots would take effect. The maximum range was around 1,200 yards, but very few shots would land where they were wanted (or not wanted, if on the receiving end).

the trumpeters (actually buglers) and everyone else with any task intended to keep the guns in action. In total one troop fielded the perhaps surprising total of 220 horses and six mules. Guns could fire round shot (solid iron balls), spherical case and canister. Spherical case, often called shrapnel after its inventor, Major (later Lieutenant General) Henry Shrapnel, was a hollow iron ball packed with musket balls and a bursting charge. Provided the fuse was set correctly – and this was critical – the shell burst in the air and showered the target with musket balls.[*] A canister round – of the sort most probably used by Napoleon at the Tuileries in 1795 – was a cylindrical tin packed with musket balls which when fired burst open and had a buckshot effect on the target. At up to 300 yards it was highly effective. The howitzer could 'lob' and was used against targets that were entrenched or behind natural or artificial cover. It fired common shell – that is, a hollow iron ball with a bursting charge, which when it exploded sent bits of iron flying around to deadly effect. Foot artillery companies (batteries) were equipped with nine-pounder guns with a maximum effective range not much greater than the six-pounder on soft ground – about 600 yards – but up to 900 yards on hard ground where the shot could be 'skipped' – that is, bounced once or twice, taking out targets on each bounce.

The French army had evolved from a mix of the old pre-revolutionary army and the volunteers and militias of the Revolution, welded

---

[*] Shrapnel shells of very similar manufacture and effect were used during and until well after the First World War. Today the results of an exploding high-explosive artillery shell are often referred to in the vernacular as 'shrapnel' when they should properly be called 'shell splinters'. Shrapnel spent a great deal of his own money developing his shell (and numerous other inventions) and received little compensation from an ungrateful government.

together and turned into a formidable military machine by Napoleon and those who thought like him. The French musket, the 1777 pattern, was 5 feet 2 inches long, weighed just over 9½ pounds and fired a lead ball of 0.8 ounces. As it was smaller than the British calibre, British troops could, in extremis, fire French ammunition, whereas the reverse was not the case. The musket could be fitted with a 15-inch bayonet, often of inferior steel and more for show and its psychological effect than of any real use. Dominique Jean Larrey, Napoleon's chief surgeon and a pioneer of military medicine, in an analysis of wounds received in battle, found that for every 119 bullet wounds there were but five from the bayonet.

In the old royalist army the men of the regular army were, in theory at least, career soldiers who enlisted for twelve or twenty-five years, with augmentation by conscription when needed. The Revolution was suspicious of standing armies as instruments of potential oppression, and at first tried to fight its wars with volunteers, attempting, often successfully, to substitute enthusiasm and patriotism for training and experience. As the wars went on, it became clear that a formally constituted army, rather than a citizen militia, was essential,* and Napoleon's army was a mix of regulars and conscripts, in numbered regiments with a laid-down establishment. There were many reorganizations, but by the time of the Waterloo campaign a French infantry regiment of the line was officially established for four service battalions, each of six companies (one of which was grenadier and one light infantry), each company being of 130 all ranks. In addition, each regiment

---

* Trotsky came to the same conclusion during the Russian civil war following the 1917 revolution there.

had a depot battalion, much smaller than a service battalion and intended to train recruits. As it was, by the time of Waterloo many regiments had only two or three battalions and were training their men on the march.

Unlike the British infantry, a French regiment of two, three or four battalions was a tactical unit that fought under a regimental commander, usually a colonel, with each battalion commanded by a *chef de bataillon*, or major. Tactically, in the attack French infantry approached in column – that is, with each company in line in three ranks, one company behind the other – and then deployed into line just before the final charge. Manoeuvre in column was easier to control without losing cohesion, while line allowed maximum firepower to be brought to bear. The trick was in knowing when to deploy from column into line. To do it too early meant loss of control – anyone who has served in the armed forces knows how difficult it is to keep in line on a flat tarmac parade ground with the band playing, never mind doing it over uneven scrub with shot and shell whistling past one's ears. To deploy too late meant being caught between formations and unable to take any offensive action. Commanders had to be able to judge the right moment to order companies to form a battalion line and bring all 600 muskets to bear. That at least was what was supposed to happen. In practice, as the long wars wore on, the dilution in the quality of men and skimping in training meant that French infantry regularly attacked as a column, without deploying into line. This often worked: the sight of a great mass of men, advancing seemingly inexorably, with cries of '*En avant!*' and '*Vive l'empereur!*', flags flying and the drums beating the *pas de charge*, was enough to persuade a frightened Italian, Austrian, Spanish or Russian conscript to fire one un-aimed shot and then flee. It did not work against the British.

The result of French infantry deployment in line and in three ranks, combined with lack of training, was that the soldiers fired by ranks, rather than adopting the more sophisticated British methods of platoon firing. As the rate of fire was rather less – often much less with inexperienced troops – than two rounds a minute, even properly controlled firing by ranks meant a pause of at least ten seconds between firings, long enough for a determined enemy to close up to an uncomfortable distance. Fire from the third rank was never very effective, due to the difficulty of firing over and past the two ranks in front, and Larrey, who analysed 3,000 hand injuries, found that most were caused to men in the front two ranks by fire from the third.[5]

On Napoleon's return from Elba, he found that most of his old cavalry had been disbanded and had to be re-formed. Given the difficulties of finding horses and training men, it is greatly to the credit of the French that they managed to produce the numbers of cavalry that they did for the 1815 campaign – and, although it was often badly handled, it proved generally competent. French cavalry, like the British, had a plethora of titles but was divided into heavy and light. One component in the French cavalry arm, and in that of most other European powers, that the British did not have was the lancer. Lancer regiments, originally all Polish but by 1815 recruited from Frenchmen as well, were armed with a ten-foot-long lance with a steel spike on the end. Unlike the lance in general use by the First World War, which was light and had a shaft made of bamboo (British) or steel (German), this earlier weapon had a heavy ash shaft and required considerable training to develop the muscle power needed for the lancer to couch his lance and hold it steadily as he charged at and speared an enemy. Only the lancer had any chance of injuring determined infantry in square, or a soldier lying down, but if a mounted enemy managed to get past the lance point to where he could use his sword, then the lancer was in real trouble.

As Napoleon started life as an officer of artillery, it is not surprising that French artillery was generally very good, although not always as overwhelming as claimed. At Waterloo there were 246 French guns of various calibres against 157 of the Allies, but in many battles of the Napoleonic Wars there were fewer guns per division in the French army than in that of their enemies – it was just that French guns were better handled. French field artillery was based on the Gribeauval twelve-pounder and eight-pounder, although there were also some six-, four- and three-pounders. Given that the French pound weighed a little more than the English equivalent, the twelve-pounder was actually a thirteen-and-a-quarter-pounder by British measurement and the eight-pounder only very slightly smaller than the British nine-pounder.* Heavier though the twelve-pounder field gun was, its maximum effective range was still only around the same as that of the British nine-pounder – 600 yards – although it did of course fire a heavier projectile.

The Prussian army of 1815 was not the all-conquering army of Frederick the Great, nor the formidable machines of 1870, 1914 and 1939. The Frederician system was finally shown to be obsolete by the overwhelming defeat of the Prussians at the twin battles of Jena and Auerstädt on 14 October 1806, which led to the loss of Prussian territory east of the Elbe, the imposition of a massive

---

* The French pound, the *livre usuelle*, introduced in 1812, was defined as being equal to 500 grams. The British pound was (and is) 453 grams.

indemnity and the occupation of Prussian towns by French troops until it was paid. Outdated tactics, obsolete equipment and officers who were far too old were the main factors that led to the Prussian debacle, and in the ensuing years the Prussian state and army poked into every tiny corner of its military system to see what had gone wrong and how it could be put right. Under reformers such as the Hanoverian Scharnhorst and the Saxon Gneisenau, nearly every aspect of the Prussian military system was examined and brought up to date or abolished.

Commissions were now open to all comers, not just the nobility; universal military short service replaced conscription for life or wholly professional recruitment; promotion was based on merit rather than seniority; regimental equipment and accoutrements would henceforth be the property of the state, not of the regimental colonel; a more liberal disciplinary code was introduced and flogging was abolished; a properly organized logistic service was founded; a new 1809 pattern musket was introduced; officer training, and particularly staff officer training, was brought up to date; an army reserve was established (in secret, to get around maximum strengths imposed by the French); and the standing army was to be backed up by a *Landwehr,* a part-time militia, and the *Landsturm*, a home guard. Organizationally the infantry was to be composed of regiments, which as in the French army would be tactical units, each with two battalions of musketeers, one battalion of light infantry skirmishers and two companies of grenadiers. Battalions had four combatant companies and a training company. The combatant companies had an establishment of five officers and 185 men, but in peacetime 120 private soldiers were on long leave, available for recall when required, and only fifty remained with the colours.

The cavalry was also overhauled – the type and size of horses were standardized and the organization of a regiment settled at four squadrons each of six officers and 162 Other Ranks, of whom seventy-two would be on long leave. Reform of the artillery was more protracted as the equipment was more expensive and took longer to obtain, but it was eventually formed into foot batteries of six-pounders and horse batteries of six-pounders and howitzers. Some of the guns were British, others of Prussian manufacture. By the time of Waterloo some twelve-pounder guns were also in service.[6]

The result was that, by the time of the Waterloo campaign, although the Prussian army was made up very largely of recruits and inexperienced *Landwehr* units, their men were of high morale and genuinely motivated by patriotism and hatred of the French, and there were enough experienced officers and NCOs to provide a cadre of real leadership and tactical know-how.

Holland had been the French-dominated Batavian Republic from 1795 to 1806 and then the Kingdom of Holland, ruled by Napoleon's brother Louis, the father of Napoleon III, until incorporated into metropolitan France in 1810. Belgium, having been the Spanish Netherlands and then the Austrian Netherlands, was absorbed into France in 1795. In November 1813 French troops had withdrawn from Holland, leaving garrisons in Antwerp, Bergen op Zoom and Arnhem, and William of Orange, who was declared sovereign prince, with his capital in Amsterdam, began the difficult task of forming a national army. As most Dutch units were away serving in the French army, the initial recruits were a motley bunch: a battalion in England formed from Dutch prisoners of war was hastily incorporated, and when the Prussians captured Arnhem, it was discovered that the 5th Battalion of the French 123rd Regiment of the Line was composed of Dutchmen, who were also enrolled. After Napoleon's first abdication in 1814, Holland and Belgium together became the Kingdom of the Netherlands in the Allied camp and a member of the Seventh Coalition. The formation of a national army continued, and the intention was to have thirty battalions of infantry, ten squadrons of cavalry and ten batteries of artillery backed up by a militia and a home guard. By 1815 the Dutch-Belgian army consisted mainly of units that had served Napoleon until a year previously, some of them in the Imperial Guard, the elite of the French army, and was thought to be of doubtful loyalty. It was accustomed to using French equipment and tactics, although some French artillery was being replaced by guns of British manufacture. Many regiments still wore their French uniforms, with an orange cockade in their hats to indicate the change of allegiance, and some of the newly raised units had a bewildering array of weapons, firing ammunition of different calibres. In fact, the summer of 1815 caught the army of the Netherlands in mid-reorganization, and only two divisions of infantry and three cavalry brigades would be available to Wellington for front-line duties, although others would man garrisons to release regular troops for combat duties.

These, then, were the armies that would fight Waterloo – the campaign that would decide the future of Europe.

3

THE COMMANDERS

The results of the Waterloo campaign would hinge on the decisions of three great men: Napoleon Bonaparte, Arthur, Duke of Wellington and Gebhard von Blücher.

We have already seen how Napoleon rose through the ranks of the French army before becoming emperor in 1804, and while he undoubtedly had a global perspective politically and a strategic one militarily, he understood the common soldier too. Today all armies award medals to all ranks. These are either decorations, in recognition of good service or leadership in action or for a specific act or acts of gallantry, or they are campaign medals. The latter are awarded to every soldier (or sailor or airman) who has served in a particular theatre, campaign or battle. These are a source of great pride and worn, in most armies, on the left breast. On formal occasions the actual medal will be worn, suspended by a ribbon unique to that medal; otherwise the recipient will wear the ribbons only, arranged in a row or rows. Thus, what is displayed on a man's chest is his history – where he has been on active service and whether or not he has been decorated.

Not only are medals highly prized, they are also cheap to

produce, thus for governments they are an easy way to reward and recognize service. Napoleon, as first consul, introduced the Légion d'honneur to award meritorious service. It was divided into five classes and entitled the recipient to wear a medal, with a star or sash, depending on the grade, and it also came with a pro rata monetary award. By the time of the Bourbon restoration in 1814 there were around 40,000 members of the Légion and Louis XVIII did not risk alienating them by scrapping it, but he did try to devalue it and replaced Napoleonic and revolutionary symbols with Bourbon ones. Campaign medals were issued for all of Napoleon's major battles, and some of the minor ones, usually those where the consul or emperor was personally present. When an intimate derided the medals as mere baubles, Napoleon is quoted as saying, 'It is by baubles that men are led… the soldier needs glory, distinction and reward.' He was quite right. All other nations copied the Napoleonic medals system, including, eventually, the British.

Napoleon was unquestionably imbued with strong natural leadership qualities, but he was also a consummate actor who made full use of the tricks of showmanship. Before inspecting a body of troops, he would enquire of the commander which of the soldiers had served in a Napoleonic battle. He would be told that, say, the third from the left in the rear rank and the sixteenth from the right in the front rank had been with him at a particular battle. Then, strolling along the line of men drawn up to receive him, Napoleon would suddenly dive into the ranks and seize the relevant soldier by the cheek: 'You were with me at Austerlitz – Jean-Claude, is it not? What a day that was – how have you fared?' The more intelligent would have realized that the emperor could not possibly remember the thousands of private soldiers who had passed under his command, but it went down well all the same. There is no question that Napoleon's soldiers loved him and most would have happily died for him. He loved them too, up to a point, but he was often profligate with their lives. Apart from his first Italian campaign and the abortive expedition to Egypt, when the small numbers of his forces made him husband them carefully, he thought little of hurling his divisions into a frontal attack if that was the quickest way to achieve victory. If he lost 42,000 men killed, wounded and taken prisoner, as he did at the two-day battle of Wagram in July 1809, he had the whole of Europe whence to conscript more. By 1815, however, those great reserves of manpower were no longer available to him, and he could rely only on those troops that could be raised from mainland France.

Napoleon's British adversary in the campaign was Arthur Wellesley, first duke of Wellington. Born in 1769, Wellington was a younger son of an Irish peer, the second baron and first earl of Mornington, a composer and professor of music at Trinity College, Dublin. The name had originally been Colley, or Cowley, but Arthur's grandfather had changed it to Wesley (or Wellesley) on inheriting the estates of a cousin, Garret Wesley (or Wellesley). Like most of the Anglo-Irish, the Wellesleys owned vast tracts of land, most of it incapable of supporting anything other than a few very hungry goats and a donkey or two and mortgaged up to the hilt. They owned a property in County Meath – Dangan Castle, more a large country house than a castle and now an overgrown ruin – and a house in Merrion Street, a fashionable quarter of Dublin, just behind what is now the Irish parliament.* Garret Wellesley died when Arthur

---

* The Dublin house is now a very smart hotel, and residents are told with pride that the room they are staying in is the one in which the future Duke of Wellington was born. At one time or another virtually every room in the hotel has been so described, but you can't blame them for trying.

was twelve years old and the family then moved to England, taking Arthur out of the diocesan school in Trim, County Meath, and placing him in a seminary in Chelsea. In 1781 he went to Eton, where he seems to have achieved little or nothing scholastically, although he did say in later life that it had taught him two things: never to get involved in something he knew nothing about, and never to speak in Latin.* Family money soon ran out and Arthur was removed from Eton to make room for his academically much more promising younger brother. Thereupon his mother took him to Brussels, in what was then the Austrian Netherlands, where he learned to speak French, albeit with a Belgian accent, before he was sent off for a year to a military finishing school in Angers in France. There, in the last years of the *ancien régime*, in what was in effect a finishing school for the sprigs of the minor nobility and where a large number of the pupils were British, he was taught equitation, military fortification, drawing and dancing, and learned to speak French with a French accent.

After spending the year 1786 in Angers, young Arthur was now ready to find a way of earning a living. As a younger son, the family estates, such as they were, were not his birthright; as a gentleman, trade was out of the question (even if he had known anything about commerce, which he did not), and enquiries as to posts in politics or the administration of government failed to elicit offers of employment. Finally, in March 1787, two months short of his eighteenth birthday, he joined the army, not through any soldierly vocation, but because there seemed to be nothing

---

* Although when he was appointed Chancellor of Oxford University in 1834 – despite a very obvious lack of any academic credentials – his acceptance speech had to be delivered in Latin, which he almost certainly had someone else write for him.

else open to him: his mother is reported to have said that her 'ugly duckling' was 'fit only for powder'. At this stage he was thought to be socially awkward, gauche even, of delicate health, dreamy, musical and indifferently educated. Commissions then were purchased, as were subsequent promotions (this system will be looked at in detail in chapter 4); suffice it to say that Arthur had to borrow the money and in his early years he was constantly in debt, although he was always careful not to become dangerously so.

Arthur Wesley (as he then spelled it) was commissioned into the 73rd Highlanders, a regiment in which he never served as family influence secured him a post as aide de camp (ADC) to the Lord Lieutenant (governor general) of Ireland. Nor did he ever grace the officers' messes or the parade grounds of the 76th Foot, the 41st Foot, the 12th Light Dragoons, the 58th Foot or the 18th Light Dragoons, on the books of all of which regiments he was held as he purchased his way up the ranks of the army. A lieutenant nine months after he was first commissioned and a captain in June 1791, he spent the entire time based in Dublin Castle as one of a number of ADCs. The purpose of an ADC, then and now, is to ensure that his master can get on with the job for which he is trained (or not trained) and paid to do without having to worry about his own personal administration. In peacetime the requirements were not onerous. An ADC had to be unmarried, in order to devote his full attention to the job, socially adept in order to assist with entertaining, have a good memory and an eye for detail, be tactful and be able to think on his feet and smooth away any obstacles to his master's progress. At worst he might be employed as little more than a dog walker and social ornament; at best he might be taken under his master's wing and initiated into the art of higher command and administration.*

It was while he was an ADC that Arthur made his entry into politics, when he became the MP for Trim in the Irish parliament.† Trim was a 'pocket borough' with a restricted electorate, which nevertheless had to be cosseted and cajoled. Arthur did little of note as an MP but was not, unusually for the time, susceptible to bribery; and he was sympathetic to the majority Roman Catholic population, which suffered under severe restrictions including the requirement to pay tithes to the established (Anglican) church of which they were not, of course, members. It was during this time too that he began to mature, and went through a brief period of misbehaviour and riotous living not untypical of youth then and now. He was a relatively successful gambler, liked a drink and is supposed to have been fined five shillings by the Dublin magistrates for beating up a Frenchman in a brothel (as one would). In April 1793 he purchased the rank of major in the 33rd Regiment but, despite this elevation, a proposal of marriage to Kitty Packenham was turned down by her family, on the not unreasonable grounds that Arthur had no money and fewer prospects. While Arthur did

---

* Officers of the British army (and probably everybody else's too) are reported on by their superiors every year. The report assesses the officer's progress during the past year and makes recommendations as to their fitness for promotion and suitability for employment in certain roles, including that of ADC. This author's reports generally reported on him favourably, until it came to the question of suitability as an ADC, when all reports said 'No'. On one occasion the 'no' was underlined. He never wanted to be an ADC anyway.

† Surprisingly, perhaps, it has only been since 1928 that officers have been forbidden to stand for parliament or become involved in politics in any way. Officers of the Territorial Army are still permitted to stand for parliament and are not required to resign if elected.

eventually marry Kitty (and the marriage was not a happy one), the spurning of his overtures at this stage had a salutary effect on him. He is reported to have burned his violin and sworn never to play it again, and at last joined a regiment for duty.*

By the time he joined the 33rd Foot in Cork as a major in 1793, Arthur had acquired some social polish and some understanding of the rumbustious world of politics, was heavily in debt, mainly to his elder brother Richard but to others also, had been turned down as a prospective husband, and had done no soldiering worthy of the name. He had little understanding of how a battalion of infantry actually worked, nor any understanding of what the army calls 'interior economy' – the administration of stores and funds. Sparsely educated in the formal sense though he may have been, Arthur had considerable wit and innate intelligence. As a newly arrived major in the regiment, he was fortunate in that the other major of the 33rd (battalions were established for two) was John Coape Sherbrooke. Sherbrooke was described as 'a short, square, hardy little man, with a countenance that told at once the determined fortitude of his nature. Without genius, without education, hot as pepper, and rough in his language, but with a warm heart and generous feelings; true, strait forward, scorning finesse and craft and meanness.'7 He was five years older than Arthur, had been commissioned eight years before him, but was six months his junior in the rank of major. He had been on active service abroad and had commanded a company for ten years. If he did resent the arrival of Wesley as his senior, he was quickly won over, for he became the newcomer's mentor and helped him greatly

---

* It is, however, difficult to see what relevance violin playing could have had on his prospects – unless of course he was a very bad player and insisted on playing in the company of others.

as Arthur tried to pick up in weeks and months what Sherbrooke had taken over a decade to absorb.

Arthur's first task in the battalion was to sort out its accounts, which had been allowed to get into a dreadful state, largely as a result of the lack of interest in matters administrative shown by the Colonel of the Regiment, Lord Cornwallis, who was in India.* Tedious and painstaking though the task of going through several years of imperfectly kept paperwork was, it taught the young officer a great deal about the internal workings of a battalion – something that enabled him to avoid being bamboozled in later years. In September 1793 Arthur bought the lieutenant colonelcy of his battalion. He was now the commanding officer at twenty-four years of age and perforce learning very quickly indeed.† Youth is not and was not a barrier to competence in high rank, but unlike

---

* The Colonel of the Regiment was (and still is) a senior officer, usually one who has served in the regiment, with the remit of looking after its interests. At this time he was enormously powerful, effectively the proprietor, paying the officers and men and providing their uniforms and other necessaries out of grants from the government for that purpose. He had the final say on such matters as dress and appointments of officers. By 1815 his powers had been considerably reduced, and peculation and personal profiteering almost eliminated. Today he has no dealings with public money but still has the final say on officers joining and directs policy in regard to private, regimental, funds.

† In today's British army an officer could expect to be a senior lieutenant or recently promoted captain at twenty-four, but that is the penalty of a peacetime army with a laid-down career pattern. In both world wars it was not unusual for battalion commanders to be in their twenties. In the First World War Harold Alexander, later Field Marshal Earl Alexander, commanded a battalion of the Irish Guards at the age of twenty-four, was a lieutenant colonel aged twenty-six and a brigadier general at twenty-seven, while in the Second, Michael Carver, later Field Marshal Baron Carver, commanded a regiment of tanks (battalion equivalent) at twenty-eight and a brigade at thirty.

The Duke of Wellington by Thomas Heaphy (1775–1835). Invited to accompany the army in the Peninsula from 1813, Heaphy painted most of the senior officers and many of the soldiers. Officers were charged according to the size of the painting – full length, three-quarters length, head and shoulders, head – and Heaphy did very well out of his commissions. His portraits are considered to be the most lifelike of contemporary artists, and this one was painted in 1813.

Napoleon Bonaparte. Also by Thomas Heaphy, although this time without a sitting by the subject and presumably unpaid. Painted in 1813, by Waterloo Napoleon had put on weight and looked much older.

Field Marshal Prince Gebhard von Blücher. Commander of the Prussian Army during the Waterloo campaign and seventy-three in 1815, his relationship with Wellington was crucial to the success of the battle. While he rarely appeared in full dress uniform and medals, that is how he was visualised by ally and enemy alike. (Henry Alken, 1815)

Ligny. Looking north towards the church at Ligny from La Tombe, the prehistoric burial mound used first by General Zeithen as he brought in the Prussian rearguard, and then by Napoleon who moved from Fleurus. The main Prussian position is beyond the church along the ridge on the skyline.

Gemioncourt Farm. Gemioncourt from the south. Built around the early 1600s, it was the headquarters of Bijlandt's Brigade at Quatre Bras until it was captured early on. A brief attempt to recapture it failed and it remained in French hands until the end of the battle.

The Death of the Duke of Brunswick. Unusually for professional soldiers of the time, the Duke hated all things French in general and Napoleon in particular. He was hit trying to rally his cavalry at Quatre Bras, carried off the field and died shortly afterwards. (Diterich Monten, 1815)

Above left: Papelotte Farm. On the extreme left of Wellington's position at Waterloo, it was held throughout the day by Saxe-Weimar's Dutch-Belgians. Heavily damaged during the battle, it was largely rebuilt after it.

Above right: La Haie Sainte. A farmhouse forward of the Allied centre with a roadblock of upturned carts, it was held by a battalion of the King's German Legion against repeated attacks until about 1800 hours, when, out of ammunition, they were forced to withdraw.

The Battle of Waterloo. One of the few contemporary paintings of which the artist might just possibly have seen the ground, rather than drawing from his imagination. La Haie Sainte is on the left and La Belle Alliance on the right, although the scene of Highlanders in the valley seeing off French cavalry is entirely allegorical, and may be due to the artist confusing the Waterloo and Quatre Bras battles. (Published by Richard Holmes Laurie, 1819)

The Marquess of Anglesey leading the 7th Hussars. Henry Paget, not the Marquess of Anglesey until after Waterloo, where he was Earl of Uxbridge, was in overall command of the allied cavalry but led his own regiment with great skill in the retreat from Quatre Bras to Waterloo, where in the closing stages of the latter battle he lost a leg. (Charles Turner Warren, 1819)

French cavalry charging Highlanders at Waterloo. Steady troops in square had little to fear from cavalry, and it is unlikely that the horsemen ever got as close to the square as is depicted here. The failure of the French command and control systems to support the cavalry with artillery and infantry cost them dear. (William Heath, 1836)

The Battle of Waterloo. The almost insatiable desire of press and public to be informed of the great battle led to all sorts of dubious artistic endeavour hastily employed to show what war was like, or what the artist thought it was like.
(W. T. Fry, supposedly after Denis Dighton, 1815)

Above left: The Tree of Hougoumont. One of the very few surviving trees of the wood to the south of Hougoumont Farm. The bullet holes made by the Guards' muskets can be seen clearly.

Above right: The French Right Flank. The area to the right of the French position at Waterloo was a maze of sunken roads. Infantry could have crossed them, cavalry could have got in but not out and guns could only be manhandled across with very great difficulty. This made any attempt by Napoleon to envelop Wellington's left flank very unlikely.

The Battle of Waterloo. Prussian infantry on the right of the picture and French infantry on the left, probably somewhere in the vicinity of Plancenoit in the late afternoon. Artistic license shows the opposing forces far closer than they would actually have been. (Dunkler, 1816)

Arthur Wesley, those who achieved it had generally started learning their trade a lot earlier than he.

Lieutenant Colonel Wesley's first taste of active service, after a few false starts when various planned forays were cancelled, was when the 33rd Foot formed part of the Duke of York's abortive expedition to Flanders in 1794. For all sorts of reasons, many not the fault of the 'Grand Old Duke', the campaign was a disaster: it failed to capture the port of Dunkirk and ended in retreat, during one of the worst winters until then recorded, across Holland to Bremen, where the Royal Navy was once again called upon to remove a beaten British army for deployment elsewhere. During the retreat Wesley commanded a brigade of three battalions, including his own, not because of any perceived ability but simply because, young though he was, he was the senior lieutenant colonel of the three. At this time and briefly thereafter, battalions were established for two lieutenant colonels, and John Sherbrooke, who had purchased that rank earlier in the year, could safely be left to command the 33rd. Despite his lamentable lack of experience, Arthur did well as a brigade commander – possibly because many of the other officers were well below par – and it began to dawn on those who cared to look (and to himself) that here was some inherent military talent. Years later he was quoted as saying about the Flanders expedition that at least he had 'learned how not to do it, which is always something'. One should be wary of extrapolating backwards, for many of the statements attributed (some of them correctly) to Wesley/Wellesley/Wellington were made in his later years with the benefit of hindsight, but there can be little doubt that he must have pondered long and hard on the lessons of the campaign and his first experience of war.

After he had embarked his battalion and himself aboard troopships bound for the West Indies in the autumn of 1795 – a posting cancelled after weeks of being tossed about by heavy seas and gales in the Atlantic – the 33rd were disembarked to Lymington. Arthur was doubly lucky: he had escaped drowning in the storm, a fate that befell a number of his contemporaries as ships of the expedition sank, and he did not go to the West Indies, where the chances of surviving yellow fever were not great. Then, in 1796, the 33rd were ordered to India. It was at this point that Arthur made a decision that would shape the history of Great Britain, Europe and indeed the world. Up to now he had not committed himself wholly to a military career. He retained his seat in the Irish parliament and his appointment as an ADC at Dublin Castle, and still put out feelers for a post in the administration of government. As the Lord Lieutenant of Ireland was no longer Lord Westmorland, the friend of the Wellesleys, the only job that he was offered was Surveyor General of Ireland, but as that office was already occupied by Kitty Packenham's uncle, he turned it down. If he stayed with his battalion and went to India, he would have to abandon any hope of political preferment and could only pursue a military career in the long term. And that is what he did. He resigned his seat in parliament, settled his affairs, and set off on a frigate to catch up his battalion, which had departed on slower troopships two months before, rejoining it at Cape Town in September 1796. This commitment is sometimes painted in damascene terms, but it was more probably good, sound pragmatism. Arthur needed gainful employment and had failed to find it elsewhere, so he would have to settle for the army; and given that he had no alternative, he would take the army seriously and soldier to the best of his ability.

Promoted to colonel just before leaving England, Arthur and the 33rd reached Calcutta in February 1797 after an eight-month journey. Fifteen months later, in May 1798, Arthur's eldest brother

Richard Wellesley, Earl of Mornington, arrived in India as governor general, and Arthur changed his name from Wesley to Wellesley to conform. Had we never heard of Arthur, Richard would still merit a paragraph or three in British history – perhaps even a page. He was academically bright – brilliant, some said – and, although shortage of money, his father's death and his own succession as the second earl had made him leave Oxford without taking a degree,* he was highly thought of by influential English politicians. After a short time in the Irish House of Lords, he was successively MP for the English constituencies of Bere Alston, Windsor and Old Sarum.† Appointed early to office, first as Junior Lord of the Treasury and then to the Indian Board of Control, he was a Pittite and in favour of free trade, a friend of William Wilberforce and opposed to slavery, and in favour of Catholic emancipation. He also had a rather jolly French mistress, whom he eventually married.

At this time British India was divided into three presidencies: Bengal, Madras and Bombay, each with its own governor. The governor of Bengal was the senior and also governor general of the whole, with the right to overrule the other two governors if necessary. Richard was a believer in the forward policy – that is, that Britain should become the dominant power in India and should either enter into treaty relationships with those native states that were prepared to be guided by the British, or defeat militarily those who were not, drive out their French advisers and annex their territory. He laid the foundation for the British Raj.

The eight years that Arthur Wellesley served in India were the making of him as a soldier and as a commander. Between his first

---

* Although in his first year he won the chancellor's prize for Latin verse.
† He could sit in the House of Commons in Westminster because his earldom was in the Irish, rather than the English, peerage.

battle prior to the storming of Seringapatam, where he became lost and disorientated during a night attack on an outlying water course and village – and when, had his brother not been the governor general, he might have ended his career in court martial and disgrace – to the subjugation of Mysore and the final pacification of the Mahrattas, he had risen from colonel to major general, had repaid his debts from prize money awarded as a result of successful sieges, had been knighted, and had received numerous presentations and loyal addresses. Far more importantly, he had learned the significance of coalitions and how to work with difficult allies, how to administer an army in an undeveloped country where terrain and climate conspired against him, and the importance of health and hygiene (and in an age of stupendous overindulgence in the demon drink, he himself was by now but a moderate imbiber). All these lessons would be put to good use against the French in Portugal and Spain.

After a six-month voyage, Arthur arrived in England in September 1805. He was seventy-fifth in seniority as a major general – although many of those above him on the Army List had not held an appointment for some time and were unlikely to do so again – and the best that he could be offered was command of a brigade on the south coast.* It is sometimes alleged that Wellesley was regarded with some disdain as being only a 'sepoy general' and that those who had served in India were generally looked down upon by the military establishment, but this was not necessarily so.† While most of the full generals on the Army List may well have

---

* The Army List, published annually (sometimes six-monthly) by government, contained (and contains) the names and details of all the officers in the army by regiment, rank and seniority.
† A sepoy is an Indian private soldier of infantry. The derivation is Persian and variants are found in Arabic, Hindi, Urdu and Nepali.

had little regard for experience that they lacked, generals who were still active, like Craig, Bentinck, Clarke and Cornwallis, had served in India – Cornwallis returned and died there in October 1805 – as had many of the younger lieutenant generals. The only criticism – if it was a criticism – that might have been levelled at 'Indian' officers was that, owing to distance, they were unable to dabble in domestic politics or benefit from or exercise patronage. Certainly Castlereagh – then the Secretary for War and the Colonies and a member of the Board of Control for India, whose great-uncle had been governor of Bombay – respected Wellesley and frequently sought his advice, not just on matters Indian but across a broad spectrum of military planning and international relations.

After a brief foray into politics when he was returned as the member for Rye in the House of Commons and a stint as Chief Secretary for Ireland, Wellesley commanded a division in the expedition to Copenhagen in 1807. Napoleon had just signed the Treaty of Tilsit with the Russian Tsar and the Baltic was now a French lake. The Danes, although neutral, had a small but modern and efficient fleet, which if snaffled by the French could undo the maritime supremacy that the Royal Navy had underlined at Trafalgar. The British made an offer to hire the Danish ships and, when this was turned down, demanded that they be handed over for the duration of the war. After another refusal – an indignant one this time – the British burned Copenhagen and sank the Danish fleet. They had done it once before, in 1801, and on both occasions it was certainly illegal, but – as in the sinking of the neutral Vichy French fleet at Mers-el-Kébir in June 1940 – necessity makes criminals of us all.

Next, in 1808, Lieutenant General Wellesley was sent off to Portugal, and it was his two campaigns here, in 1808 and again between 1809 and 1814, that saw him emerge not just as the foremost British general but as the only one in all the Allied coalitions who had consistently beaten the French. From a junior lieutenant general in 1808, he emerged from Iberia as a field marshal and a duke, taking the name Wellington after lands that the family was thought to have once held in Somerset.

It is tempting to draw parallels between Napoleon and Wellesley. Both were born in the same year, and both were the product of feckless fathers and domineering mothers; both were born in the outer fringes of their nations, and both rose through sheer ability and a minimum of patronage. But in reality they were very different. Napoleon was an opportunist, a gambler, a taker of chances and, for all that his soldiers loved him, he was careless with their lives. He was not only the head of the army but the head of state too, so there could be no conflict of interest. Wellington, by contrast, knew that Britain only had one army and that, if he broke it, there was not another to be had. He planned meticulously and well understood the importance of logistics – of being able to feed, house, tend and transport an army. Unlike many of his contemporaries, he did not look down on intelligence as being somehow underhand; rather, he made full use of it, and if no intelligence service existed, he created one. Despite a scanty formal education, he was a thinker, forever pondering on what the enemy was doing or might do. He always understood the political imperatives within which a military commander had to act. Unlike Napoleon, who saw no reason why a conquering army should pay for anything, Wellington knew that an army could be kept in the field in a foreign land only if the population tolerated it. Here was the big difference in the Peninsula: the French became an army of occupation rather than an army fighting a war; the British, by treating the locals properly and paying for what they wanted, had the wholehearted support of the vast majority of Spaniards and could concentrate on fighting the war rather than having to watch their backs.

Because Wellington, despite some reverses in Spain, had been consistently opposed to and generally victorious over the French, he was the obvious commander for the Anglo-Dutch army for the Waterloo campaign, and this was the view not only of the British government but of the Allies too. After Napoleon's abdication in 1814, Wellington had been briefly British ambassador in Paris, and then part of the British delegation to the Congress of Vienna, where the victorious powers met to decide the future shape of Europe. He was given the choice of remaining in Vienna or taking command in the Netherlands. Unsurprisingly, he chose the latter and arrived in Brussels on 11 April 1815.

The commander of the Prussian army in Flanders, Field Marshal (*Generalfeldmarschall*) Gebhard Leberecht von Blücher, Furst (prince) von Wahlstatt, was cut from very different cloth. The description 'larger than life' is much overused, but it does fit Blücher admirably, and if he appeared as a character in a novel, he would be considered a gross exaggeration. Wild in his youth, energetic and full of vitality until the day he died in 1819, subject to extraordinary hallucinations that nevertheless did not detract from his ability to command troops, he was born into genteel poverty in December 1742 in Rostok on the Baltic, then part of the Duchy of Mecklenburg. He was a younger son, so the family's infertile lands were not for him and at the age of sixteen he joined the Swedish cavalry. Captured by the Prussians during the Seven Years War, he made a marked impression, for his captors invited him to join their army and for the rest of the war he served as a captain (*Rittmeister*) in the Prussian Red Hussars. He then fell out with King Frederick II ('the Great'), largely for delivering judgements that were often sound but given in an intemperate manner and totally lacking in tact. Out of the army, he took to farming, becoming reasonably successful, until Frederick died in 1786 and Blücher was recalled as a major.

By 1801 Blücher was a lieutenant general, and, although captured in the disastrous retreat from Auerstädt in 1806, he was exchanged for the French Marshal Victor, who had been captured by the Prussians. He was violently opposed to peace with France and a vocal supporter of the reform and modernization of the Prussian army that followed. When Prussia returned to the fray in 1813, Blücher played a prominent part and defeated Napoleon at the Battle of Leipzig in October of that year, his fourth battle against the emperor and the first that he had won. Promoted to field marshal and created a prince after Napoleon's abdication in 1814, he was furious on arriving in Paris to find that the French had named a bridge over the River Seine after their victory over the Prussians at Jena and announced that he would blow it up, only relenting under extreme pressure from the other Allied commanders.

A quaffer of copious quantities of gin and brandy, Blücher would swig coffee, munch raw onions and smoke a huge meerschaum pipe as he rode along. His nickname among the troops was 'Marschall Vorwärts', a tribute to his liking for constant, immediate and headlong attacks. His addiction – and the consumption of gallons of coffee every day does produce an addiction – led to short hallucinatory episodes, and on occasion he would announce that he was pregnant, once telling Wellington that he was carrying the foetus of an elephant and that the father was a grenadier of the French Imperial Guard. But Blücher was brave, often to a fault, loyal and a man of his word, and the Waterloo campaign could not have been won without him.

The commander of the other Allied army at Waterloo was considerably less experienced in either war or battle. As we have seen, the United Kingdom of the Netherlands had been created after Napoleon's 1814 abdication by combining the French imperial province of Holland (previously the Kingdom of Holland ruled by Napoleon's brother Louis), Belgium (previously part of France and before that the Austrian Netherlands) and the prince-bishopric of Liège. The 43-year-old William, Prince of Orange-Nassau, became King William I in March 1815. William was a despot, of the reasonably enlightened variety, and one of his first acts as king was to assure Wellington, on the latter's arrival from Vienna, that the entire Netherlands army would be at his disposal. There was one condition: the crown prince of the Netherlands, also William, would command the Dutch-Belgian troops and was also to have a senior Allied command.

The Orange-Nassau princely house had fled Holland when the French invaded, and the younger William had been educated in Berlin before joining the British army in 1811, when he was instantly promoted to lieutenant colonel and appointed aide de camp to Wellington in the Peninsula. A full colonel the same year, he returned to England in 1812 to become an ADC to the Prince Regent and be promoted to major general in 1813, at the tender age of twenty-one. It is probably unnecessary to say that his military abilities were limited to looking smart at dinner parties and balls, and he was known as 'Slender Billy' or 'Sweet William' to those who liked him and as 'Stinking Billy' or 'the young frog' to those who did not. Unfortunately he had deluded himself that he was a real general, with unfortunate consequences during the campaign for some of those nominally under his command.[*]

No commander, however competent, can command an army all by himself: he needs a staff. The purpose of the staff, or staff officers, is to put the commander's ideas into practice. Napoleon decides to march on Moscow. The staff work out how many troops are required to be supported by how many guns; how many wagon loads of kit must be collected; what routes the various units are to use; how much spare ammunition will be needed; where the rations are to come from; where hospitals should be established – and all the other myriad details that need to be resolved before a single man can move. The staff have always come in for criticism, usually unfairly, for when things go wrong it is easy to blame the anonymous 'them', sitting in their comfortable tents, chateaux, caravans or dugouts, rather than accepting a portion of the blame oneself.[†] The staff have a number of branches dealing with various aspects of war – operations, movement, stores, medical, promotions and appointments, manning, intelligence and the like – with officers dedicated to each of those branches. Heading the staff is, under varying titles depending on nationality, the chief of staff. Responsible for seeing that all aspects of the army work efficiently, the chief of staff is the commander's right-hand man,

---

[*] William was a closet homosexual, or possibly a runner under both rules, and was blackmailed for it. He later proved a popular and effective king as William II from 1840.

[†] This author has been both a staff officer and at regimental duty. While on the staff he fulminated that the units had no understanding of the wider picture, and when commanding troops he raged that the staff had no conception of the conditions at the sharp end. He was usually wrong in both incarnations. It has ever been thus.

and it is essential, if the business of the army is to be conducted as it should be, that the commander and the chief of staff have complete trust in one another, and if possible complement each other.

Until 1814 Napoleon's chief of staff was the incomparable Louis Alexandre Berthier. Born in 1753 and one of the few senior officers of the Bourbon army to remain in France and to survive the Revolution, he had joined the royalist army in 1766, initially as a surveyor responsible for making maps, and then successively as a cavalry and an infantry officer. Singled out as having a good eye for detail, from 1787, as a lieutenant colonel, he was mainly employed as a staff officer and was the equivalent of a brigadier general staff when the Revolution broke out. He was suspended for a time by a Directorate suspicious of why this well-bred, albeit not actually aristocratic, officer should want to serve the republic, but reinstated in 1795. He came to the attention of Napoleon in the first Italian campaign and was the first to be made a marshal of the empire after Napoleon's coronation in 1804. From 1805 until the first abdication he was Napoleon's chief of staff, turning the emperor's broad strategic direction into clear and detailed directives. While Napoleon gave him little credit for it, it was Berthier's efforts that played a large part in Napoleon's victories and mitigated the results of his defeats. He would never allow the emperor to write directly to a subordinate – Napoleon's handwriting was notoriously bad and almost unreadable, which would have a direct effect on the result of the Battle of Ligny during the forthcoming campaign – but would rewrite the emperor's instructions and then send them by two or three different routes to their recipients. In his final exile, Napoleon admitted that 'No one could replace Berthier'. Like most of his colleagues, Berthier swore allegiance to Louis XVIII at the first restoration. Unlike them, however, he did not turn his coat yet again and rejoin his old master, but accompanied the king as he fled to Ghent, and then went to his wife's castle at Bamberg in east Germany. There, on 1 June 1815, he was leaning out of a third-floor window watching Russian cavalry moving west when he fell to his death. Both suicide and murder have been suggested. The truth almost certainly is that he simply slipped and overbalanced.

The loss of this superb staff officer, with his prodigious capacity for hard work and his ability to reduce the fog of war to the essentials, was severe. Had Berthier been at Napoleon's side, the campaign might well have been waged in a different way, and, although Napoleon could – probably would – have still lost the war, he might have been able to arrive at a negotiated peace rather than the complete and utter defeat that he actually suffered. As it was, for the Waterloo campaign Napoleon chose as his chief of staff Marshal Nicolas Jean de Dieu Soult. He was born in 1769, the same year as both Napoleon and Wellington, but there any resemblance ends, for Soult had little education and enlisted as a private soldier in the Bourbon infantry at the age of sixteen. At the outbreak of the Revolution he was a hard-bitten sergeant. With the execution or exile of so many of the officers of the army, the opportunities for Soult and men like him were immense, and he was soon commissioned and showed considerable tactical cunning in the early campaigns of the French republic. By 1794 he was brigadier (*général de brigade*) and by 1799 major general (*général de division*), and he was created a marshal, the seventh in seniority, by Napoleon in 1804. In Italy and later in the Iberian Peninsula he proved a perfectly adequate field commander, and an inveterate plunderer; he also possessed the ability to re-form remarkably quickly a beaten and dispersed army – something at which he had lots of practice in Spain and Portugal, where he was regularly defeated by Wellington. He fought a good delaying campaign in the Pyrenees and southern France in 1814, and on the restoration joined most of the other marshals by signing up for King Louis and becoming his minister for war, until declaring for Napoleon once again on the emperor's return from Elba.

Soult was, though, a totally unsuitable choice as chief of staff. He was competent as a field commander, but through no fault of his own he had never been trained as a staff officer, nor did he understand the management of a campaign – something quite different from the mere fighting of it. His inexperience in an unfamiliar appointment would show up starkly during the coming campaign.

Wellington, too, was without his long-time chief of staff and had to make do with what he could get.* His first choice would have been the man who had been at his side for most of the Peninsular War, George Murray, chief of staff from 1809 to 1814 with only one year out. Murray had served with Wellington in Denmark, had been John Moore's chief of staff as a lieutenant colonel in the retreat to Corunna, and was delighted to serve Wellington in the same capacity, as a colonel in 1809, a brigadier general in 1811 and a major general in 1812. A man of great ability who could motivate and enthuse those under him, Murray was punctual in an age when many were not, had a good eye for ground and was said to have

---

* The title of the senior staff officer in many armies of this period, including the British and Prussian, was Quartermaster General (QMG). This is confusing to modern ears as the QMG today deals with the procurement of supplies and equipment, rather than with operations. Originally there was no operations staff officer, his duties being discharged by the commander, but as the QMG's responsibilities included movement, and getting troops to the right battlefield at the right time was bound up with fighting the battle, the QMG became responsible for operations as well. To avoid confusion this book uses the modern 'chief of staff'.

a memory like an elephant's.* He was completely in Wellington's confidence and had the rare ability to see inside his chief's mind and anticipate his wishes, turning them into unambiguous operational orders and then ensuring that they were carried out. Alas, despite his wishes and those of Wellington, Murray was not available in 1815, for he had been sent to Canada as a lieutenant general at the close of hostilities in 1814 and could not return in time.

As it was, on his arrival in Flanders Wellington found that the chief of staff of the Anglo-Dutch army was Major General Sir Hudson Lowe. Lowe was an immensely experienced officer, both operationally and on the staff, but Wellington had little time for him, considering him to be 'a damned old fool' (he was the same age as Wellington) who couldn't read a map. Lowe was despatched to Genoa, to take command of a scratch force that was to cooperate with the Austrians, and replaced by Colonel Sir William Howe DeLancey. While we cannot comment on his map-reading ability, Wellington does seem to have been rather unfair to Lowe, who had been favourably reported on by, among others, John Moore and who seems to have fulfilled every task he had so far been given in a perfectly satisfactory manner. But Lowe had not served Wellington before whereas DeLancey had, and Wellington always liked to surround himself by those he knew – those who understood the great man's way of working and whom he had trained to operate in the way that he wished.†

---

* As elephants spend most of their time eating or defecating, this author has never understood why they should be thought to have superb memories. What is it that they have to remember?
† Lowe married DeLancey's sister after the Waterloo campaign, by which time DeLancey was dead. He would have a more favourable place in military history had he not upset Napoleon, and almost everyone else, as governor of St Helena during Napoleon's exile there.

DeLancey was born in New York in 1778, but as his family had been royalists, their land and property were confiscated by the victorious rebels and they had had to flee to England. DeLancey joined the army at the age of sixteen as a cornet (a cavalry rank equivalent to second lieutenant) in the 16th Light Dragoons and became a lieutenant the following year and a captain in the 80th Foot the year after that. Having survived yellow fever in the West Indies, he became a cavalryman once again, in the 17th Light Dragoons this time, and then a major in the 45th Foot in 1799, aged twenty-one.* With a keen intellect and good organizational abilities, DeLancey was soon spotted as suitable for the staff, and from 1802 until his death at Waterloo he was employed solely in that capacity. He was on Wellington's staff in the Peninsula from 1809 until the end of the war as, successively, Deputy Assistant Quartermaster General, Assistant Quartermaster General and Deputy Quartermaster General.† For those few readers who may be unfamiliar with nineteenth-century staff appointment titles, this meant that DeLancey worked for George Murray and moved up from being three steps below him as a major, to two steps as a lieutenant colonel and finally as his immediate deputy as a colonel. He was knighted at the close of hostilities in 1814 and sent to Flanders as deputy to Sir Hudson Lowe, before succeeding to the post of Quartermaster General (chief of staff) when Lowe was effectively sacked.

Meanwhile, the appointment of chief of staff to Blücher was a brilliant decision by King William of Prussia. The old field marshal

---

* In today's British army a really bright boy who was clearly going places could be a substantive major at thirty. Most achieve that rank between thirty-two and thirty-four.
† In modern terminology, SO3 G3, SO2 G3 and DCOS.

was an inspirational leader, full of energy despite his years and raring to have a go at the French. What was needed as a chief of staff was a cooler head, one that could translate Blücher's *Vorwärts* into practicality and act as a restraining hand on his master's enthusiasm, should that get out of hand. August Neidhart, Graf (count) von Gneisenau had just the qualities needed to counterbalance the army commander's sometimes unconsidered aggression. He had considerable experience both as a field commander and as a staff officer. He had served in a German regiment in the British army in North America during the revolution there, after which he transferred to the Prussian service and was an influential member of the movement to reform the Prussian military system after the defeats of Jena-Auerstädt. He became Blücher's chief of staff as a major general in 1813 and their relationship was an excellent example of how the commander–chief of staff symbiosis ought to work: each trusting the other totally, each reinforcing the other's strengths and compensating for their weaknesses. Unlike the British system, Prussian army regulations stipulated that, should the army commander be incapacitated, the chief of staff would succeed him, and Gneisenau was well capable of discharging the functions of a commander-in-chief, as would be demonstrated during the campaign.

Similarly, the appointment of the right man as chief of staff to the Prince of Orange was vital: the prince lacked the experience to command anything more than a sentry box and the chief of staff would in effect command the army, but he would have to be sufficiently tactful not to allow the prince to realize as much. The officer selected was Jean Victor, baron de Constant Rebecque. A Swiss, he was the third generation of his family to serve in the Dutch army. Originally commissioned as a second lieutenant in the

French (Bourbon) Swiss Guard, he narrowly escaped with his life when the mob stormed the Tuileries in 1792. He then took service with the Dutch, and when that nation was overrun by France, he alternated between the Prussian and British armies, being awarded an honorary doctorate from Oxford during one of his stints with the latter. As a major Rebecque became staff officer (essentially a minder) to the Prince of Orange when the latter was an ADC in the Peninsula. In 1813 he became a Dutch lieutenant colonel and a colonel later in the same year. After Napoleon's 1814 abdication he was given the task, as major general, of organizing the army of the new United Kingdom of the Netherlands. As most of the Dutch officers and nearly all the Dutch regiments had served in the French army, the new army of the Netherlands was organized according to the French, rather than the British, system, and while Rebecque, as a highly competent and intelligent officer, was himself familiar with the British way of doing things, this did create some difficulties for Wellington in commanding a multinational army.

In addition to a commander's personal staff, it was normal to attach a liaison officer to Allied armies. At Wellington's headquarters was Major General (*Generalmajor*) Philipp Friedrich Carl Ferdinand Freiherr von Muffling,* while his opposite number at Blücher's side was Colonel Sir Henry Hardinge. Both men were eminently suitable for their role, which was to keep each commander aware of the doings and views of the other. Muffling, another Saxon aged forty in 1815, had entered the Prussian service at the age of fifteen and joined the general staff in 1804 in the

---

* Roughly equivalent to the British 'baron' (and sometimes addressed as such), *Freiherr* is the second order of German nobility, ranking above *Ritter* (equivalent to a knight) and below *Graf* (earl in Britain, count elsewhere), and is normally hereditary.

survey department, responsible for mapping. He moved to the operational staff in 1806, when he served Blücher in the campaign of that year, and he served him again in 1813, by which time he was a major general. He did not get on with Gneisenau, partly because the latter blamed the defeat at Jena on poor mapping, but as he spoke English, was highly experienced and had established an excellent relationship with Wellington, he was well equipped for the job.

The thirty-year-old Henry Hardinge was equally capable, and the right candidate to liaise with Blücher. The son of a rector, he had joined the Queen's Rangers in Canada as an ensign in 1799 at the age of fifteen,* before transferring to the 4th Foot as a lieutenant in 1802. A captain in 1804, he attended an eighteen-month course at the senior department of the Royal Military College at High Wycombe from 1806. This was the recently established forerunner of the staff college, to which very few officers went, not least because it was not compulsory – it was also fee-paying and many of the lectures and items on the reading list were in French. Having passed the final examination at High Wycombe, Hardinge joined Wellesley (as he still was) in Portugal as a staff officer under Murray and then served Moore in the same capacity all the way to Corunna. After a short spell in England, he was promoted to major and then joined the staff of the Portuguese army – which was commanded by a British officer, William Carr Beresford – and became a (Portuguese) lieutenant colonel. On Wellesley's return to Portugal in the spring of 1809, Hardinge was detached to him to act as his Portuguese staff officer and was then promoted to lieutenant

---

* The minimum age for a commission was sixteen, but this did not apply to colonial regiments.

colonel in the British army. Present at most of the major battles of the Peninsular War, he stayed on the staff until 1814, when he took command of a Portuguese brigade for the last few battles in southern France. He was one of the military representatives with Wellington at the Congress of Vienna and was knighted in January 1815.

These, then, were the men who would plan and direct the coming campaign.

4

THE OFFICERS

Between the storming of the Bastille in July 1789 and 1793, when France declared war on just about everybody, 75 per cent of the officers of the pre-revolutionary French army had gone: executed or thrown into prison if they were unlucky, or having fled abroad if they were less so. Of the 300 generals, only five remained; they were viewed with grave suspicion and only one, Kellermann, survived into the Napoleonic period. Général de division Adam Philippe, comte de Custine, might have realized that his title would mark him out as a target for the class warriors of the Directorate. He had served in the royal army in the Seven Years War and in the American Revolutionary War and was governor of Toulon when the French Revolution broke out. When as commander of the Army of the North he was considered not to have acted with sufficient vigour against the Austrians in Belgium in 1793, he was recalled to Paris, accused of treason, and guillotined. His successor was Jean Nicolas Houchard, who had begun his military career at the age of sixteen in the Royal German Regiment and was noted for having put down an anti-French uprising in Corsica with considerable, and effective, brutality. Houchard defeated the Prince of Orange at Menen and the Duke of York at Dunkirk, but he too could not drive out the Austrians. Summoned to Paris, he met the same fate as his predecessor. While executing senior officers considered to have failed is one way of encouraging the others, as Voltaire put it, the result was a reluctance to do anything without orders from the centre and a further haemorrhaging to England or Prussia of pre-revolutionary officers. Killing generals was eventually seen to be counterproductive, as was the presence of representatives of the Committee for Public Safety with each army formation. These latter were there to ensure the loyalty of the army but, having no military experience, they frequently interfered and were often themselves responsible for disasters, for which, of course, they blamed the generals.

With the exception of a very few officers of the old royal army who survived the excesses of the Terror, there was no pool of trained leaders for the army of the republic. The solution was to promote senior NCOs who had served the Bourbons, and volunteers of the various revolutionary armies and militias who had exhibited some talent. Napoleon as First Consul reopened the military colleges, but while these would churn out a plentiful supply of second lieutenants, it would be many years before there could be a fully trained officer corps, and in the meantime the army would rely on ex-sergeants.

Napoleon created twenty-six marshals, the corps and army commanders. Of this number, eleven had been Other Ranks in the royal army, seven had begun their military careers as volunteers in revolutionary formations, and only eight had already been officers before the Revolution, and of those only one, the aforementioned Kellermann, had been a senior officer. Sergeants and captains are essential – you cannot run an army without them – but they are not interchangeable. In very broad terms, officers form policy and direct it, while sergeants carry it out. The training, mindset and experience of officers and sergeants are very different, and with rare exceptions they cannot easily do each other's jobs. Not only were the bulk of the French army's senior officers in 1815 ex-NCOs, but also there was no pool of trained staff officers, the military managers who ensure that a campaign runs as the commander wishes or hopes. French marshals – and French officers – displayed great personal bravery and were afraid of nothing, but they often lacked strategic and tactical awareness and were unable to detach themselves from the immediate situation to look at the bigger picture. It was this lack of trained staff officers that was the major weakness of the Napoleonic army.

André Masséna was a typical Napoleonic promotion. Born in 1758, the son of a small shopkeeper, he was orphaned at an early age, became a cabin boy on board a merchant ship and then enlisted in the Bourbon army aged seventeen in 1775. After fourteen years' service, he was the equivalent of a company sergeant major. He left the regular army on the outbreak of the Revolution and was elected lieutenant colonel of volunteers, while manning a vegetable stall and engaging in a little smuggling on the side. By 1793 Masséna was *général de brigade* and came to the attention of Napoleon in Italy when he was promoted to *général de division*. He became a marshal in 1804. He fought in numerous campaigns in northern Europe and in Portugal and Spain, with great gallantry but little finesse. At the Battle of Busaco in Portugal on 27 September 1810, he persisted in throwing divisions up a steep escarpment against Wellington's Anglo-Portuguese troops well sited in a prepared defensive position. Each time Masséna's men were thrown back in confusion, and each time he would send them back again. He made no attempt to avoid frontal attacks by manoeuvring to a flank and the result was overwhelming defeat. Similarly, at Fuentes d'Onoro in May 1811 his only thought was to mount headlong attacks, and when he eventually realized that he could turn Wellington's right flank, it was too late – another defeat.

At regimental level, too, in 1815 ex-NCOs were well represented among the captains and majors, many of them ex-NCOs of the Napoleonic, rather than the royalist, army, for every man in the former genuinely did have a marshal's baton in his knapsack if he survived and he was good enough. Here the problem was less acute as the company and battalion commanders had simply to obey orders, and the scope for individual initiative was limited. Typical of these men was Captain Jean-Roch Coignet. Born in poverty in 1776, he dabbled in horse-coping before enlisting in 1779. A corporal in 1807, a sergeant in 1809 and, having taught himself to read and write, commissioned as a second lieutenant (*sous lieutenant*) in 1812, Coignet fought in forty-eight battles, survived the retreat from Moscow and, now a captain, was wagon-master (transport officer) at Napoleon's headquarters for the Waterloo campaign.[8] There were many like him.

Napoleon's chief of staff was, as we have seen, an ex-sergeant, Soult. As his deputy and operational commander, he had Michel Ney, born, like so many players in this campaign, in 1769, the second son of a barrel-maker. Ney enlisted in the royalist Colonel Général des Hussards regiment in 1787 and was promoted to the equivalent of regimental sergeant major in 1792, the year before King Louis was sent to the guillotine. Commissioned later in the same year as a *sous lieutenant* and then elected as a captain of volunteers, he was a brigadier in 1796, a major general in 1799 and a marshal in 1804. As a fighter of battles, he was hugely experienced:

he was wounded five times, had been a prisoner of war of the Austrians, and commanded the rearguard in the dreadful retreat from Russia in 1812. He led the group of marshals that persuaded Napoleon to abdicate in 1814. Known to his soldiers as *Le Rougeaud* because of his red hair, he was a superb battalion, brigade and even divisional commander, but he lacked the intellectual capacity to manage a major campaign.

Napoleon's corps commanders for the Waterloo campaign were Major Generals Jean-Baptiste Drouet, comte d'Erlon, commanding I Corps, fifty years old, an ex-corporal of the royalist army who had been elected captain in 1793 by revolutionary volunteers; Honoré Charles Reille, II Corps, forty, who at fourteen had become a private in the National Guard; Dominique Vandamme, III Corps, forty-five, a sergeant in the royalist army when the Revolution broke out (it was he of whom Napoleon remarked that, if there were two of him, he would order one to hang the other); Étienne Maurice Gérard, IV Corps, forty-two, who had joined the Revolution as a volunteer in 1791; Georges Mouton, comte de Lobau, VI Corps, forty-five, who was one of fourteen children of a baker and who had enlisted as a private at the onset of the Revolution; Rémi Joseph Isidore Exelmans, II Cavalry Corps, forty, who had enlisted as a private aged sixteen in 1791; François Étienne Kellermann, III Reserve Cavalry Corps, forty-five, and the son of Marshal Kellermann, the only pre-revolutionary general to have prospered under the republic and empire; and Édouard Jean-Baptiste Milhaud, IV Reserve Cavalry Corps, thirty-nine, the son of a peasant who had been elected *sous lieutenant* during the Revolution. Initially more a politician than a soldier, Milhaud called for the death of the king, became an enthusiastic exponent of the Terror and a protégé of Marat, and was lucky not to go down with Robespierre. He was very much part of the coup that brought Napoleon to power as First Consul, after which he concentrated on matters military and, perhaps surprisingly given his background, became one of the more competent cavalry commanders. Commanding the artillery was Major General Charles Étienne François Ruty, forty-one, an officer cadet at the artillery school who had been commissioned in 1793 and spent his entire career in the artillery.

All these men were enormously experienced; they had fought all over Europe and bore the scars of numerous battles. They genuinely believed in Napoleon, were tremendously brave and had great personal charisma, but most were terrified of their commander-in-chief and emperor, were reluctant to deviate from orders once issued, even when it became obvious that the situation had changed, and lacked the training and education to take a strategic view rather than an immediate, tactical one. The officers of Napoleon's army during the Waterloo campaign were therefore a mix of senior officers who had happily turned their coats twice, those on half-pay or no pay who had been discharged upon the restoration, a few who had managed to avoid being discharged, and the cadets at officer schools who were commissioned on Napoleon's return after only one month's training. The senior officers could, and did, argue that on his abdication Napoleon had released them from their oath of loyalty to him, but this did not cut much ice with those more junior officers who had been unemployed for eleven months, and there was an underlying current of mistrust, which often meant that genuine errors, accidents or incompetence were presumed to be treachery.

While the French army of Napoleon was classless, the same was not true of the British army. There, most commissions and promotions in the cavalry and infantry, up to and including the rank of lieutenant colonel, were obtained by purchase, a system that continued until 1871. While it may appear scandalous to modern eyes that command of the king's soldiers could be obtained by buying it, the system was not as iniquitous as it might seem. The logic was similar to that applied to someone joining the board of a trading company, when he would be expected to buy shares in that company. While the origins of purchase are obscure, it seems to have begun to be formalized after the restoration of Charles II, when the raising, training and equipping of regiments was farmed out to notables, who in order to recoup their outlay offered commissions in those regiments for a fee. By 1815 it had long been regulated by the state, rather than by individuals. It was the army that had executed King Charles I, the army that had brought his son back from exile and the army that had deposed James II. Purchase gave the officer a stake in the system and a commitment to the existing order, which he was therefore less likely to attempt to overthrow, and it prevented the king from packing the army with his favourites, as James II had tried to do.* In theory at least, the purchase system prevented parliamentary manipulation of the army, but as many senior officers were also members of parliament, interference by ministers or patrons could not be discounted entirely.

The Duke of York, second son of King George III, had an inglorious career as a field commander, but this was not by any means all his own fault, and when his father appointed him commander-in-chief of the British army, against the advice of most

---

* It did him little good. John Churchill, later first duke of Marlborough, who was raised from obscurity by James, made a general and given all sorts of financially rewarding sinecures, turned on his master once it was to his advantage to do so.

of its generals, he became one of the great military reformers. In the Flanders campaign of 1793–5 he had been painfully aware of the ills besetting the army and, once ensconced in Horse Guards,* he began to put them right. There would be no more child colonels: modern godfathers lay down a pipe of port for their godsons (or given the price, more probably a bottle); then it was not uncommon to buy a lieutenant colonelcy. For some time the minimum age for a commission, widely ignored, was sixteen; now it would be enforced, with an upper age limit of eighteen.† Applications for commissions would be made to the commander-in-chief through his military secretary, a serving officer, rather than, as previously, through the Secretary at War, a political appointee who was often notoriously corrupt. There would be a laid-down length of time that an officer had to serve in one rank before purchasing the next one, and military colleges would be opened, even if hardly anyone went to them.

A young man wishing to join the army as an officer had to be able to read and write to a reasonable standard and be certified by an officer of the rank of major or above, or by a magistrate or a person of similar standing, as being suitable in all respects to hold a commission – an oblique way of ensuring that the candidate did not eat peas with his knife. Armed with his references, the young gentleman applied to the military secretary and was placed on a waiting list. Once a vacancy occurred, whether by death, retirement or promotion, then the young aspirant was required

---

* Army headquarters and the office of the commander-in-chief, so called because the building looked on to Horse Guards Parade in London.
† Today the minimum age for entry to the Royal Military Academy Sandhurst is eighteen, and the maximum, with a few exceptions, is twenty-six.

to lodge the laid-down price of an ensigncy (for the infantry) or a cornetcy (for the cavalry) with an accredited agent. There were around seventeen agents – the number fluctuated slightly – each responsible for a group of regiments, and in addition to dealing with the purchase of commissions they administered regimental funds, ensured that officers and men got paid, and managed any other financial transactions affecting the regiment. For purchase they were the stake-holders. If the vacancy arose because an existing holder of a first commission was promoted, then the agent credited that officer's account and the candidate was 'gazetted' as a commissioned officer – that is, his name was listed in the *London Gazette*, which since 1665 has been (and still is) the British government's official journal of record in which certain statutory notices must appear.

Once in post, an officer could then, subject to certain restrictions, purchase his way up the ladder until reaching the rank of lieutenant colonel. He could only purchase a promotion if there was a vacancy; he had to be certified by his commanding officer as fit for promotion, and the Duke of York had laid down that an officer must serve at least two years as a subaltern (ensign/cornet and lieutenant) before being promoted to captain, and that he must have at least six years' commissioned service before becoming a major.* By 1809 this had been further extended to three years as a subaltern, seven years' service before promotion to major, including at least two as a

---

* Today, again with a few exceptions for specialists or officers commissioned from the ranks, an officer will spend five years as a subaltern (second lieutenant and lieutenant), and on average a further five as a captain before promotion to major. There are examinations for promotion to captain and to major, and officers for promotion to major are selected by a board. University graduates spend only two-and-a-half years as subalterns.

captain, and nine years' service to lieutenant colonel. When a vacancy occurred in a regiment, it was first offered to the most senior in that regiment of the rank below. If that officer wished to and could afford to purchase, then he lodged the difference – 'the step' – between his existing commission and the one he was to be promoted to with the agent and was duly gazetted in his new rank. If, for example, a major either retired or purchased a lieutenant colonelcy, then the senior captain could move up to major, the senior lieutenant to captain and the senior ensign or cornet to lieutenant. If the senior did not wish or could not afford to purchase, then the vacancy was offered to the next senior and so on. If no one could purchase, then the vacancy could go outside the regiment. However, despite the experience of the young Arthur Wesley, promotions were more usually kept within the regiment – although the Duke of York reserved the right to appoint commanding officers from the pool of available lieutenant colonels.

It was possible for an officer to change regiments by swapping places with an officer of the same rank in another regiment, although both now went to the bottom of the seniority list of their rank in their new regiment. Very often the exchange would be motivated by one officer not wishing to serve in a particular station whither his regiment was to be posted, while the incomer might want to serve there or, more likely, have accepted a sum of money to agree to the exchange. When an officer retired, he could 'sell out' and in doing so realize the full value of his commission and thus provide himself with a capital sum to invest or live off.

The cost of commissions and subsequent promotions varied between arms of the service. The Foot Guards were the most expensive, followed by the Household Cavalry, which was more expensive than the line cavalry, who cost more than the line infantry. The official rates in force at the time of Waterloo were as follows:[9]

Rank	Foot Guards		Household Cavalry		Line cavalry		Line infantry	
	Full price	Step	Full price	Step	Full price	Step	Full price	Step
Lieutenant colonel	£6,700	£400	£5,200	£950	£5,350	£1,100	£3,500	£900
Major	£6,300	£3,300	£4,250	£1,150	£4,250	£1,100	£2,600	£1,100
Captain	£3,000	£1,500	£3,100	£1,350	£3,150	£1,785	£1,500	£950
Lieutenant	£1,500	£600	£1,750	£150	£1,365	£262.50	£550	£150
Ensign (inf) Cornet (cav)	£900	£900	£1,600	£1,600	£1102.50	£1102.50	£400	£400

These sums mean little unless we can relate them to salaries at the time and to present-day prices. Army pay at the time was expressed as a daily rate (as it still is) and the annual salaries for officers of the line infantry were:

Lieutenant colonel	£369.56
Major	£310
Captain	£191.62
Lieutenant	£118.62
Ensign	£95.81

Officers of the Guards and the cavalry got higher pay than those of the more humble line. In 1815 a Guards lieutenant got £142.71 per annum compared to the lieutenant of the line's £118.62. Between 1793 and 1815 the pay of the Guards, the cavalry and lieutenant colonels of the line remained unchanged, while other officers of the line saw their pay raised by almost 50 per cent for subalterns, 11 per cent for captains and 20 per cent for majors.

A comparison with income tax may provide an indication of the real worth of these salaries. Income tax was introduced by Prime Minister William Pitt in 1799 to pay for the war, with the promise that the tax would be for ever abolished after it.* It was agreed that only the

---

* Ho ho.

comfortably off should pay it, and anyone earning less than £60 per annum was exempt. At £60 it started at two old pence in the pound, a rate of 0.83 per cent, and increased gradually until those earning £200 and above paid two shillings in the pound, or 10 per cent. Thus it can be seen that the lieutenant and the captain are not badly off, while majors and above could be described as well off.

The total net outlay of £3,500 to reach the rank of lieutenant colonel (spread over a number of years) equated to 9.47 years' salary in that rank. The same number of years' salary in that rank in 2012 would be £668,213, a huge sum even if lieutenant colonels today are (slightly) better paid in real terms than their nineteenth-century equivalents. Thus, another role of the army agents was to lend money to officers to purchase first commissions or promotions. The interest to be paid on the sum borrowed depended upon how secure the loan was thought to be: in peacetime the surety was the officer's commission, but as the commission was not an inheritable property and died with the holder, rates in wartime were higher. The bank base rate throughout the period we are interested in was 5 per cent,[10] so it is reasonable to estimate an interest rate of, say, 6 per cent in peacetime and perhaps 10 per cent in war. To repay this in time of peace was of course possible, but far from easy, and many officers languished as lieutenants and captains unable to find the wherewithal to progress further. In wartime there were opportunities to amass riches legally by taking part in the successful capture of an enemy town or fortress or baggage train. Any monies or saleable property captured were divided up, with the major portion going to the state and the rest divided pro rata among the captors, rather in the way of prize money in the Royal Navy. In 1799 Colonel Arthur Wellesley commanded the reserve brigade in the storming of Seringapatam in the Second Mysore War. His share of the booty was £4,000, more than enough to repay his various creditors who had loaned him the money to buy his way to lieutenant colonel.

A constant curse to those who had to administer the purchase system was the payment of 'over regulation' prices. Here an officer who wished to retire or purchase promotion would demand a sum in addition to the laid-down price. This was entirely illegal and the Duke of York laid down that any officer caught asking for or paying anything over the regulation price was, on conviction by court martial, to be cashiered and to lose his commission – and therefore be unable to realize any money by selling it – with half the value going to the informant. Despite this copper's nark's charter, the practice went on.

In October 1808 Lieutenant John Orrok, serving with the 33rd Foot in India, wrote to his father that a Major Quin had said that he would sell out provided that he got £5,000 in addition to the full price of his commission. The regulation price for a majority was £2,600 and the difference between a major's and a captain's commission, the step, was £1,100. Captain Lambton would contribute £3,000 on top of the step and would get the major's vacancy, while Orrok would find £2,000 over and above the step of £950 and get Lambton's captain's vacancy. Although Orrok was seventh in seniority of lieutenants, none of those above him could afford to purchase. Orrok did say that there was a lieutenant of the regiment, now in England, who did have the money, but as he had gone home under arrest, he was probably not a contender.[11] Despite the blatant illegality of this transaction, Orrok was encouraged to find the money by his commanding officer, Lieutenant Colonel Arthur Gore.* In contrast, Captain Robert

---

* Gore had taken over command of the 33rd from Arthur Wellesley, and as a major general was killed in March 1814 at Bergen op Zoom.

Crauford – 'Black Bob', the famous commander of the Light Division who, by then a major general, was killed at the storming of Ciudad Rodrigo in 1812 – was offered £2,500 on top of the regulation amount for his captaincy, which he refused, insisting that he would accept only that amount sanctioned by the sovereign.[12]

While purchase was the norm, there were all sorts of exceptions. There was no purchase in the Royal Artillery or the Royal Engineers. While officers of the infantry and cavalry might be expected to learn their trade as they went along, those who took charge of large amounts of explosive, either for putting in cannons or for blowing things up, and who needed to understand technical matters, like placing siege guns or building bridges, had to know what they were up to. Candidates for commissions in those arms therefore attended the Royal Military Academy at Woolwich, opened in 1741, for a course lasting between eighteen months and two years, engineers spending an extra six months. Candidates had to be between the ages of fourteen and sixteen on entry, be of a minimum height of 4 feet 9 inches, and be 'well grounded in vulgar fractions, able to write a good hand and have gone through the Latin Grammar'.[13] It was recommended, though not compulsory, that entrants should have some knowledge of the French language. Thereafter promotion was by strict seniority, which might seem a fairer system, but it had grave disadvantages, one being that, whereas purchase allowed men of real ability to rise to high rank while they were young enough and fit enough to do it justice, many of the artillery and engineer officers were, while not quite dribbling down their waistcoats, far too old, far too fat and far too unfit to be of much use. As officers of the Royal Artillery and Royal Engineers took their initial seniority as subalterns from their positions in the final examination before commissioning, a difference of one or two places could mean a wait of several years when it came to promotion – a powerful incentive to study. The problem of senior officers being far too old to be of much use meant that the officer who was in practice, if not in name, Wellington's artillery commander in the latter stages of the Peninsular War was Alexander Dickson, a 36-year-old substantive captain, local major and lieutenant colonel in the Portuguese army to give him some clout. The post would normally have been filled by an officer of at least major general's rank. Similarly, his chief engineer was Richard Fletcher, a major, local lieutenant colonel and finally a substantive lieutenant colonel before being killed at the siege of San Sebastián in 1813.*

First commissions might be granted free of purchase when new regiments were being raised, and an officer from the militia who transferred to the regular army bringing a set number of recruits with him might be granted a free commission.† Lieutenant John Kincaid, adjutant of the 1st Battalion 95th Rifles at Waterloo, a Scot who had been a lieutenant in the North Yorkshire Militia,

---

* Substantive rank was permanent and could not be taken away except by royal command. Acting rank gave the holder the pay and privileges of the rank, but he could be required to revert to his substantive (lower) rank if moved to a post not established for the higher. Local rank was granted for a specific purpose, sometimes short-lived, and carried the privileges but not the pay.

† The militia was a home defence force, intended to allow regular troops to be used abroad. Commissions were granted by the lord lieutenant of the county free of purchase, and the Other Ranks were compulsorily raised by ballot, to provide a laid-down number of Protestant men for each county. The last officer to avail himself of this method of joining the regular army was John French, later Field Marshal Earl French of Ypres, commander of the British Expeditionary force from 1914 to December 1915. He joined the Suffolk militia in 1870 with that in mind, although by the time he actually transferred, purchase had (just) been abolished and the requirement to bring recruits with him had long lapsed.

obtained a free commission in the 95th in 1809 as a second lieutenant by bringing volunteers for his militia unit with him.* Queen's pages – teenage sons of the gentry selected to wait upon the queen and carry her train on formal occasions – were granted free first commissions in the Guards, and free commissions were also awarded to those who excelled in the passing-out examination from the Royal Military College, which was located at Great Marlow from 1802 until 1812, when it moved to Sandhurst. Graduates of the college not granted free commissions took first priority for purchase. Orphans of officers killed in action could also be granted free first commissions at the discretion of the commander-in-chief.

A sergeant could be awarded a free first commission, either for gallantry or for continuous good service. Contrary to popular opinion now, there were quite a lot of them, and at Waterloo around 10 per cent of the officers at regimental duty had been commissioned from the ranks.† They were particularly in demand as adjutants in line battalions. Today the adjutant is the battalion staff officer, responsible for ensuring that the commanding officer's policy is put into practice as well as overseeing ceremonial and discipline. What is now ceremonial drill, where battalions form divisions, march past in column of companies and form into line before halting, was in 1815 tactics – the evolutions necessary on the battlefield to bring the unit to the right place at the right time and deliver maximum fire on the enemy. This required a knowledge of

---

* Kincaid's *Adventures in the Rifle Brigade* and *Random Shots of a Rifleman*, originally published in 1830 and 1835 and reprinted numerous times since, give some of the best accounts of soldiering in King George's army, from Walcheren to Waterloo.
† This is about the same percentage as is found in a battalion of British infantry of the line today: two quartermasters and the MTO (mechanical transport officer).

a large number of words of command and an ex-sergeant might often be much more knowledgeable of the commands and of the actions to be taken on them than an officer from a conventional background.

In wartime a commissioned ranker might progress up the ranks free of purchase by leading a forlorn hope. When a fort or a fortified town was being besieged, there were three ways for the attackers to gain entry: over, under or through. 'Over' meant escalade, the placing of ladders against the walls for the attacking troops to climb up – a very dangerous method if the defenders were at all awake – but it was by escalade that the first British troops went into Badajoz in 1812. 'Under' meant tunnelling under the walls and setting fire to the pit props, thus collapsing the tunnel and the walls above it – a long and difficult undertaking and usually impossible if the objective was built on rock, as Ciudad Rodrigo, taken in 1812, was. 'Through' meant hammering away at the walls with siege guns – 24- or 32-pounders – until a breach was created, through which the attackers could gain entry. Once a breach had been made and the engineers deemed it 'practicable' – which meant that it could be ascended by a soldier without using his hands – a small body of men was needed to seize and hold the breach to allow the main body to enter and take on the defending garrison. That body was known as the 'forlorn hope', an apt term from the Dutch *verloren hoop* ('lost hope'), and the officer commanding it was promoted one rank free of purchase if he survived, which he frequently did not. At Badajoz the last words of Major Peter O'Hare, 95th Rifles, as he led the forlorn hope against the breach, were: 'A lieutenant colonel or cold meat in a couple of hours.' For O'Hare it was cold meat, whereas the 22-year-old Lieutenant John Gurwood of the 52nd Light Infantry, who commanded the forlorn hope at Ciudad

Rodrigo, got away with a slight head wound, collected his captaincy and was with his regiment at Waterloo.*

Again, the commissioned sergeant might be promoted into a vacancy caused by death, but once peace was declared, very few had the money to progress further, and in the 1820s and 1830s there were numbers of very elderly lieutenants and captains who, because they had not bought their commissions, could not, under the rules then extant, sell them until they had completed twenty-five years' service. While on active service an ex-NCO could fit in and be respected for his knowledge and ability; in peacetime many found it difficult to fit into the officers' mess and, according to evidence given by Wellington to a committee of inquiry in 1842, many turned to drink.

Another method of obtaining a free commission was 'recruiting for rank', whereby a man who raised a company's worth of men was granted a captain's commission. Only resorted to when the army was desperate for recruits (in other words, quite often), it was highly unpopular among officers who were already in the service, as it allowed the new entrant to supersede all those already holding lieutenant's and ensign's rank. Meanwhile, a somewhat last-gasp approach to getting a free commission was to enlist as a gentleman volunteer. These were young men, unable to raise the money for a commission or to obtain a free one, who served as private soldiers without pay (although messing with the officers) in the hope of showing sufficient ability to obtain an ensign's vacancy arising by death. In time of peace this was not, of course, a swift

---

* In 1837, as a retired colonel, he published the collected despatches of the Duke of Wellington, twelve volumes plus an index – an enormous task, the strain of which was thought to have been the cause of his suicide in 1845.

method of becoming an officer and there appear to have been very few, if any, such men still in the army at Waterloo.

A peculiarity of the system was the holding of double rank by officers of the Guards, who as the monarch's personal troops held both regimental rank and army rank. This meant that captains in the Guards who were serving with their regiments were company commanders and paid as captains; when employed outside the regiment, however, they were lieutenant colonels and treated and paid as such. Similarly lieutenants were captains or majors in the army, depending upon seniority, and ensigns lieutenants, while majors were colonels in the army and lieutenant colonels major generals. This can be confusing, as it is often said that 'six Guards lieutenant colonels were killed at Waterloo', whereas there were but four battalions of Guards at Waterloo, and a battalion is commanded by a lieutenant colonel. In fact one of these lieutenant colonels was a captain by regimental rank and an ADC to Wellington, while the other five were company commanders in their Guards battalions with the regimental rank of captain. Double rank was abolished in 1871 as part of the series of army reforms undertaken by Edward Cardwell, Gladstone's Secretary for War from 1870 to 1874.

As commissions and promotions were strictly regulated by Horse Guards, the only influence over promotion a commander in the field could have was when an officer was killed in action and when he sent an officer home carrying despatches. As a commission was not inheritable property and died with the holder, the vacancy could be filled free of purchase, and custom dictated that, when this happened on active service, the local commander of the forces could fill it with a deserving officer of his choice. Technically the commander could promote anyone, provided he was qualified by time and recommendation, but in practice it usually went to the next senior. The more senior the deceased officer was, of course, the more free promotions flowed from his death, hence the regular toast in officers' messes was (and still is) 'Here's to a sudden plague and a bloody war'. While such promotions had to be approved by Horse Guards, approval was hardly ever withheld. After a successful battle the commander-in-chief would write a detailed report of the action, which would be taken back to England and delivered to the government and the king. By tradition the officer bearing the despatch received a promotion of one rank, free of purchase, and commanders would usually select a promising officer who lacked the cash to buy his next rank.

Once an officer reached the rank of lieutenant colonel, there was no more purchase and promotion was strictly by seniority. Provided a man lived long enough, he would become a general, although this is not as serious as it might appear, for while he might achieve high rank, he was not necessarily employed, and if he was not employed, he did not draw the pay. Before Wellesley's first foray to the Peninsula in 1808 he was a major general. The government, and Horse Guards, considered that the expedition merited a lieutenant general in command. There were, however, twenty-eight major generals senior to Wellesley, and the seniority principle was sacred, in that it removed any possibility of patronage or corruption. The answer was to promote them all, which happened, and to employ but a few – indeed, only Henry Lord Paget, a cavalry officer and later the Marquess of Anglesey, was to play any major part in the war.* The important thing was to get to

---

* He wrote an excellent history of the British cavalry, a task repeated by his present descendant, George Charles Henry Victor Paget, Marquess of Anglesey (*A History of the British Cavalry, 1816–1919*, 8 vols, Leo Cooper, London, 1973–96).

lieutenant colonel as fast as possible, which with luck and ability would ensure employment as a more senior officer when young enough to exercise command as such.

Again contrary to modern popular opinion, the officers of Wellington's army (or more properly King George's army) were not drawn from the aristocracy. With the exception of the Guards and a few of the smarter cavalry regiments, the bulk of the officers were of the middle classes. They were not the products of the public schools (that comes in the Victorian era) nor of the universities; rather, they were educated in grammar schools and the sons of professional men: doctors, lawyers, clerks in holy orders,* minor landed gentry. Around 20 per cent of all officers in the period 1790 to 1830 were Scottish, which had very little do with the martial qualities of the Scots – great though those may well be – but a great deal to do with education in Scotland being much better than that in England.† A survey conducted in 1818, after Waterloo but still probably relevant to the period, looked, inter alia, at the occupations of army officers' fathers and found that the largest of the groups of occupations featured was that of army officer, so in a sense army officers were members of a self-perpetuating oligarchy.

A cursory look at the Army List for 1815 appears to negate the statement that officers were not of the nobility. Many generals are peers, most colonels are knights, but with a few exceptions, peerages and knighthoods were earned by military service, rather as Junker status originally was in Prussia. A colonel would often be knighted or awarded the Commander of the Order of the Bath

---

* This author has always been puzzled by the number of sons of the clergy who became officers then and still do so today – perhaps it is a reaction to turning the other cheek and not swearing.
† Some things don't change.

(CB), while a major general would certainly be knighted and a successful general elevated to the peerage. Colonel Wellesley became Colonel Sir Arthur Wellesley KB (Knight of the Order of the Bath) in September 1804; Lieutenant General Sir Arthur Wellesley became Viscount Wellington of Talavera in August 1809; as a general he became Earl Wellington in February 1812 and Marquis Wellington in September of the same year, and as a field marshal he became the Duke of Wellington in May 1814.

Many officers were Roman Catholics. While Catholics had been permitted to join the army as Other Ranks since 1741 (and did join long before that), they were still debarred by law from holding any 'office of profit under the crown', which meant that they could not hold commissions in the Royal Navy or the army and could not become members of parliament or civil servants. These laws had been in force since the so-called Glorious Revolution of 1688, when the Catholic king, James II, had been deposed and replaced by his daughter Mary and son-in-law William of Orange, who were Protestant.*

The army, however, was a pragmatic organization that wanted men who could do the business, and if these happened to be Catholics, well, that was fine provided that they did not make it too obvious. Every few years an act of indemnity would be passed

---

* It is this author's view that, despite the restrictions flowing from the Test Acts and the Act of Succession, England was not anti-Catholic, but anti-foreign, which is not the same thing. The Reformation of the 1530s was much more to do with control – who ruled England, the king or the pope? – than theology and was only the culmination of a centuries-old English suspicion of a French-dominated papacy. What did for James was not his Catholicism – his immediate successors were protestants – but his production of a son late in life out of his Catholic second wife, Mary of Modena, giving rise to a fear of a foreign-dominated succession. There has, after all, only ever been one English pope.

through parliament indemnifying the army for breaking the law by commissioning Catholics, usually put through in the dead of night when not many MPs were about and tacked onto some piece of legislation on a subject that nobody was interested in, such as whatever was then the equivalent of renewable energy. Thus, as one of the few outlets for a Catholic gentleman was the army, there developed in Catholic families and Catholic schools a tradition of finding officers for the army – a tradition that continues to this day, although there is now, of course, no bar to Catholics holding any office except that of prime minister and monarch. In 2012 Roman Catholics made up just over 8 per cent of the population of the United Kingdom, but 20 per cent of the officers of the army, with Downside, Douai, Ampleforth, Stoneyhurst and other Catholic schools providing a steady stream of Sandhurst entrants.

Anachronistic though it seems to us now – as it did to some even then – the British system did produce an effective officer corps. Of course there were idle officers, incompetent officers, even cowardly officers, but they were very few and by 1815 had mostly been weeded out, either by peer pressure, persuasion, movement to non-operational theatres or – rarely – outright sacking.* In the early days of the Peninsular War there had even been cases of officers who were not trusted being found dead after a battle with a musket ball in the back. The men who became officers had been brought up to believe that they were destined to lead – in society, in politics, in the church, in the management of estates or in the army – and it would never have occurred to them that they were not meant to

---

* Sacking was difficult because a commission was personal property that could not easily be taken away. In Spain even Wellington was reluctant to dismiss senior officers he considered incompetent, often asking the Duke of York to find them another job in Britain or Ireland.

do so. They had an inbuilt self-belief, and in an age when very few Jacks considered themselves as good as their masters, the social class system was replicated in the officer–man relationship in the army. British general officers were more able to think strategically than their French equivalents because their mental horizons were not constrained by time spent in the ranks or – at least in the early days of the Revolution – by fear of execution if they got things wrong. Similarly, Wellington's junior officers were less dependent upon the army to make a living than were their French opposite numbers, and were thus more prepared to use their initiative, even if this often merited a stern rebuke from the duke. Furthermore, an examination of the origins and backgrounds of British army officers in the years running up to Waterloo shows that they were exactly the same kind of people who join as officers now, the difference being that today's officers get there after rigorous selection and intensive training, and at a much older age, and do not get knighted unless they are very senior indeed.*

The British army had never been large enough to need the corps level of command – the commander in the field could easily command the limited number of divisions directly – but now that Wellington was to command an Allied army – one that included Dutch-Belgians, Hanoverians and others – it was divided into three corps. Two corps would be largely infantry with artillery in support, and the third would include all the cavalry. Wellington appointed the Prince of Orange to command I Corps, thus fulfilling the agreement with the king of the Netherlands that his son would have a senior command. This was the corps that

---

* Today around one in three lieutenant generals (of whom there are few) receives a knighthood. In 1815 all active lieutenant generals in the Army List were knights of one sort or another.

Wellington considered would do most of the fighting and where he himself would spend most of his time: the duke was well aware of the prince's inexperience and had no intention of allowing him to do anything on his own initiative.

To command II Corps Wellington selected Lieutenant General Lord Hill. A Shropshire man, Rowland Hill (Baron Hill since the end of hostilities in 1814) was forty-three in 1815 and one of sixteen children, six of whom, including himself, served in the war, in either the British or the Portuguese service. He purchased an ensign's commission in the 38th Foot in 1790, aged eighteen. The following year he became a lieutenant by purchase and in 1792 transferred to the 53rd Foot, being promoted to captain without purchase in 1793, having raised an independent infantry company. In 1794 he assisted Thomas Graham,* later General Lord Lyndoch, in the raising of the 90th Foot, and became a major and then the commanding officer of the battalion as a lieutenant colonel, both promotions free of purchase. A colonel in 1798 and a major general in 1805, he served in Egypt and on Sir John Moore's staff, and commanded a brigade in the rearguard during the evacuation from Corunna. He joined Wellesley's army in Portugal in 1809 and served throughout the

---

* Graham, born in 1748, was a Scottish landowner whose wife was painted by Gainsborough. He had no connection with the army until he took his wife to the continent for her health, where she died in 1792 (probably of 'consumption' – tuberculosis). His resentment at the treatment of his wife's coffin by drunken French revolutionaries fanned a spark of military interest into a flame of patriotism, and he raised the 90th Regiment at his own expense, for which he became its colonel – a temporary commission. Despite his taking part in several campaigns, Horse Guards would not deviate from the rules and refused to make his commission permanent. Only after his performance on the retreat to Corunna and a supposedly dying wish expressed by Sir John Moore did the Duke of York relent and Graham became a major general in 1810, backdated to 1803. He was a very competent divisional commander under Wellington in the Peninsula.

war, first as a brigade and then as a divisional commander. His concern for the welfare of his men and his disapproval of strong language led to the nickname 'Daddy Hill', which was something of a misnomer, as while he was certainly assiduous in looking after his troops, he could also be ruthless in pursuit of a military objective. A lieutenant general in 1811, knighted in 1812 and ennobled in 1814, he was one of the few generals whom Wellington trusted in an independent command, knowing that he would adhere strictly to the instructions given him and not divert on a private frolic of his own – something that far too many officers had been inclined to do, although by now most had learned the folly of interpreting the duke's orders to suit their own preferences.

Commanding the cavalry corps was Lieutenant General the Earl of Uxbridge. Despite his title, he was not the scion of a long line of noble ancestors; he was born Henry William Bayly in 1768, eldest of twelve children, inheriting the title of Baron Paget from a distant relative, changing his name and being elevated to the earldom of Uxbridge in 1784. On the outbreak of war with France, he raised a regiment, the 80th Foot, mainly from his own Welsh tenants, and purchased his way rapidly through the permanent ranks, becoming a lieutenant colonel in 1795 when he was twenty-seven and in command of the 7th Light Dragoons. Despite his meteoric rise to the command of a regiment, he showed real ability – not always the prerogative of cavalry commanders of the time – and had some experience, having commanded an infantry brigade in Flanders in 1794, as the (temporary) colonel of the regiment he had raised. He did well under Sir John Moore in Spain and in the retreat to Corunna, and along with another cavalryman from the Welsh borders, Sir Stapleton Cotton (later Field Marshal Viscount Combermere), was probably the most competent cavalry commander of the time. That he did not serve under Wellesley/Wellington in the Peninsula is often attributed to his having deserted his own wife and run off with that of Wellington's younger brother, a great scandal at the time, but is more likely due to his being senior to Wellington.* By 1815, when Wellington had become a field marshal and Uxbridge was still a lieutenant general, that difficulty no longer applied.

To command the artillery Wellington would have liked to have had one of his Peninsular artillery commanders, but none was available and he got Colonel Sir George Adam Wood.† Wood graduated from the Royal Military Academy at Woolwich at the age of fourteen in 1781, and it is indicative of a system where promotion was by strict seniority rather than by purchase that, despite serving in numerous campaigns with distinction, he remained a second lieutenant for nine years, a lieutenant for ten, and a captain for six until finally reaching the rank of lieutenant colonel in 1808, aged forty-one and after twenty-seven years' commissioned service. He was knighted in 1812 and, having served in the north European campaigns of 1813 and 1814, was promoted to brevet colonel.‡ As

---

* Both became major generals in 1802 and lieutenant generals in 1808, but Uxbridge was five places higher up the list (although he might have had to wait a lot longer had Horse Guards not wanted to promote Wellesley and thus all those major generals senior to him).

† Dickson, his preferred artillery officer, was in America but did get back just in time for Waterloo. As he had perforce reverted to his substantive rank of captain, he was but the second-in-command of a troop (battery) of six guns at the battle – somewhat of a comedown after commanding 8,000 men, 4,000 horses and 200 guns in the Peninsula. Wellington did, though, give him command of the siege train that supported the Prussians in the advance into France after Waterloo.

‡ Brevet promotion was a way of recognizing ability: the man got the rank and the allowances (but not the pay) but remained employed in posts of his previous rank (in this case lieutenant colonel). It was abolished in the British army in the early 1960s.

Wellington did not know Wood and anyway had decided views on artillery, Commander Royal Artillery in fact had little discretion.

The Prussian army did things differently. Prior to the post-Jena reforms, although there was no purchase, commissions in the army were restricted to Germans of noble families, and for the Junker class it was compulsory for their sons to serve in the army. In the reformed army, however, commissions were open to all candidates of merit, thus giving the middle classes, hitherto excluded, a stake in the system. In reality, patronage and family connections did count a great deal, but the Prussian training system ensured that officers did by and large know their business, and indeed it was the officer corps that held together an otherwise very inexperienced army during the Waterloo campaign. Unlike any other army of the time, the Prussians paid serious attention to the training of staff officers, and, although the Great General Staff was not formed until 1814, staff training had been going on in earnest at the Academy for Young Officers of the Infantry and Cavalry in Berlin since 1808. Graduates of the academy were posted as 'adjutants' – staff officers – to every formation and would become, as von Moltke would enunciate in a later era, the nervous system of the army. As during the French occupation the Prussians were forbidden to form divisions, they had very large brigades – between eight and ten battalions, compared to the British three or four – with commanders selected by seniority. This latter was not as deadening as it may sound, for admission to the higher ranks of the Prussian army (colonel and above) was dependent upon education.

For the Waterloo campaign the Prussian army took under its wing the armies of other north German states, many of which had been occupied by the French for many years and were now absorbed by Prussia. Not all were happy to be under Prussian command – indeed, the Rhinelanders, who thought themselves the most cultured of Germans, considered the Prussians as not far short of barbarians – and the Saxon contingent would cause so much trouble that it would be sent home long before the battles.

Blücher's army was divided into four large corps. I Corps was commanded by Lieutenant General (*Generalleutnant*) Hans Ernst Karl von Ziethen. Forty-five years old, he had proved himself both as a cavalry leader and as a staff officer (for which he was promoted early to major). He was a colonel at Jena, a major general from 1813 and a lieutenant general in 1815. The holder of the *Pour le Mérite*,* the highest military honour, and the Iron Cross (both first and second classes),† he was one of the few senior officers not to be downgraded after the disasters of 1806.

Major General Georg Dubislav Ludwig Pirch commanded II Corps, and is usually known, in the Prussian fashion, as Pirch I, to distinguish him from his younger brother, Pirch II, who was a brigade commander in I Corps. Born in Magdeburg in 1763, Pirch came from a long line of officers of the Prussian army. An ensign in 1780, captain in 1795 and major in 1797, he had spent most of his time up to then on the staff, which partly explains his

---

* Founded by Frederick the Great in 1740, the *Pour le Mérite* was awarded to military officers for 'exceptional personal achievement'. It is often (erroneously) compared to the Victoria Cross, which can only be awarded for gallantry in the face of the enemy. A civil version was instituted in 1842, which is still extant. The military version died with the abdication of the last Hohenzollern king-emperor in 1918.
† Founded by Frederick William III of Prussia in 1813 as a gallantry award, it was abolished, along with all other German military decorations, in 1945. Recent attempts by the German army to reinstate it have failed, due to (incorrect) allegations that it was a Nazi medal. If only people would study history…

slow promotion to captain (when he was thirty-two), although it is unclear whether this was due to commanders not wanting to lose their staff captain (which they would if he was promoted) or because he had not had the opportunity of showing what he could do in command of troops in the field. He was captured at Jena in 1806 and spent two years as a prisoner of war, before being promoted to lieutenant colonel on release and given command of a regiment. He was a colonel in 1812 and became a major general in 1813. Holder of the *Pour le Mérite* and both classes of the Iron Cross, he took command of the corps in May 1815 when the previous commander, Lieutenant General Ludwig von Borstell, was court-martialled and sacked for protesting about the treatment of mutinous Saxon troops.

The commander of III Corps was Lieutenant General Freiherr Johann Adolf von Thielemann. A Saxon born in Dresden in 1765, he had the distinction of attracting praise for fighting both for Napoleon and against him. When Saxony opposed France until 1806, Thielemann, who had joined the Saxon army in 1782, fought the French, and when Saxony allied herself to France in 1806, he fought for France, being promoted from colonel to major general and then lieutenant general in the same year, 1810. He led a cavalry brigade at Borodino in the Russian campaign of 1812, drawing high praise from Napoleon and the award of *Freiherr* from the king of Saxony. In 1813 he obeyed the orders of his king and handed his troops over to the French, but he himself decamped to the Prussians and fought for them in the 1813 and 1814 campaigns, before becoming a lieutenant general in the Prussian army in 1815.

IV Corps was commanded by one of the most senior generals in the Prussian army. Junior only to Blücher in Flanders and senior to Gneisenau, the chief of staff, General (*General der Infanterie*)

Friedrich Wilhelm Bülow, Graf von Dennewitz, was born in 1755 and joined the Prussian army as a cadet aged thirteen, and was commissioned in 1773. Twenty years later he was still a captain, but when war came and he won the *Pour le Mérite*, he started to move up. A colonel commanding a regiment (equivalent to a British brigade) in 1807, a major general in 1808 and a lieutenant general in 1813 commanding a brigade, in 1814 he was made a general by the king of Prussia, who also ennobled him as *Graf*. He was known as a fine military commander but excessively direct, lacking in tact, forthright in his views and quick-tempered, which would not make him easy for Gneisenau to deal with. Oddly, perhaps, as the characteristics would not seem complementary, he was a noted musician.

The Prussians had huge problems in finding sufficient cavalry for the campaign, particularly finding enough horses. Inevitably, horse-copers doubled their prices once they knew that the army was interested, and at one stage the Prussians had to threaten Polish vendors that, unless they charged a reasonable price, their horses would be commandeered.* Partly as a result of this there was no Prussian heavy cavalry in the Army of the Lower Rhine, only light dragoons, hussars and uhlans (lancers). Prussian organization tables gave each corps a cavalry brigade (these, like the infantry brigades, were much larger than their British equivalents) and each infantry brigade usually had two squadrons under command for scouting and escort duties. There was thus no central cavalry reserve available to Blücher in the way that there was to Napoleon

---

* The Poles always had a soft spot for Napoleon and provided him with some of his best troops. He was the first to give them a constitution and, although the Grand Duchy of Warsaw was a French client state, it gave the Poles a lot more independence than they had had hitherto.

and Wellington. Unsurprisingly, the Prussians also had problems in finding enough horses for their artillery, but the command was exercised by an experienced officer, 36-year-old Prince Friedrich Wilhelm Heinrich August of Prussia, a cousin of the king who, as part of the root-and-branch reform of the Prussian army, had been responsible for the modernization of the artillery arm.

An interesting aspect of Prussian, and later German, militarism (and had Mark Brandenburg and Prussia not been militaristic, they would not have survived) can be garnered by looking at the names of the Prussian commanders at regimental level and above in the 1815 campaign. Bock, Falkenhausen, Kleist, Krafft, Lettow, Luck, Lützow, Manstein, Schulenburg, Schwerin, Seydlitz, Steinmetz, Stülpnagel, Sydow, Treskow, all preceded by 'von', are only some of the names that appear in Blücher's army, and they appear again in 1870, in 1914 and in 1939. The Germans have always been fine soldiers, perhaps the best soldiers in Europe, and that there has been an hereditary caste of officers to lead them is one of the major reasons.

5

THE SOLDIERS

During Napoleon's first incarnation as emperor, his army was multinational. The backbone was of course French, but there were regiments of Dutch, of Belgians, of Hungarians, of Italians, of Poles and of Germans of the Confederation of the Rhine. Now those contingents were all serving the Allies, and with a few exceptions – Poles, a few Hungarians and the odd German – the army was entirely French. Rather more than half the soldiers were veterans, either those serving in the reduced army of the Bourbon restoration or discharged veterans who had served Napoleon before his first abdication and had rejoined as soon as they could – there were around 75,000 of the latter. Others were prisoners of war released from Dartmoor, from hulks in the Thames, and from Spain or Russia. Around 200,000 former prisoners of war had returned after April 1814, although many of them were medically unfit to serve.

Unusually for a French army, less than half the Army of the North, as the French army for the forthcoming campaign was titled, were conscripts. The pre-1789 Bourbon army was made up of professionals, many of whom were not French at all but Swiss, who signed up for between eight and twenty years. Conscription, the 'blood tax', was introduced by the Revolution. It was always unpopular and evasion was rife. Although violent resistance, with the beating up of gendarmes sent to enforce it, had declined, deserters and evaders could usually count on being given food and shelter, particularly in rural areas. Technically every male aged between eighteen and forty had to register and those unmarried between twenty and twenty-five years of age (extended to thirty after the return from Elba) were eligible to be called up, but as not all were needed, the requisite number was drawn by lot in each area. As First Consul and then emperor up to 1814, Napoleon, or rather his administration, called up around 2.5 million Frenchmen, of whom only around 1.3 million actually served. Not all the absentees were 'no shows': some failed the rudimentary medical examination (or paid doctors to fail them), some availed themselves of forgers who sold discharge certificates, some married after registration, and some did not meet the height requirement. A man drawn by lot could avoid service by paying a fine, which varied from 1,800 to 4,000 francs, or £76 to £160 at the exchange rate of the time, and then finding and paying another to take his place. Although both revolutionaries and Napoleon saw conscription as spreading the burden of war evenly across the nation, in fact only the poor were actually conscripted. On his return from Elba, Napoleon promised not to reintroduce conscription, but when his peace overtures came to naught, he had little option, describing it as much detested but ensuring the safety of the state. The class of 1815, those born in 1797, could produce 150,000 men if all were embodied. In practice, in the entire Napoleonic period, around one in fifteen of eligible rural inhabitants was actually embodied, and around one in seven in urban areas, where evasion was more difficult. In peacetime – effectively only the short-lived Peace of Amiens from March 1802 to May 1803 – the period of conscription varied from one year to five years, whereas in wartime it was indefinite – effectively until the end of hostilities.

While the old soldiers were reasonably well equipped, the conscripts called up in April and May of 1815 lacked everything except what they stood up in when they joined their regiments. The factories of France performed magnificently to produce uniforms, equipment and weapons. In Paris alone, 1,250 uniforms and 1.5 million cartridges were being turned out every week. By the time the campaign began, most men had at least a pair of boots, a blue jacket and a shako. While regiments of the line were established for depot battalions to train the new recruits, there was little time to do so and most regiments took their recruits straight into existing companies of the line with an old soldier detailed to train them. Inevitably, the veterans had little time for the newcomers: bullying was rife, many were cheated out of the few sous they had when they arrived, many were the innocent peasants sent to the quartermasters' stores with instructions to collect a long stand, and most stood open-mouthed at the veterans' tales of glory and derring-do in campaigns waged and battles fought, no doubt suitably embellished. It was the same in all armies – and still is in some.

As the pre-revolutionary army had been relatively small, there were few purpose-built barracks, and the Directorate had made use of churches, convents and monasteries from which the rightful inhabitants had been evicted. Recruits found themselves herded into these insanitary, cramped accommodations with tiny windows and expected to share a palliasse on the stone-flagged floor with at least one other; and as the original furniture had been looted or used as firewood, there was nothing to sit on but piles of straw – not that recruits got much time for sitting. A more healthy option was a tented camp, and many of the units in and around Paris were so accommodated, as were those men of the recently expanded National Guard who had been absorbed into the army. But life in barracks, whether in convents or tented, was not healthy and most soldiers were glad when they were ordered to march away to the front. Meanwhile, training for the post-Elba recruits could only be rudimentary: route marches to harden the feet and accustom the back to carrying the weight of one's kit in white leather equipment, some basic instruction in battlefield drill movements and firing practice with the musket. As powder and shot was expensive, men were issued with wooden pegs in place of flints, so they could practise loading and firing without actually doing so.

The normal establishment for the line infantry company and cavalry squadron was five sergeants, ten corporals, 104 privates and two drummers or buglers. The NCOs were always regulars and usually had considerable service; indeed, in many cases promotion, although theoretically on merit alone, was by seniority. In the royalist army NCOs' rank was denoted by what sort of aiguillette the man wore, or the colour of lace in his epaulette, but this was confusing in a citizen army and a much simpler and more obvious system was introduced where corporals wore a red chevron, point uppermost, above the cuff, sergeants a gold one and sergeant majors two gold ones, a system soon copied in principle by the British. On the face of it, the soldiers' pay was reasonably good, provided it actually appeared. A regular sergeant in the infantry received 1.69 francs per day, or £24.67 per annum, while a regular private's yearly emoluments amounted to £9.05. This compares with a captain's annual salary of £111.80 – rather less than a British captain's £191.62 – and a whopping £1,600 for a marshal.* Conscripts got considerably less.

Discipline in the French army of Napoleon was less indiscriminate than it had been in the early revolutionary armies. Men could be executed by firing squad, but this seems to have been inflicted on officers suspected of disloyalty rather than on soldiers for purely military offences. Some of the punishments of the old Bourbon army lingered on, however. The *Crapaudine* required an offender to have his leg strapped up tight to his body and to be left in the lying position for a prescribed period, while *Barre* involved tying the man to a gun carriage in the open and denied food and water; or a man could be sentenced to *Silo*, or confinement in unpleasant conditions, which might be no more than a hole hastily dug in the ground. While in some aspects of military discipline French soldiers, representing as they did a wider spectrum of society than did their British equivalents, were better behaved, the incidence of rape was considerably higher in the French service. This may be because the British soldier on the loose tended to search for and consume large quantities of alcohol first, before his thoughts turned to women, while French ambitions were the other way round.

The elite of the Napoleonic army was the Imperial Guard. Originally formed to protect the Directorate, it metamorphosed from Consular to Imperial, and despite being downgraded and reduced in size by the restored monarchy, it had managed to retain its traditions and élan – albeit that much of it was not on display, at least not while royalists were looking. Once Napoleon returned, the

---

* A marshal was normally a corps commander. His equivalent in the British army, a lieutenant general, received £1,383 and, unlike the marshal, was not likely to be able to boost this by looting.

Guard was restored in status, if not quite to its original size, which had been almost one third of the army in 1813/14. Qualifications for entry to the Guard were strict. For the Old Guard men must have had ten years' service, including operational service, and be graded 'excellent'. For the cream of the cream, the 1st and 2nd Regiments of Grenadiers of the Old Guard infantry and 1st and 2nd Regiments of Horse Grenadiers, men had to be at least six feet in height (although in the latter stages this requirement was often relaxed by a couple of inches or so, particularly for the cavalry when heavy horses were hard to come by). Mutton-chop whiskers and moustaches were compulsory, as was a pigtail tied by a black ribbon. Both horse and foot wore tall bearskin caps with a metal plate bearing the eagle and Napoleonic insignia, and they were the only part of the French army to retain the greasing and powdering of the hair. The Guard was almost an independent army of its own, with integral infantry, cavalry, artillery and engineers, and was divided into Old, Middle and Young depending on length of service; the Young Guard provided the light infantry battalions, although it is unclear whether the term 'Middle Guard' was an official nomenclature or simply the colloquial term for the third and fourth regiments. Prior to Napoleon's first abdication, the Guard also had a training function, with regiments of the line rotating through the Guard, then returning to the line with standards improved, but there was not time to reintroduce this custom before Waterloo.

Private soldiers in the Guards were paid more than sergeants in the rest of the army – 912.50 francs, or £36.50 a year – and regimental commanders of the Old Guard were brigadiers rather than colonels. They had a uniform of higher quality, and considerably greater cost, than anyone else's and even had a special musket with highly polished bands and butt plates. Not only was the pay of the Guard considerably better than for units of the line, but also rations, barracks and all sorts of allowances and privileges were far superior to anyone else's, which not unnaturally gave rise to considerable resentment and jealousy. To the rest of the army the men of the Guard were 'the Immortals', who did not die because they did not fight. This was somewhat unfair as the Guard was always kept back as a reserve, to pluck victory, or at least a draw, from impending defeat, or to administer the final breakthrough if the battle seemed to be about to go either way. When they did fight, they fought with great bravery and an almost fanatical tenacity, with a personal loyalty to Napoleon rather than to the state. For the forthcoming campaign, the Guard mustered twenty-two battalions of infantry, four regiments of cavalry and ninety-six guns, twelve-pounders and eight-pounders, and it would be the Guard who were the last to lay down their arms at Waterloo.

The British army has never found it easy to recruit and, although there was no conscription for the regular army, that is not to say that there were not other means of compulsion – many of them economic. The authorities had to rely on persuasion, and occasionally coercion, to attract sufficient men to fill the number of units needed to fight the war. Britain had an empire, which needed garrisons spread all over the world, so the army was always, on paper at least, larger than that required solely to fight the French. Recruiting was not, as it is now, a central responsibility, but was devolved to regiments, which adopted a number of ways of enticing men to join. The simplest and most common method was to send recruiting parties around the towns and villages to appeal to patriotism, greed, escapism, love of adventure or simple economics in order to find the number of men needed. Each party would normally consist of a sergeant, a drummer and two or three old soldiers, and there was an officer in overall command for the county.

One of the most common myths about the British army of the period is that its ranks were filled by criminals, ne'er-do-wells, simpletons and others from the lowest strata of society, lured into the service when drunk or deceived into accepting the king's shilling by subterfuge. While there were undoubtedly some of those types in each regiment, there were also men who were motivated by the attractions of a military life or by the prospect of adventure or who wanted to see the world. Recruiting parties did frequent the ale houses because that was the social centre of the life of those whom they hoped to enlist, and there were certainly cases of men being plied with drink to persuade them to join. The qualifications were relatively few: the man must not already be in the Army of the Reserve (Militia, Volunteers, Fencibles, Yeomanry), be no older than thirty-five for the line infantry and cavalry, or twenty-five for the Guards and the artillery, and at least 5 feet 4 inches tall (5 feet 8 inches for the Guards and artillery). Within twenty-four hours of a man agreeing to enlist, he had to be taken before a magistrate and declare that he wished to do so of his own free will, that the decision was taken when sober and that he had not been subject to any threats. This was one of the reforms put in place by the Duke of York to stamp out old practices such as slipping a coin into a man's beer tankard so that he had in law 'taken the shilling' and had therefore enlisted, or getting a man so drunk that the recruiting sergeant could claim he had agreed to enlist despite the man having no recollection of it.

Once a man had confirmed that he really did want to be a soldier, he had to be passed by the doctor. The medical requirements were lax in the extreme. While the potential recruit was supposed to be examined for all sorts of ailments, including ophthalmia, ruptures, rheumatics and 'damaged limbs', many of the conditions that would bar a man from joining now – poor eyesight, deafness, flat feet, lack of intelligence, wetting the bed, etc., etc. – were passed over, with the only medical requirement stringently applied being that the man had to have four front teeth, two on the top and two on the bottom. This was because the loading drill for the musket required the ripping open of the cartridge with the teeth; if a man did not have any front teeth, he could not load a musket and was therefore useless. In an age when dental hygiene was hardly thought of and the cure for toothache was to pull out the offending tooth, young men with few or no teeth were common. Even with medical examinations that were extremely lax, up to 30 per cent of volunteers were rejected for medical reasons.[14] The population of the British Isles in the early years of the nineteenth century was inherently unhealthy.

Once past the magistrate and the doctor, a man could enlist for either seven years or twenty-one, the seven-year option being a wartime-only concession. It is an indication of the insecurity of civilian life felt by potential recruits of the time that between 1811 and the end of the war only 10 per cent signed for the shorter period. The recruit was entitled to a bounty of ten guineas (£10.50) if he signed for seven years and fourteen guineas (£14.70) if he signed for twenty-one. Two guineas was paid once the man signed, or made his mark, the rest when he arrived at the training depot or his regiment. Recruiters had to keep an eye out for 'bounty jumpers' – men who took the two guineas and then disappeared, only to perform the same trick with another recruiting party. Those who were caught were tried by court martial (as they had signed, they were subject to military law) and those who had pushed their luck too many times risked being executed by firing squad.[15]

Many of the recruits – perhaps most – did come from the lower orders of society but that did not make them bad soldiers, and nor does it now. Men from an environment with no structure welcome boundaries; they like to know where the line is drawn, what they are permitted to do and what is forbidden. Men rejected by society, men who could not find a job in civilian life, men desperately trying to eke out an existence at a time of economic retrenchment – all found that the army became their family: if nobody else wanted them, at least the army did. Men performed their duties – and in the final analysis stood and died in the ranks – not for king and country, for king and country had done nothing for them, but for the regiment, for their mates, for their own officers whom, by this stage in the war, they knew and trusted, and out of sheer professional pride.

That said, there were undoubtedly a proportion of real bad hats, men who were incorrigible and who could only be kept under some sort of control by brutal discipline and frequent application of the lash. John Colborne, who served throughout the Peninsular War and at Waterloo in command of the 52nd Light Infantry, thought that there were around fifty men in every battalion who were hardened criminals; some of these would have been given the choice by the magistrates of joining the army or going to jail, others were drunkards, thieves, smugglers and forgers, similarly incapable of reform. These, he said, were the men who initiated every act of vandalism, who instigated the looting, who bullied and exploited the local peasantry, and whose example led otherwise well-behaved soldiers into crime.[16] Sometimes ex-criminals could be an asset: poachers were much in demand to snare rabbits and catch birds when rations were short; and when Wellington discovered that on advancing into France in 1814 the French would not accept Spanish silver dollars, he was able to find forty 'coiners' (forgers of the currency, a capital offence) from the ranks who could melt down Spanish coins and produce French silver five-franc pieces (so accurately did they do their job that even today an expert cannot tell their products from the genuine article). But most military crime had – and still has – its origin in the over-consumption of alcohol.

One of the problems in the early days of the war with France was that the regular army was in direct competition for recruits with the Army of Reserve and its various types of unit – the Militia, the Fencibles, the Volunteers and the Yeomanry. By 1815 there were two types of militia. The Regular Militia, established by various Militia Acts of 1802, 1803 and 1808, was a conscript force composed of eligible males (aged eighteen to thirty and, theoretically at least, Protestant) selected by ballot. On payment of a fine ranging from £20 to £30, a man could find a substitute to do his service for him. The Regular Militia were full-time, could serve only in the United Kingdom and were intended to be a home defence force to allow regular troops to be sent abroad. Men served for five years, after which they were exempt until their turn came round again. The finding of substitutes was widespread: of the 26,085 men embodied in 1810, only 3,129 were those who had been drawn at the ballot; all the rest were substitutes.[17] The Local Militia, originally founded in 1808 when there was an (unrealistic) fear of invasion, was a voluntary part-time force restricted to service within its own county; its members were required to carry out twenty-eight days' military training a year. The Fencibles were part of the regular army, composed of full-time volunteers, but their regiments were required to serve only within the United Kingdom. The Volunteers were exactly that: a part-time force established in 1808 whose members were exempt from conscription into the Regular Militia. Although increasingly absorbed into the Local Militia, the Volunteers lingered on long after Waterloo and eventually became the Territorial Force, the Territorial Army and, from 2013, the Army Reserve. The Yeomanry were part-time local cavalry, first raised during the invasion scare of the 1790s. Some of its regiments found their own horses, and it was generally officered by the landed gentry of the area. It was frequently used to restore law and order in an age when there was no properly organized police force.

When the militia was originally established, its members were forbidden to enlist into the regular army, but this rule was rescinded in 1805 and from then on the militia was one of the best sources of recruits; indeed, by Waterloo almost 50 per cent of private soldiers were ex-militiamen. A militia soldier could not join as a regular until he had served one year in the militia, and the great advantage for the regular army was that they not only got a better type of recruit but he had already received military training. In many cases a militia regiment would be paraded and representatives of various regular regiments who sought recruits would extol the advantages of their various corps and hope to persuade the listeners to join – as many of them did, although more often than not they joined not their supposedly local regiment but another, perhaps on the 'grass is greener' principle. One of the attractions of transferring from the militia to the regular army was the bounty, which was larger than that for recruits who had no military training and varied from £16 to £40 depending on the state of army manning at the time.

Another, albeit much less satisfactory, method of obtaining recruits was by privatizing the process to civilian contractors, who for a fee would provide the numbers needed. Known as 'crimpers', many of the persons who got the contract by submitting the lowest tenders were of very dubious natures and on the borders of criminality. It was in their interests to obtain as many men as possible in the shortest time at the lowest cost, and this included bribing doctors and magistrates to pass men who were totally unsuitable for military service. The men were often of very poor quality, and crimpers were not above kidnapping vagrants and orphans and keeping them under lock and key before persuading or forcing them to take the shilling and then cheating them out of much of their bounty. Once enlistment from the militia was authorized, however, the responsibility for finding recruits was much less likely to be contracted out to crimpers, and by 1815 they had virtually disappeared.

Although most regiments had in theory a local affiliation to a particular county, this had little effect on its composition. Regiments recruited where they could and a majority of recruits came from the disadvantaged parts of the kingdom where there were few alternatives as an escape from poverty. There were very large numbers of Irish soldiers, and not only in Irish regiments. When Thomas Graham, assisted by Rowland Hill, raised the 90th Perthshire Regiment of Foot, many of its soldiers did indeed come from Perthshire, but in 1796, of a total strength of 746 Other Ranks, 165 were English and ninety-five Irish.[18] At Waterloo in the 71st Highlanders eighty-three men were English and fifty-six Irish.[19] Looking at the muster rolls of the regiments that embarked for the Waterloo campaign, a very large number of the men have Irish names. Some may, of course, have been of families long resident in Liverpool or in other colonies of Irish émigrés, and some may have enlisted under false names, but from contemporary accounts it does seem that at least 20 per cent and perhaps considerably more of the soldiers of the British army at this time were Irish, and Catholic. (The Protestants of the North do not appear to have enlisted as readily as their economically less favoured southern countrymen.) Although it was an offence for a soldier to attend a Catholic church service in England (but not in Ireland), Wellington had always allowed his men to attend when abroad, provided, he said, that they were not there 'merely to gawk'. There can be little doubt that it was the religious make-up of his army that persuaded the Protestant Anglo-Irish Wellington to support Catholic emancipation and to force it through against the wishes of the king and much of the nobility when prime minister in 1829.

The other group over-represented in the ranks of the army were the Scots, and while many were indeed soldiers of economic necessity, they tended to be better behaved and more amenable to discipline than the Irish, who had a distressing tendency to get drunk and indulge in mindless violence.* Scottish society was less mobile than that in England and many Scottish regiments were still officered by local men, whom the soldiers knew. It was said that, if a Scottish soldier misbehaved, the worst punishment that could be inflicted was to have his name posted on the door of the kirk back home.

The army at the time was not, therefore, in any sense representative of the nation, in the way that Napoleon's army was, although it was composed of a wide spectrum of backgrounds. Apart from the criminal element, there were apprentices running away from a hard master, boys fleeing over-strict parents, farmhands bored behind the plough, swains crossed in love and

---

* See page 111, second footnote.

those escaping a forced marriage, shop assistants, shepherds, weavers, the urban unemployed and, in at least one case, a failed actor. There were even a few gentlemen rankers: men of education and breeding who had fallen on hard times, usually through gambling or drink or both, and who enlisted as the only alternative to starvation or to escape their creditors. Only a very small number made good, but they could be useful as writers of letters for their illiterate comrades, or as company clerks (one per company) – although few were employed as such owing to the temptation to embezzle the company funds, keeping the accounts of which was the responsibility of the clerk.

Once a recruit had been formally attested, he was marched to his regimental depot, or if he was an ex-militiaman, direct to his regiment if it was in the United Kingdom or to a holding unit to await drafting if it was overseas. The standard of training in depots varied widely. In some it was very good, staffed by officers and NCOs who knew their business; in others it was at best rudimentary and at worst brutal and uncaring and staffed by rejects, invalids and those who wished to avoid active service. The recruit had to learn military discipline, to obey orders without question, to perform tactical movements, to maintain his equipment, to march carrying around forty pounds' weight in addition to his weapon and ammunition,* and to handle his weapon. Unlike European armies, the British paid serious attention to musketry, with regular range practice both as individuals and in platoon firing.

A man who proved himself capable, loyal and professionally competent could be promoted to NCO rank. There was one

---

* About the same weight as is carried by an infantry soldier today, although now it is much better distributed about the body.

sergeant major in a battalion. Equivalent to the regimental sergeant major (RSM) of today, he was the most senior NCO in the battalion,[*] and the commanding officer's right-hand man in all matters relating to welfare and discipline and promotion of Other Ranks. The establishment of a company included one colour sergeant, three sergeants and three corporals. The rank of colour sergeant was instituted in 1813, and he was the equivalent of today's company sergeant major and company quartermaster sergeant rolled into one. Although colour sergeants supposedly acted as escorts to the colours in battle, this task was more usually delegated to sergeants who had annoyed the sergeant major, as it was one of the more dangerous positions to hold in action. The British had copied the French method of indicating rank by chevrons, but in the British case with the point downwards. The sergeant major wore four chevrons on his upper arm; the colour sergeant a single chevron surmounted by crossed swords, the union flag and the royal crown; the sergeant three chevrons; and the corporal two. The rank of lance corporal had not yet been introduced, although many regiments recognized a need for a transitional stage between private and NCO and had appointed what were known as 'chosen men', who acted and were paid as senior privates but would become corporals when a vacancy arose.

The pay of a soldier varied depending upon what arm of the service he joined. The cavalry were paid more than the infantry and the Guards more than the line. Annual rates of pay for the infantry of the line – the bulk of the army – at the time of Waterloo were:

---

[*] Not yet a warrant officer – that does not come until 1879.

Sergeant major	£54.75
Colour sergeant	£42.55
Sergeant	£32.92
Corporal	£23.94 to £26.93 depending on length of service
Drummer	£20.54
Private	£17.95 to £20.95 depending on service

Soldiers in the Guards got an extra old penny per day (£0.41, or £1.49 per year) and corporals and privates in the cavalry were paid around double that of the line infantry.

To put those pay rates into perspective, in 1815 a shipwright in Plymouth might earn £86 a year, a mason in London £82 (but in Glasgow only £51), a skilled carpenter £45.50, a cotton weaver in Belfast £35 (but a linen weaver in England £19.50), a fully trained merchant seaman £33 and an unmarried farmhand £15.33.[20] These figures do not, however, tell the whole story, for they assume that the man was employed for the entire year. In fact the wages of carpenters and masons were expressed as daily rates, so from the salary given Sundays and any days not worked must be deducted. Similarly some occupations – farmhand and sailor, for example – were provided with free board and lodging, and agricultural workers were normally paid a bonus over the harvest. Nevertheless, after deductions for his food (£2.33 per year) and 'necessaries' – those items of clothing and equipment not provided free by the service (£2.93 per year) – and one shilling (£0.05) per year towards the upkeep of Chelsea Hospital, a private soldier, who was paid for Sundays and was accommodated, was not badly off compared to his peers in civilian life. And unlike his peers, he could qualify for a pension of £7.50 a year after fourteen years' service, and, depending on rank, anything between £36.50 for a sergeant major to £18.25 for a private after twenty-one years. Men invalided out of the service through wounds before reaching the point at which a pension was payable got between £3.72 and £11.20 a year depending upon the degree of disablement.[21]

Discipline in the army was regulated by the Mutiny Act of 1803, which gave a legal basis for the various Articles of War that were to be applied in the United Kingdom, and not just overseas, as had been the case hitherto. On the face of it, the offences listed and the possible punishments were draconian: after a trial by court martial, a wide variety of offences ranging from mutiny to desertion, from plundering to striking a superior, from disobeying orders to aiding the enemy, could attract the death penalty, although some only if committed on active service. This would be inflicted either by firing squad or by hanging. The one organization that could sentence a man to death and carry it out on the spot was the provost, the ancestors of the military police, if they caught a man in the act of committing a capital offence. In practice it was rare to inflict the supreme penalty. Wellington did not execute deserters, unless they took service with the enemy, nor did the provost often hang plunderers on the spot, however much Wellington would fulminate against looting (on the grounds that it would alienate the local population and turn them against the British). In the Peninsula one man was executed for buggery, and as this is an activity that requires two participants, we can assume that the other was a civilian and thus not subject to British military law.

The form of an execution was prescribed in great detail. The units of the man's brigade were formed up in hollow square, and there was a procession of a fatigue party carrying the man's coffin, followed by the prisoner escorted by men of his own regiment, then a chaplain, then the firing party of (usually) twelve soldiers of the man's regiment commanded by a sergeant, with the provost marshal bringing up the rear. The whole entourage paraded along the line of assembled troops while the band played the Dead March from Handel's oratorio *Saul*. The prisoner was then placed on the open side of the square, his hands tied behind his back, blindfolded and ordered to kneel. Orders to the firing squad, positioned ten paces away, were normally given by hand signals, and should the condemned not be killed instantly, he would be finished off by the provost marshal with a pistol. The body was then placed in the coffin and the whole parade slow-marched past the body, with recruits ordered to pass as close as possible to it – presumably as a warning about their future conduct.[22]

While soldiers could be imprisoned, this was rare – a man in jail escaped duty and was out of danger, which may have been what motivated him to sin in the first place – and the most common punishment was flogging. Men could be sentenced to receive up to 200 lashes by a general court martial, 150 by a district court martial and 100 by a regimental court. Again, the man's battalion was paraded and the miscreant tied to a 'triangle', originally made of sergeants' halberds, but as by 1815 many sergeants no longer carried halberds, it was often purpose-made of wood. The sentence was carried out by drummers using a 'cat of nine tails', a whip with a short wooden handle and nine knotted cords each sixteen inches long, and a medical officer was in attendance. The punishment was usually inflicted on the man's back, but in the case of a man who had recently been flogged and whose back was in no state to take any more, it might be on the buttocks. The strokes were counted out loud by the drum major, and after every twenty-five lashes the drummer was changed. In some regiments the man flogged was required to pay the cost of the cat used to lash him, and in the case of a really nasty recipient drum majors would alternate right- and left-handed drummers to administer the punishment more thoroughly.

British infantry soldiers wore scarlet tunics and light-grey trousers. In practice, with contracts for uniforms let to contractors who submitted the lowest tenders, the quality varied enormously, and mostly it was bad. After a few weeks' campaigning the scarlet tunic was more of a rusty brick-red, and the trousers bore the stains of the scarlet dye that had begun to run in the first shower of rain. Boots were not issued as right or left boots but as boots, and the man made his own lace holes with a nail or an awl if he could not persuade a cobbler to do it for him.*

Worst of all was the web equipment. This was a mass of straps and buckles that held the man's cartridge pouch, bayonet frog, water bottle, bread bag and knapsack. It was made of white buff and had to be kept white by applications of pipe clay; it looked very smart on parade, but with its straps and cross-belts pulled tight it was hugely uncomfortable and restrictive in movement, unless worn loose, which in most units after years of war it was, at least when not on parade. The standard issue Trotter pack, called after its inventor, was made of lacquered canvas stiffened with leather. Although Mr Trotter, based in Soho, was a supplier to the army (and was hauled before various parliamentary committees on several occasions and accused of corruption in regard to his methods and products), it was up to the colonel of the regiment to select a supplier, although all patterns were roughly the same as Trotter's. All could be polished and made to look very smart indeed,

---

* One of the many scandals involving army procurement revolved around a consignment of boots delivered to the army in Spain in 1810, which fell apart after the wearers waded a stream. The contractor had soled the boots with cardboard painted black.

but depending on the supplier ranged from merely uncomfortable to agonizing to wear, and many old soldiers suffered from 'Trotter's Chest', a respiratory ailment caused by long years of the chest being restricted by the straps of the pack. Old soldiers were also easily identified by tiny black pockmark-like specks on the right cheek, caused by the ignition of the powder in the pan when firing the musket.

Also at Waterloo as part of the British army was the King's German Legion. When George I ascended the British throne in 1714 as the first of the Hanoverian dynasty and the nearest male Protestant relation to Queen Anne, who died with no surviving children, he retained the electorate of Hanover. Hanoverian troops served under British command at Gibraltar and at one stage in India. In 1803 France invaded Hanover and absorbed that state into the kingdom of Westphalia, to be ruled over by Napoleon's youngest brother, Jérôme. Napoleon hoped and expected that the Hanoverian army would enlist in the Légion Hanovrienne but was disappointed, as apart from a few, the majority opted to continue the war from England and were removed by the Royal Navy. Until it was decided what to do with them, it was first proposed to billet them on the Isle of Wight, as English law forbade the stationing of foreign troops on the mainland of the United Kingdom. When it was argued that, foreign though they might be, they were subjects of the same king, they were first stationed in Bexhill, in Sussex, then Lymington, in Hampshire, and then in various towns on the south coast. They formed the King's German Legion, some of the British army's best troops, and served throughout the Peninsular War. As time went on, the supply of Hanoverian recruits dried up and eventually any German was allowed to join, but standards were not allowed to slip. Commanded by their own officers and equipped, dressed and paid exactly as British troops, they were in the process of being converted back to the Hanoverian army when Napoleon returned from exile, and at Waterloo they provided two light and eight line battalions of infantry, four regiments of cavalry and eighteen guns.

Other Germans to fight under British command were the newly constituted Hanoverian army, with seventeen battalions of infantry, a regiment of cavalry and twelve guns, and the Brunswick contingent. Karl Wilhelm Ferdinand, Duke of Brunswick and Luneberg, was mortally wounded at the Battle of Jena-Auerstädt, and when the French included Brunswick in the kingdom of Westphalia, the new duke, Friedrich Wilhelm, went into exile in Austria. When Austria returned to the fray in 1809, the duke mortgaged his principality of Oels, raised a contingent of troops and fought his way across French territory to the mouth of the Weser, from where he and his men were evacuated to England by the Royal Navy. As they were cut off from their source of recruits in Brunswick and as the best Germans joined the King's German Legion, the Brunswick-Oels were reduced to recruiting what they could get – prisoners of war, Poles, Dutch and indeed any European who spoke German. They had a reputation for deserting, but fought well in the Peninsula, and at Waterloo they provided eight infantry battalions, one regiment of cavalry and sixteen guns. Finally the Nassau contingent provided eight infantry battalions at Waterloo. Not to be confused with Orange Nassau, which fought as part of the Dutch army, Nassau was a German state in the Confederation of the Rhine. As the Nassauers were suspicious of Prussian motives, they elected to fight under the British rather than the Prussians.

Although from 1815 the Kingdom of the Netherlands included Belgium, the Dutch and the Belgian armies had different origins and at Waterloo were still separate, with Belgian units looking to the Belgian Legion, raised by the Austrians, and the Dutch looking to the traditions they had inherited from the French. As we have seen, both nations had been under French control for nearly twenty years and had fought for Napoleon for most of that time, so loyalties were mixed. The situation was not helped by the blue of the tunics that the new army of the Netherlands would wear – the colour was too easily mistaken for French blue – nor, of course, by the fact that some units had not yet received their new uniforms and at Waterloo were still in French kit, with merely the addition of an orange cockade on the hat. Organization, tactics and badges of rank were French, but on closer inspection Dutch units could be seen, confusingly perhaps, to wear the Austrian shako, while Belgian ones wore one similar to that worn by the British. Most of the rank and file of the army of the Netherlands were conscripts, while most of the senior NCOs were professionals. The language of the Dutch units was Dutch and that of the Belgians French, which did not ease communication to or between the two.

The soldiers of the Prussian army in the Waterloo campaign were largely untried, although they had a cadre of experienced officers and senior NCOs to stiffen them. The Prussian army recruited on the *Krümper* system. Designed to allow them a far larger pool of trained manpower than the occupying French permitted, this system was based on conscripting men for a relatively short period, discharging five men from every company each month and taking in five new recruits. Prussian infantry companies were 150-strong, so a man would serve for thirty months before discharge to the reserve. A similar system operated for the artillery and the cavalry. This meant that the Prussians could keep to their treaty with France, which limited the Prussian army to

42,000, while in reality evading its restrictions. The system was proven when for the Waterloo campaign the Prussians mustered 130,000 men, around half of the units being *Landwehr*, or militia manned by men who had completed their thirty months' service with the field army. Many of them were rusty and some had spent most of their thirty months in barracks, but all were motivated by a genuine patriotism, and while there was mass desertion after Ligny, those that remained were not at all disconcerted by the results of one defeat and the prospect of another.

Discipline in the Prussian army of 1815 was far removed from the brutality of the Frederician age, where men could be executed for what would have been considered minor offences elsewhere, flogged unmercifully, made to sit upon a saddle horse with weights tied to their feet, or forced to 'run the gauntlet' between a double file of soldiers, each of whom would batter the unfortunate as he tried to make his way between them. Now Prussian soldiers could be shot, but only for very serious offences such as mutiny. They were not subject to flogging but instead could be caned, but this was done in private and either on the back or on the buttocks. The Prussians regarded the British disciplinary process as cruel in the extreme.

About 14,000 of the Prussian army that was stationed in Flanders were of the Saxon contingent. Saxony had been the last German state to continue to fight for Napoleon, and many Saxons disliked and distrusted Prussians and had no wish to be under their command. Equally, many Prussians were suspicious of Saxon loyalty. Blücher was increasingly concerned that the Saxon contingent might change sides and decided to break it up and place Saxon brigades in Prussian corps. The reorganization was insensitively handled, and in May 1815 the situation erupted into a full-blown Saxon mutiny. Some Saxons even attacked Blücher's quarters, and the grand old man had to flee via the back door. Blücher told the king of Saxony: 'I shall restore order even though I be compelled to shoot the entire Saxon army.'[23] Order was swiftly restored and only four Saxons were executed by firing squad. One of the most seriously affected Saxon battalions was paraded before their comrades and their regimental standard burned in front of them. As the standard had been personally embroidered by the queen of Saxony, this did little to improve Prussian-Saxon relations, and the entire contingent was sent home.

Here, then, were the men who would fight the campaign of Waterloo. Their training and motivations varied widely, as did the methods and traditions of their armies. Many had no experience of intensive warfare, while others had fought all over Europe and beyond. Whatever their different backgrounds and ambitions, the vast majority fought bravely for a cause in which they believed, and all would fight under commanders who were not only experienced in war, but who were also well aware that for them this campaign could have only two outcomes: glory and riches for the victors, defeat and ignominy for the losers.

6

BATTLE JOINED

After 2 June 1815, when the Congress of Vienna officially declared Napoleon to be an outlaw, there could be no doubt that there would be war. Napoleon had always known that there would be, but had to go through the motions of seeking peace to placate those sections of French public opinion that did not want a return to the years of struggle. Now that war was inevitable, Napoleon's plan was to strike at the only armies that were in position on the French frontiers, those of the Anglo-Dutch and the Prussians. If he could catch them before they had time to join, then he would outnumber each and could defeat them separately. If they were allowed to join, however, the combined army would greatly outnumber the Army of the North and the result could be entirely different. For all the enormous efforts to raise and equip new French formations, the army was brittle. It was patriotic, fired by loyalty to the emperor and made bitter by the treatment meted out during the brief restoration period, but there remained an atmosphere of distrust between those who had stayed loyal to the emperor and had been unemployed or worse until Napoleon's return, and those who had taken an oath to the Bourbons and had done well by it. Napoleon needed

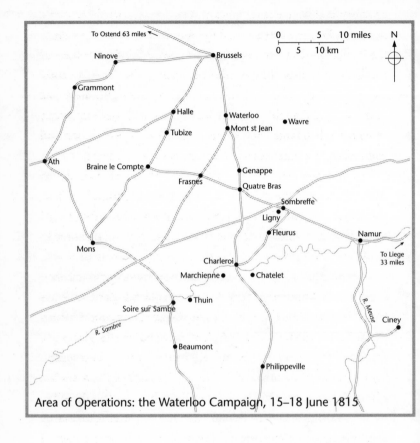

Area of Operations: the Waterloo Campaign, 15–18 June 1815

a victory, and he needed it quickly. Any unnecessary delay would not only give the Austrians and the Russians time to get closer to the French borders but it would also allow suspicion to fester and encourage royalists at home and waverers in the army. An early victory, however, would consolidate his position in the army and in the state, and might well provoke a rebellion in Belgium, many of whose inhabitants had not been unhappy as Frenchmen and women, and were not especially enamoured of now being Dutch.

Napoleon's plan was to strike north at the junction of the Anglo-Dutch and the Prussian forces and towards Brussels, seizing the crossroads and the lateral roads that linked the two Allied armies. Then, by preventing his two opponents from combining, he would defeat them one by one. His first opponent would probably be the Prussians, as Blücher was far more aggressive than the generally cautious Wellington, but by advancing in two wings with a reserve following up along a central axis, Napoleon retained the flexibility to attack either Allied army and use the reserve to administer the coup de grâce if required. Surprise was essential: the French army had to be well into Belgium and have possession of the vital roads between Wellington and Blücher before the Allies woke to the fact that they were under attack. It would, of course, be impossible to conceal the movement of such large bodies of troops; what was important was to conceal where and when the attack was to take place.

From mid-May Napoleon had been asking for reports on the state of the rivers and canals in the area between Charleroi and Mons, and the engineers had been told to collect bridging equipment, so it is clear that from then he had determined to go on the offensive rather than fight a defensive battle on French soil. While the main thrust would be north through Belgium, the defence of the rest of France could not be neglected and the emperor ordered dispositions to guard against the early arrival of the Russians and Austrians or anyone else who might decide to join this seventh Allied coalition. Generals Clausel and Decaen would command 14,000 men between them at Bordeaux and Toulouse to watch the Spanish frontier; Marshal Suchet with 23,000 men and Marshal Brune with a pathetic 5,000 were based in Lyon and the Riviera to block any Austrian advance from Italy; General Lecourbe with 8,500 in the Jura would watch for any movement by the so far neutral Swiss; and General Rapp with 23,000 based at Strasbourg would look east to guard against Russian or Austrian deployments. Marshal Davout would command in Paris with a garrison of 20,000 men, and General Lamarque would have 10,000 men along the River Loire to deal with any royalist uprising in Brittany. Additionally, there were another 30,000 or so soldiers scattered in frontier fortresses and garrisons around the country.

The army that Napoleon had taken from the Bourbons had been around 200,000-strong, around 100,000 veterans and ex-prisoners of war had rejoined, and the 1815 conscripts would, eventually, produce 150,000, so, when all the defensive formations are deducted, Napoleon had – on paper at least – around 305,000 men available for offensive action. His difficulty was that many of the former prisoners were in no physical condition to cope with the exertions of campaigning, and only a very few of the 1815 class of conscripts could be ready in time for operations in June – and if the plan to knock Britain and Prussia out of the war before the Russians and Austrians could make themselves felt were to work, he could not afford to wait longer than June. In the event, Napoleon was able to find around 123,000 men for the Army of the North, albeit only by including the garrisons of the fortresses on the Belgian border. But now the campaign could begin. It would consist of two pairs of linked battles: Quatre Bras and Ligny on 16 June 1815, and Waterloo and Wavre on the 18th.

Some of Napoleon's appointments are difficult to fathom. Suchet, created a marshal in 1811, was one of the more competent French generals in the Peninsula, being not only an effective soldier but one who understood that respect for local culture and religion was essential to gain if not the support, at least the acquiescence, of the population. Aragon, where Suchet commanded, was the only province of Spain where there was not a vicious guerrilla war waged against the occupiers. He would have been a far more effective field commander than d'Erlon. Again, Davout had shown himself to be a good commander of armies, and would seem to have been a better choice than Grouchy for command of the right wing. One can only suppose that it was Davout's skill as an organizer and his total political reliability that persuaded Napoleon to leave him as minister for war and governor of Paris, with the added responsibility of organizing, training and despatching the latest intake of conscripts.

On 6 June orders went out to the various commanders detailing the deployments for the coming campaign. As surprise was essential, from 7 June the frontiers were closed with no one allowed in or out of France, mail was stopped, fishing boats were forbidden to leave port, and French sympathizers in Belgium – of which there were many – began to spread false rumours as to the whereabouts of the emperor and the movements of various military units. The army would concentrate within striking distance of the Franco-Belgian border south of Charleroi. The two corps that would make up the left wing, d'Erlon's I Corps from Lille (sixty miles away) and Reille's II Corps from Valenciennes (thirty miles), would make for Soire-sur-Sambre; the right wing, Vandamme's III Corps from Mézières-en-Vexin (eighty miles) and Gérard's IV Corps from Metz (130 miles), would concentrate at Philippeville, while the reserve of the Imperial Guard under Mortier and Lobau's VI Corps bivouacked north and south of Beaumont respectively. The four corps of reserve cavalry, under Grouchy, would be spread between Beaumont and Walcourt, a distance of about nine miles and essential if sufficient fodder for all the horses was to be found.

There were problems in assembling so many men in so many units at the right places at the right time and with all their equipment. Partly this was caused by Soult's lack of staff experience. He sent movement orders to the corps commanders by the hand of one messenger only (Berthier would have sent three, all by different routes), and messengers got lost or delayed. He forgot to send any orders at all to Exelmans' cavalry corps, who fortunately were in the area anyway and only realized that something was up when other units arrived. Despite all this, by 14 June all were in position, poised across a frontage of twenty miles and without the Allies having any inkling of Napoleon's intentions.

The emperor himself left Paris at 0400 hours on 12 June, and got to Laon, eighty-seven miles away, by midday. He covered another seventy-two miles to reach Avesnes-sur-Helpe on 13 June and twenty-five to arrive at Beaumont on 14 June. Napoleon had travelled 184 miles in less than three days, in a coach over roads that were little more than tracks, deeply rutted and unsympathetic to the rudimentary suspension of the imperial vehicle. He had had little sleep and exhaustion must have played a part in his performance over the next four days, although French contemporary sources claim that he was in the best of health. Having reached Beaumont, he addressed the reserve and representatives of the other corps in a typically Napoleonic oration with appeals to *l'honneur*, *la gloire* and the need to defend *la patrie* against the depredations of the English coalition, which had spurned his offers of peace. He then ordered the advance to begin on the next day, 15 June, with Ney – who had not yet reached the army but was reported to be on his way – commanding the left wing, Grouchy the right and the emperor himself the reserve. Grouchy was the most recent member of the marshalate, having been promoted by Napoleon in April 1815 as a reward for putting down a royalist rising in the Midi where he captured the Duke of Angoulême, nephew of Louis XVIII. Grouchy was an ex-captain of the pre-revolutionary Bourbon army and unquestionably a competent, above-average even, commander of cavalry, although he had served briefly in the artillery and also had had command of infantry. The problem was that he was too steady, too ponderous, too unimaginative when what was needed was initiative, dash and a lightness of touch.

On the other side of the hill, as Wellington used to say, the Prussians and the Anglo-Dutch were spread out over a distance of around 150 miles and a depth of between twenty and forty miles. Blücher had his headquarters at Namur, on his lines of communication with the German states and Prussia, with Bülow's IV Corps at Liège, twenty-five miles away to the east-north-east, Thielemann's III Corps at Ciney, thirteen miles to the south-east, Pirch and II Corps with Blücher at Namur, and Ziethen's I Corps north of Charleroi on the Prussian extreme right and in contact with Wellington's left. Wellington's headquarters were in Brussels with his reserve of two British divisions and the Brunswick and Nassau contingents; the Prince of Orange's I Corps had its headquarters in Braine-le-Comte, fourteen miles south-south-west of Brussels; Hill's II Corps was based on Ath, thirty miles away to the south-west; and the cavalry was stationed between Grammont and Ninove, fourteen miles off to the east. Additionally there were garrisons, mainly Dutch, along the British lines of communication back to the ports of Ostend and Antwerp, through which reinforcements and supplies would come, and through which Wellington would evacuate his troops if he had to. Both Allied armies were deployed with a view, first, to invading France when the Russians and the Austrians were in position; second, to defending against an attack from France – which was initially not considered likely; and finally, to securing lines of communication to the Channel coast for the British and to Berlin for the Prussians. Napoleon, from his intelligence sources inside Belgium, knew the rough disposition of the Allied armies, and he knew that the boundary between the Anglo-Dutch and the Prussians ran just west of Charleroi. He calculated that each army would need at least a day to concentrate and three days to join. He did not intend to give them those three days.

Both Allied commanders had problems. Blücher had his unruly Saxons and a very inexperienced rank and file, while Wellington was commanding an army that spoke four different languages, used a variety of weapons, all with their own ammunition requirements, and had different organizations and tactics as well as widely divergent standing operating procedures. There were arguments over seniority and chains of command, and a certain coolness on the part of the Prussians over the position of the German states that provided contingents for Wellington – contingents that the Prussians felt should be with their fellow Germans. The duke had had to exercise all his considerable diplomatic skills to persuade Blücher that a joint invasion before all the Allies were in position would not be a good idea, and he had to expend even more effort to stop the Prince of Orange mounting an invasion of his own with the army of the Netherlands. Given that an invading force's lines of communication would get longer and longer and would have to be guarded, and that garrisons would have to be left in towns and fortresses in rear of the advance, such an enterprise would not have succeeded and would have run out of troops before a main battle – probably somewhere north of Paris – could be joined.

Wellington had far more hangers-on than he needed, as just about everybody in England at a loose end wanted to get in on the act. He said that he had an 'infamous' army and also 'a very inexperienced staff'.[24] This was not the Peninsular army, a highly trained and honed killing machine, for in the usual manner of British governments then and now much of that had been disbanded with no thought to the morrow, and much of what had been retained was in America, where the war begun in 1812 had just ended. That said, the inexperience of the British troops may have been somewhat exaggerated – no doubt to put pressure on the government at home to raise more troops. In fact, of the thirty-one British infantry battalions under command, sixteen had been in the Peninsula, and of the other fifteen, all but four of their regiments had had at least one battalion there. The Peninsular veteran battalions would, of course, have had a fair number of inexperienced recruits, but there would have been a hard core of officers, NCOs and senior privates who were well accustomed to fighting (and beating) the French. Similarly, in the normal process of cross-posting between battalions, those battalions whose regiments had been represented in the Peninsula would have had at least some experienced men. Of the sixteen British cavalry regiments present, all of the light cavalry (nine regiments) had been in the Peninsula, and of the seven heavy regiments, two

(2nd Life Guards and 1st Dragoons) had been there, although again they would by now have had a goodly sprinkling of recruits.

In the days leading up to the opening of the campaign proper, it was obvious that something was brewing: Ziethen's patrols reported seeing the smoke from thousands of camp fires away to the south, and Wellington's cavalry reported movement of large bodies of troops going west to east. But, although there were some deserters from the French, none of them was privy to any definitive information as to what was going on. There was a report that the emperor was at Avesnes on 13 June, as indeed he was, but was this really him or was it a double intended to confuse? And if it was him, was he contemplating an attack towards Brussels, or a wide outflanking move to cut the British off from the Channel ports? No one realized that the whole of the Army of the North was but a few miles from the Franco-Belgian border, and ready to strike.

At 0300 hours on the morning of 15 June the soldiers of France struggled out of their billets and bivouacs and fell in by regiments and squadrons. Gun wheels were wrapped in sacking to cut down the noise on the cobbled roads, then removed when the artillery moved onto beaten earth tracks; the usual leisurely breakfast was forgone and men stuffed four days (some sources give the unlikely total of eight days) of bread in their voluminous goatskin knapsacks. The army moved off in three columns, twelve regiments of cavalry and the engineers with their bridging equipment to the fore. All had begun well but there were problems of traffic control, with units running into the backs of those in front; movement was much slower across the hilly country with its dirt roads and woods than had been planned. Reille in the left-hand column met stiffer resistance than expected against men of Major General Steinmetz's

Prussians, part of Ziethen's corps, at Thuin on the Sambre, and he also had to fight for Marchienne, nearer Charleroi. Only when Napoleon himself brought forward the Guard did Ziethen order a fighting withdrawal. The right-hand column, led by Gérard's IV Corps, suffered dismay and confusion when, on reaching Châtelet, the commander of his leading division, Major General Louis August Victor Bourmont, said he was going forward to reconnoitre and promptly deserted to the Prussians.

Bourmont had started military life as one of the last officers to be commissioned in the royal Garde Française. On the outbreak of the Revolution, he joined the Chouanerie, a royalist guerrilla group in the Vendée, but when he was suspected of involvement in a bomb plot against Napoleon in 1800, things got too hot for him and he fled to Switzerland. An amnesty in 1807 saw him join Junot's staff in Portugal and he served on, becoming a major general in 1814. On Napoleon's first abdication, he enthusiastically declared for the Bourbons and then offered his services to Napoleon again. Bourmont made no secret of his dislike of Napoleon personally and was regarded with considerable suspicion by many French officers, who advised Napoleon not to employ him. That he was employed was a reflection of Napoleon's wish to heal old sores and unite the nation – reasonable enough, but to put him in command of the lead division was perhaps a gesture too far.

As he galloped towards the Prussian positions, Bourmont ordered his ADC to return to the French army with a letter that he had prepared. In it he assured the emperor that what he did was done to save the shedding of French blood and that he would not fight in the ranks of the enemy. He was eventually brought before Blücher, who treated him as a 'dirty dog', and his revealing of French plans was of little help now that battle had been joined. Blücher had anyway already ordered the Prussian army to concentrate at Sombreffe, about seven miles east of the Charleroi–Brussels road. His chief of staff, Gneisenau, had sent out gallopers to take the orders to the corps commanders, and while his intentions were very clear to Ziethen, Pirch and Thielemann, his orders to Bülow were couched in such a polite and diplomatic fashion that they gave no indication of any great urgency. Gneisenau was, of course, junior to Bülow, who had a notoriously quick temper, and given the tone of the despatch, Bülow saw no need to hurry. This would have a considerable bearing on the result of the first major clash of the armies.

Despite its problems, the advance for the French had gone reasonably well. The first great physical obstacle, the River Sambre, was crossed with ease – the Prussians had not blown the bridges – and at about 1530 hours Marshal Ney arrived and took command of the left wing. The three columns pressed on, and by last light Grouchy's right wing, prodded by the emperor himself, had reached Fleurus, two miles south-south-west of Ligny, having covered twenty miles from its start point against stiff delaying action from Ziethen. Ziethen's own command post in a windmill at Fleurus was now occupied by Grouchy, while he took post on top of an Iron Age burial mound, La Tombe, further north. The French left wing had fought its way through Charleroi with relative ease and made good speed through Gosselies, driving the Prussians out by early evening. Ney then pushed the cavalry forward up the main Charleroi–Brussels highway to Frasnes-lez-Gosselies.

On 15 June, once Blücher became aware that his outposts were under attack, he sent a message off to Wellington in Brussels. There is considerable disagreement among historians about exactly when this message was received. Conspiracy theories abound, but there can be no reason to doubt Wellington's own report in which he says that it was not until 'the evening of the 15th' that he first became aware that the French had crossed the border south of Charleroi.[25] Realistically, the report of the first clash at Thuin at around 0600 hours (at the earliest) would have been sent to the regimental and then to the brigade headquarters, probably taking an hour; from there the news would have gone to Ziethen's corps headquarters, another hour; then to Blücher at Namur, twenty miles as the crow flies, probably nearer thirty as the messenger trots and canters,[*] say four hours at best, taking us to midday. There the information would have been evaluated, and when it was confirmed as genuine, a message to Brussels would have been sent along the communication route of the Roman road to Quatre Bras and then north along the high road, a distance of forty miles, or five hours for a horseman, who would have arrived in Brussels no earlier than 1700 hours. Those who think it could have arrived much earlier are not familiar with the military method of passing information, nor of the distances that a horse and rider could realistically cover in the conditions of the time. Even the use of a system of post horses, where the rider could change horses every ten miles or so, could only have shortened the journey by two hours at most.

Among the Dutch outposts and the cavalry patrols along the portion of the frontier for which Wellington was responsible, it was clear that something was up. The question was what. Minor clashes and skirmishes had been commonplace during the past few weeks, so was this just another or did it presage something more serious? And was the sound of cannon-fire merely the Prussians at target practice, as was their wont? In the event, General de

---

[*] And no, it is not possible to gallop a horse for thirty miles.

Constant Rebecque, the Prince of Orange's chief of staff, ordered a heightened state of alert and sent some units to their alarm posts, while the prince set off for Brussels to dine with Wellington, who was still ignorant of any crossing of the border. Dinner then was taken around 1500 hours, much earlier than today, partly on account of a general wish not to dine by candlelight (supper, on the other hand, was eaten by candlelight and often a substantial meal). Both commanders, and command and staff officers within reach of Brussels, were invited to a ball given by the Duchess of Richmond, wife of Charles Lennox, fourth duke of Richmond. A Scottish aristocrat, Lennox had joined the army as an ensign in 1785, and, although now a general, he was not on the active list and had held no command since being commanding officer of the 35th Foot in 1789.* Although holding the appointment of governor of Hull and of Plymouth, he in fact lived in Brussels and the ball was held in his house in the rue de la Blanchisserie.†

As soon as Wellington received the news from Blücher, he ordered the Anglo-Dutch army to concentrate at Nivelles, five miles west of the Charleroi–Brussels high road and fifteen miles south of Brussels. In hindsight, the initial concentrations of the two Allied armies was playing into Napoleon's hands, for they were moving away from the French axis of advance and enabling Napoleon, if he moved swiftly enough, to get between them and implement his plan of defeating both individually. But nobody had hindsight in 1815. Wellington's concern was his supply (and withdrawal) route

---

* He had risen to lieutenant colonel by purchase in four years, before the Duke of York's reforms, which stipulated at least seven and then nine years' service before attaining that rank. Thereafter he was promoted by seniority but never held a command (and hence did not draw pay).
† And not, as present-day inhabitants of Brussels claim, in the Hotel de Ville.

back to the Channel ports and home. While it certainly looked as if there was a French thrust towards Brussels, was this but a feint? Where was the real point of attack, and could it be that Napoleon was manoeuvring to the west, in the direction of Mons, in order to cut the British off from the coast? A concentration at Nivelles would allow Wellington to counter any such move, and until he was absolutely sure from where the French main thrust was coming, and where it was aimed, he would not risk his polyglot army.

Meanwhile, the cavalry vanguard of Ney's left wing of the French army, the light cavalry of the Guard commanded by Major General Charles Lefebvre-Desnouettes,* had reached the hamlet of Frasnes-lez-Gosselies and, upon pushing on beyond it against withdrawing Dutch infantry skirmishers, suddenly found themselves faced with a battery of guns drawn up on a ridge that ran at right angles across the Charleroi–Brussels road. This was a Dutch artillery battery of six six-pounders and two 5½-inch howitzers commanded by Captain Adriaanus Bijleveld, which opened a brisk fire and halted the initial French movement. As there was in fact very little behind Bijleveld except some Dutch infantry that was beginning to arrive in accordance with Rebecque's orders for a heightened alert state, the artillery commander decided to withdraw northwards towards Quatre Bras.

Quatre Bras – 'four arms' – was a tiny hamlet around a

---

* An ex-cavalry trooper, Lefebvre-Desnouettes was a major general when he was captured at Benavente, during the retreat to Corunna in December 1808, became a prisoner of war in Cheltenham, where he was joined by his wife and son, broke his parole and escaped back to France in time for the Russian adventure of 1812. After Napoleon's second abdication in 1815, Lefebvre was sentenced to death *in absentia* by the Bourbons but escaped to America. Amnestied, he set out to return to France in 1821 but was drowned when his ship sank in a storm off Kinsale.

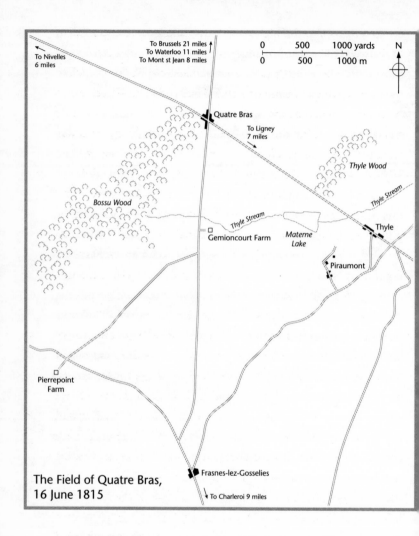

To Nivelles
6 miles

To Brussels 21 miles ↑
To Waterloo 11 miles
To Mont st Jean 8 miles

0   500   1000 yards

0   500   1000 m

N

Quatre Bras

To Ligney
7 miles

Thyle Wood

Bossu Wood

Thyle Stream

Thyle Stream

Thyle

Gemioncourt Farm

Materne
Lake

Piraumont

Pierrepoint
Farm

The Field of Quatre Bras,
16 June 1815

Frasnes-lez-Gosselies

↓ To Charleroi 9 miles

crossroads, where the high road from Charleroi running north to Brussels was crossed by the east–west Roman road that linked Sombreffe, where the Prussians were concentrating, and Nivelles, the town to which Wellington had ordered his Anglo-Dutch army. As we have seen, the road was important to both Allies as the only swift means of communication between them. Quatre Bras was vital, for if the French could take and hold that crossroads, then any Allied attempt to combine the two armies would be, while not impossible, a very lengthy and difficult process. In a very real sense, this crossroads was the objective that had to be taken, and quickly, if the overall French plan was to work at all. Now was the time to throw caution aside and drive up the high road with infantry and take the crossroads – and if the French high command had thought about it, they would have realized as much.

It was not to be. Marshal Ney acted with unusual hesitation: he sent forward one battalion of infantry to support the cavalry but little could be seen owing to the crops of standing maize and the gathering dusk. Ney had fought Wellington in the Peninsula: he had led his men up slopes against and through the British skirmishers to arrive at the top of a crest, satisfied that he had taken the position only to find the reverse slope lined by red-coated infantrymen firing their volleys at close range and dealing out death and destruction to their attackers. We can only assume that Ney thought that a single battery of guns and a few Dutch infantrymen could not possibly be all that Wellington would have placed to cover a vital crossroads. There must be more behind the ridge; to attack now in the gathering dark would be suicidal – far better to wait until the morrow. Whatever his reasoning may have been, Ney ordered the left wing to bivouac for the night. The chance of using the Napoleonic tactic of the central position and pressing on to Brussels was lost and, though none yet knew it, barring a miracle so was the campaign.

The rest of the Allied infantry brigade now moving up to Quatre Bras was temporarily commanded by Colonel Bernhard of Saxe-Weimar, the 23-year-old heir to the grand duchy of Saxe-Weimar-Eisenach, whose superior, Colonel Frederick van Gödecke, had been kicked by a horse that morning. These men were hardly comparable with the British and Portuguese infantry that Ney had faced on the ridge at Busaco. One of Saxe-Weimar's line battalions was armed with British muskets, most of which were old and had been hurriedly refurbished, another with the smaller-calibre French musket, while the skirmishers, a *Jäger* (light infantry) battalion, were equipped with four different calibres of rifles – he would have to ensure that his quartermaster was able to procure six different types of ammunition.

Wellington had insisted on attending the ball in Brussels, as his non-appearance could have been perceived as panicking. As it was, it was not until his Prussian liaison officer had brought him reports that there was fighting to the south and that Napoleon himself and elements of the Imperial Guard had been positively identified – and these reports had been further supported by the arrival of a staff officer from Lieutenant General Sir Wilhelm Kasper Ferdinand von Dörnberg, commander of the 3rd Cavalry Brigade at Mons – that Wellington could be sure that the main French thrust was indeed coming north for Brussels and not around the British right flank at Mons. Dörnberg's despatch reported that there were no camp fires to his front, such French troops that there were on the French side of the border were all national guardsmen, and all the French cavalry had moved east. Wellington now sent ADCs and orderly dragoons to order units to stand to while the chief of staff, DeLancey, prepared operational orders telling each formation where to go, concentrating the army at Quatre Bras and reversing the previous instructions to go to Nivelles.

Earlier, Saxe-Weimar's brigade had been ordered to Nivelles, but he and Lieutenant General Henri-Georges Perponcher-Sedlnitzky, commanding the 2nd Netherlands Division, decided to ignore that order and concentrate at Quatre Bras. No doubt any concern they might have had at disobeying an order was mitigated by their recall of an instruction issued by Colonel Wellesley in 1803, one in which he reminded his officers that an order may be given, which, 'from circumstances not known to the person who gave it at the time he issued it, would be impossible to execute'. Perponcher also ordered up the other brigade in his division, that of Major General Willem Frederick van Bijlandt, whose command consisted of a (French-speaking) Belgian line battalion, three Dutch militia battalions, a Dutch *Jäger* battalion and a battery of guns. These actions by Perponcher and Rebecque were critical to the forthcoming battle.

As Napoleon rode back to Charleroi to spend the night, and despite the failure of Ney to crack on up the Brussels road – something he may not even have known about, he would have been reasonably pleased with the day's progress. His army had covered thirty miles against opposition stiffer than had been expected, and his enemies' armies were not yet concentrated and a very long way from joining. He must have thought that his plan was still capable of achievement and that on the morrow he could defeat one of his opponents and then turn on the other. Orders to Ney that night instructed him to press on the following morning, and, although apologists for Ney have claimed that the contradictory nature of the various instructions he received – was he to take Quatre Bras, or to advance towards Brussels? – must have confused him, as an experienced soldier Ney should surely have realized that taking and holding the crossroads and preventing the Allied armies from joining was a priority. As it happened, of course, the Allied armies did not join at that stage of the campaign, nor did they attempt to, but had Ney shown more of a sense of urgency, the French plan might have had a chance of working.

All night British and Dutch-Belgian infantry, cavalry and guns were on the march – the reserve from Brussels, others from Nivelles and from Mons, all heading for Quatre Bras – while seven miles off to the east Prussian troops were arriving in the vicinity of Sombreffe. It now really was a race against time, for if the French bestirred themselves and attacked north towards Quatre Bras before the troops that Wellington had set in motion got there, they would easily brush aside Perponcher's one division. Wellington, having approved the orders written by DeLancey, snatched a few hours' sleep before being awakened by the arrival of General Dörnberg himself, who emphasized what his previous despatch had said. The duke and his immediate staff then left Brussels by horseback at around 0700 hours on 16 June and met the Prince of Orange at Quatre Bras. The prince had been there since around 0600 hours and was supervising the deployment of the battalions of Bijlandt's brigade, which were still arriving. He explained to the commander-in-chief that the French had as yet made no move and that – apart from some desultory firing between piquets and a minor skirmish when the Dutch-Belgians had pushed back a French cavalry patrol and regained some of the ground they had given up the previous day – all was quiet. Wellington rode around the Dutch-Belgian defence line, pronounced himself satisfied and rode six miles east over the Roman road to meet Blücher.

The Prussian commander had appreciated that the French attack would come from the direction of Fleurus and had

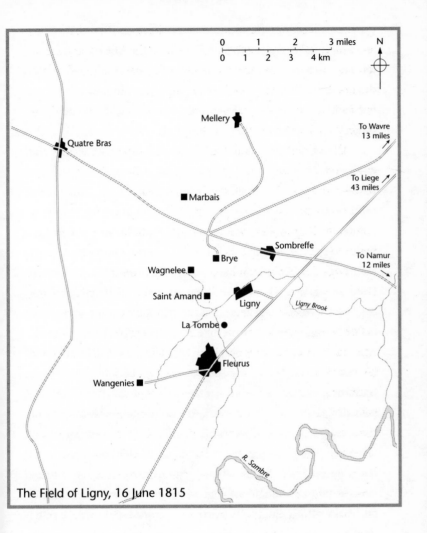

The Field of Ligny, 16 June 1815

positioned Ziethen's corps in a rough semi-circle along the Ligny brook, with his left in the village of Ligny, his centre in Saint-Amand and his right flank at Wagnelée. The brook itself was no obstacle – an infantryman could jump over it with ease – but its valley was marshy and would be a problem for artillery and wheeled vehicles. The brook would also likely slow any cavalry attack, and as a clearly visible feature it was an obvious boundary to give to the troops. Each village, hamlet and cluster of farm buildings was in the process of being fortified, with roads blocked by furniture taken from houses, overturned farm carts and felled trees, and the soldiers were making loopholes in the walls and roofs of houses, to cover all likely approaches, with gun batteries sited to support the defenders. Ziethen's, being the nearest corps to the concentration area, was first to come in, followed by Pirch's II Corps, which Blücher ordered to take post on the slope south of the hamlet of Brye where they could overlook the Ligny brook. The last corps to arrive before the action started was Thielemann's – Bülow's stately progress meant that he would not arrive until the coming battle was over – and he was positioned on the left of Pirch, between Sombreffe and Mazy, four-and-a-half miles east. Blücher therefore was covering a frontage of around twelve miles, with Ziethen's 32,000 men with a brigade of cavalry under command holding the Ligny brook salient, supported by Pirch's 33,000 and Thielemann's 25,000 on the high ground above the brook. Behind Pirch and Thielemann were two brigades of cavalry and altogether the Prussians fielded 312 artillery pieces, including some twelve-pounders. On the face of it, they should have been a match for anything the French might throw at them, particularly as there were only four bridges over the brook and its marshy valley that could take artillery.

Wellington arrived at Brye around midday. He and Blücher met at a windmill, long since demolished, to the south of the hamlet. Wellington advised the Prussian field marshal that to have the bulk of his troops formed up on the forward slope would make them a very tempting target for the French artillery, and suggested that they might be moved to the reverse slope. A reverse slope position, always a favourite of Wellingtonian defensive postures, meant that men could administer themselves and rest out of sight of the enemy and out of direct fire. Skirmishers would be in cover on the forward slope to give warning of an approach, but an attacking force could not see the troops they were supposed to be taking on until they had got to the top of the crest, tired and unsure where their objective actually was. Blücher is supposed to have retorted, 'My boys like to see their enemy', but the real reason for his deployment was almost certainly that desertion would be much harder from the forward slope, whereas to slip away would be relatively easy on the far side of the crest. Blücher was well aware that for much of the Prussian rank and file this would be their first experience of battle. Wellington assured Blücher that, if he was attacked, he, Wellington, would come to his assistance 'provided I am not attacked myself'. Conspiracy theorists have made much of this meeting, claiming that Wellington promised assistance with no qualification and then deliberately left the Prussians to their own devices. Never mind that there was no earthly reason why Wellington should have wanted the Prussians to be defeated; the conversation was recorded by both Colonel Hardinge, liaison officer from the British to the Prussians, and his opposite number Major General Muffling, to whom Wellington's statement was quite clear: he would assist if he could. And as we shall see, he could not.

Meanwhile, there was confusion in the French camp. Napoleon now seems to have been reconsidering his initial view that his first target would be the Prussians, and certainly Ney appears to have been under the impression that Napoleon and the powerful reserve would be coming to support him in pressing on to Brussels. There were indeed a plethora of orders going out to both wings, and these in the emperor's own handwriting – something that, because of its near illegibility, Berthier would never have allowed. Here we see more evidence of bad staff work at imperial headquarters, and the possible cause of Ney's otherwise inexplicable delay in doing anything on the morning of 16 June, when, had he moved in strength at first light, he could still have been well up the Brussels road, with the crossroads of Quatre Bras in his pocket, before Wellington's reinforcements had arrived.

By the time that Ney did stir himself – and well before he received Napoleon's final order, which made clear that he was to take Quatre Bras – most of Perponcher's 2nd Netherlands Division was in place. To the west of the Brussels road was Saxe-Weimar's brigade in Bossu Wood, which ran south from the crossroads as far as and just over the ridge, cut back to a distance of one hundred yards or so from the road.* They were able to overlook a large farmhouse on their right flank, Pierrepoint (now a golf clubhouse), in which the French were ensconced, and they could give covering fire to the gun battery, which was still positioned either side of the road. This looked to be a strong position – any commander was (and is) wary of

---

* A legal requirement to make things difficult for highway robbers. In medieval England the rule was one bowshot from the road.

attacking into woods – but the brigade had only ten rounds per man for muskets and rifles, and nobody was sure where their ammunition wagons had got to.

To the east of the high road were Bijlandt's battalions, some of which had been marching all night, with his headquarters and two battalions in the farm of Gemioncourt. This lay about 700 yards south of the crossroads and was a stoutly built manor house with adjoining barns; it was the property of the local diocese, and probably then around 200 years old, and it had been built for defence in an age when life in the cockpit of Europe was even more unstable than it was in 1815. Also arriving as Bijlandt's supporting artillery was another battery, giving the Dutch-Belgians a total of sixteen guns. A section of Prussian cavalry from the Silesian Hussars, who had become separated from their parent regiment and had attached themselves to the Dutch, now clattered off to Sombreffe, having discovered from Wellington where the Prussian army was.

At this stage, therefore, all that was standing between Ney and Quatre Bras was nine battalions of infantry, much of it inexperienced, and sixteen guns. Having lost his borrowed Prussian cavalry, and well aware of the preponderance of French horsemen in the area, the Prince of Orange sent an ADC to Braine-le-Comte, fourteen miles off to the east, to order up the light cavalry brigade of Major General Jean-Baptiste van Merlen, consisting of the 6th Dutch Hussars and the 5th Belgian Light Dragoons. Van Merlen had served in the French cavalry of the Imperial Guard and should, the prince thought, know how to deal with his erstwhile comrades, but it would take at least four hours before he could arrive at Quatre Bras.

Napoleon's indecision over which enemy he should attack

first was resolved by a message from Grouchy to the effect that the Prussians, rather than retiring north, were massing on the ridge of Sombreffe and preparing to offer battle. Napoleon rode over to Fleurus and from a windmill in the village scanned the Prussian position through his telescope. This was his chance: he would revert to his original plan and from around 1100 hours the emperor issued orders for an attack on the Prussians. The plan, like all good plans, was a simple one: the cavalry of Pajol and Exelmans would harry the Prussian left wing and prevent them from supporting their centre, which would be attacked by the corps of Vandamme and Gérard. Once the main body of the Prussians was under attack and unable to manoeuvre, Ney, having attacked up the Brussels road and having driven back anything approaching, would send at least one corps along the Roman road from Quatre Bras to strike in rear of the Prussian right wing. This would drive the Prussians back along the road to Liège, away from Wellington and towards Germany. Napoleon himself would stand by with the Guard ready to reinforce if necessary. As Gérard's corps was still some way back and the Guard had only just cleared Charleroi, the attack would begin at around 1430 hours. When all was ready, Napoleon would have about 51,000 infantry, 12,000 cavalry and 210 guns to pit against around 82,000 Prussian infantry with 8,000 cavalry and 312 guns – hardly the textbook stipulation of a three-to-one superiority for a successful attack, but with the Guard in reserve, Ney's support and the exposed Prussian position, it would surely be more than sufficient.

Back at Quatre Bras, Ney finally moved. At about 1400 hours he sent the three divisions and 20,000 men of Reille's corps, supported by the cavalry division of Major General Hippolyte-Marie-Guillaume Piré – around 2,000 horsemen including a brigade of lancers – and two batteries of guns, against the ridge south of Gemioncourt farm on which were Bijlandt's brigade and an artillery battery, with Saxe-Weimar's men on their right in Bossu Wood. The Dutch-Belgians fought fiercely, but eventually numbers began to tell, and although the French could make little progress against Bossu Wood – and nor, to begin with, did they press very hard on that flank – they did succeed eventually in driving Bijlandt's men out of Gemioncourt and capturing two of his guns. Some of these troops made for Bossu Wood, but most, still in their cohesive units, began to pull back north, along the high road towards the crossroads, forming square to fend off the pursuing French cavalry. The French almost scored a major coup by catching the Prince of Orange: almost but not quite, as the prince had a very good, and very fast, Arab horse, a gift from the Tsar, which got its master back to Quatre Bras.[*]

For all the thought and all the planning, luck still plays a part in military affairs, and it was good luck as much as anything else that brought Wellington to Quatre Bras from Ligny just as Bijlandt's men were streaming up the road from Gemioncourt. The duke and the Prince of Orange between them soon had the Dutch-Belgians rallied and formed once again by the crossroads, when the first men of the Allied army ordered to Quatre Bras arrived – van Merlen's cavalry that the prince had sent for earlier. This was closely followed by units of the 5th British Infantry Division commanded by Lieutenant General Sir Thomas Picton, which consisted of seven British infantry battalions and six companies of the 95th Rifles, all of whom were Peninsula veterans, four Hanoverian *Landwehr* battalions and two artillery batteries, one

---

[*] Contemporary accounts say that this was a stallion, which is unlikely. Entires are rarely sufficiently tractable to be used in an operational environment. It was probably a gelding.

British and one Hanoverian. After the Rifles, the 1st Battalion 28th Foot were next to arrive, and while van Merlen's cavalry held off that of Piré, the duke instructed Bijlandt to put his brigade into column and to advance down the road and retake Gemioncourt farm. They were to be followed up by the 28th, who would garrison the farm once the French had been driven out.

Wellington of course knew that, if a brigade could not hold Gemioncourt farm, a brigade could not retake it, and even if by some fluke they could, it could not be held by a mere one battalion, not even by a British veteran battalion. And indeed it could not, but the operation, which got to within 150 yards of the farm, traded Dutch and Belgian lives for time – time for Wellington to deploy Picton's battalions, which were arriving at the crossroads, having marched the twenty miles from Brussels. The Rifles were sent off to the east to anchor the left flank. They were told to get into position in the village of Piraumont, but found that the French were already there, so they took cover in the hamlet of Thyle, east of Étang Materne, or Materne Lake – which was not a lake at all but a man-made pond to provide water for animals, yet big enough to provide an obstacle to any French attempt to get around the Allied left flank – and in what the British called Cherry Wood, which lay north of Materne and north of the road. Safe in Thyle and in the wood, the Rifles could stop anyone coming out of Piraumont and around the eastern end of Materne, their 400 Baker rifles allowing them to kill Frenchmen at a far greater distance than the range of the French musket. It was an excellent position, which, if held, would anchor Wellington's left flank.

Considering that the right flank on Bossu Wood was secured, at least for the present, by Saxe-Weimar's men, Wellington next fed Picton's battalions as they arrived along a diagonal line from the crossroads to the Materne Lake, while the gun batteries took post either side of the crossroads. By the time that the French had beaten off the advance by Bijlandt and the 28th, there was a line of red-coated infantry stretching all the way from the Materne Lake to the crossroads. From east to west were the 79th and the 32nd Foot of Major General Sir James Kempt's brigade and then Major General Sir Denis Pack's 3/1st, 2/44th, and 42nd Foot, with the 92nd around the crossroads itself. Just behind the road stood the Hanoverian brigade in support.

At this stage of the battle at Quatre Bras, the open ground to the east of the Brussels road was planted with maize and rye, up to eight feet in height and impossible to see through. Only the officers on horseback could see or be seen, and only the tips of the men's fixed bayonets could tell an observer where they were as they tramped off to their positions. The French now launched infantry columns from the area of Gemioncourt towards the crossroads. Picton's battalions moved forward in line until they reached the edge of the rye where they could see the advancing French, and with a series of volleys of musketry at close range sent them back whence they came. This was not, however, without cost, for as the British infantry emerged from the rye, they came under canister fire from French artillery and were ordered to withdraw back to their original position, without being able to recover all their wounded. For those who had been hit by a French ball the situation now became far worse, for the burning wads from the British musketry set the stubble on fire and many of the wounded, unable to move, were burned to death.

French light cavalry and lancers could make little progress against Picton's men, partly because of the difficulty in moving through the rye and also because of the well-aimed volleys of musketry at short range. One group of lancers managed to get in between battalions and behind the 44th, who were about 300 yards east of the high road. There was no time to form square, so the commanding officer ordered the rear rank to face about and soon the musketry volleys drove off the lancers, except for one man who managed to spear the officer carrying the king's colour through the jaw and attempted to carry off the colour. That officer was Ensign Christie, a commissioned sergeant and a hard veteran of many battles. He would not let the colour go, and his escort of sergeants cut down and killed the lancer. Christie survived Quatre Bras, and Waterloo, despite a horrible and disfiguring wound. He would go on half-pay in October 1815 and live a long and honourable retirement, never having to buy a drink as long as he told the tale of his saving the colour – a tale that doubtless got more daring and more harrowing the more glasses of gin were consumed.

Meanwhile, the next group to arrive at the crossroads was the Brunswick contingent consisting of the Duke of Brunswick himself with the 2nd Brunswick Hussars of around 600 men and a squadron of lancers and five battalions of infantry. The cavalry was sent forward to keep the French horse at bay while the infantry was dispersed to back up the defenders of Bossu Wood, to reinforce the Rifles at Thyle and to strengthen Picton's line. One of Brunswick's battalions was severely mauled by the French cavalry, and a charge by his own cavalry was not pressed home. It was while the duke was trying to rally his hussars south of the crossroads that he was hit. The ball, probably from canister or possibly a French cavalry carbine or pistol, pierced his liver and knocked him from his horse. He lived for only a few minutes and command of the contingent devolved on his second-in-command, Colonel Olfermann.

As the day wore on, more and more of Wellington's troops

arrived and Ney became more and more desperate. An infantry attack supported by cavalry on the British left having failed, the marshal ordered a charge by the heavy cavalry straight up the road to take the crossroads. Major General François Étienne Kellermann, commanding III Reserve Cavalry Corps, gave this task to the 2nd (Cuirassier) Brigade of Major General Samuel François L'Héritier's 11th Cavalry Division. Cuirassiers were big men on big horses, armoured front and rear and wielding long straight swords, heavy enough to cleave a man's skull in with one blow. Kellermann personally led the charge of five squadrons, each numbering around 100 officers and men, and it nearly succeeded – indeed, had his second cuirassier brigade been present, it might well have done, but that brigade had been seriously delayed crossing the Sambre and was many miles away. That the charge failed was due to sniping from Bossu Wood by Saxe-Weimar's men, artillery fire from the British and Hanoverian guns either side of the crossroads, and finally volley fire from the Brunswick and British infantry at the crossroads. Kellermann himself was wounded and his horse killed, and he only escaped capture by hanging onto the nosebands of two of his troopers' horses and returning to Gemioncourt.

Then there was a crisis at Thyle, which the Rifles were forced to give up, falling back into Cherry Wood where they could still cover Wellington's left. It was while Wellington was at Thyle, supervising the changed deployment of the Rifles, that the Prince of Orange ordered the newly arrived 5th British Brigade of Lieutenant General Charles (Karl) Alten's 3rd British Infantry Division to advance down the road towards Gemioncourt farm to block any further French cavalry movement down the relatively good going (for horses) of the road and the cleared area between the road and Bossu Wood. The brigade commander, Major General Sir Colin Halkett, like his divisional commander lately an officer of the King's German Legion, marched his four battalions down the road and formed them either side of the road in battalion squares. This was a perfectly sensible move, and four battalions in square with full cartridge pouches were more than enough to stop any more cavalry probes, but the Prince of Orange was unhappy. Riding up to Sir Colin, he ordered him to place his battalions in line. Presumably the prince considered that a battalion in line could produce far more firepower than one in square and would be less of a target for French artillery, which was quite correct, but not the point. When Halkett demurred, pointing out that the threat was from cavalry, the prince said that he could see no cavalry – as indeed he could not, as it was forming up out of sight behind Gemioncourt farm – and repeated his order.

Today, a blatantly silly order from a superior would be circumvented,* but on 16 June 1815 this was an order coming from a senior officer, the corps commander no less, and the son of an Allied sovereign to boot, even if he was barely out of nappies. Halkett duly galloped along his battalions and ordered them into line. It was just what the French cavalry had been waiting for and they did not neglect the opportunity. The result was catastrophic. The 2/69th were overrun and their king's colour captured (the only time a colour was ever lost by a battalion under Wellington's command), while the 33rd and the 2/73rd were driven in disorder into Bossu Wood. Only the 2/30th, Peninsula veterans, stood fast. Having seen it all before, they turned their rear rank about,

---

* In this author's battalion the expression was 'agree and evade'.

delivered several regular volleys, formed square when the first rush of horsemen had passed, and withdrew in good order into Bossu Wood. By this time Wellington had returned from Thyle. He cantered up to the edge of the wood, dismounted, threw the reins of his horse to an ADC, and castigated the officers of the 33rd – the regiment that he had commanded for many years and whose colonel he had been – saying that he expected better of them. The brigade was soon re-formed, in squares this time.

While the scattering of Halkett's brigade was the low point of the battle for the Allies, Wellington's strength was increasing all the time. The shortage of ammunition was resolved by the arrival of wagons at the crossroads, and the British Guards Division was on its way. Ney had no more than Reille's corps and part of Kellermann's cavalry corps. He should have been able to throw d'Erlon's corps of 20,000 men into the operation but he could not, because d'Erlon was not available to Ney, nor indeed was he available to Napoleon.

Over at Ligny, the battle had begun shortly after the first shot had been fired at Quatre Bras. It began well enough when the French cavalry chased the Prussian mounted patrols back onto their own main body, and the infantry attacked the villages of Saint-Amand and Ligny. These were much tougher nuts than the French had expected. At Saint-Amand, after being repulsed several times – on one occasion the Prussian counter-attack was led by Blücher in person – the French secured the village only with the deployment of Vandamme's reserve division. The same story applied at Ligny, where one of the strong points at the edge of the town was only taken by trickery, when a German-speaking soldier from Alsace claimed to be deserting to the Prussians. As more and more Prussian soldiers were sucked into the battle, and as the French artillery wreaked more and more havoc on the men deployed on the forward slope of the high ground, now was the time for Ney to intervene on the Prussian right and rear. There was, though, no sign of Ney as he had not yet received the order telling him to send a corps across.

What happened at this point is the subject of much confusion: written messages have been lost, recollections contradict and all the relevant commanders blame each other. What is certain is that Napoleon wanted Ney's reserve – d'Erlon's corps – to move to Ligny to envelop the Prussian right and rear.

One theory holds that the emperor despatched the 29-year-old Brigadier General Charles-Angélique-François-Huchet Labédoyère with a message to Ney telling him to send d'Erlon. Labédoyère was of aristocratic origins but embraced the Revolution with fervour and was a great (and vocal) admirer of Napoleon. No great field commander, he was a professional ADC, serving a number of the marshals in that capacity, until as a colonel he was given command of a regiment of the line by the newly restored Bourbons. One of the first to take his regiment over to Napoleon in March 1815, he was promoted and appointed as an ADC to the emperor himself. On his way across to Quatre Bras, Labédoyère saw d'Erlon's column and rode up to its commander and told him to make for Ligny. He did not do as he should have done, which was to go to Marshal Ney first. D'Erlon duly set off, and sometime in the late afternoon the men of Vandamme's corps reported a column of troops behind the French left. Was it the Prussians? All action stopped while riders were sent out to identify them. They were of course d'Erlon's men, but in the meantime Ney, fearful that he was about to be counter-attacked, prepared to commit d'Erlon, only to find that I Corps was on its way to Ligny, without so much as a by your leave. Furious, the marshal despatched an

ADC ordering d'Erlon to return to Quatre Bras at once. On the principle of always obeying the last order, d'Erlon turned his men about and began to retrace his steps towards Quatre Bras.

Another theory has it that Napoleon sent a written message ordering d'Erlon to march on Wagnelée, on the extreme right of the Prussian position. This would make sense as a whole corps debouching on Wagnelée could certainly turn the Prussian flank and get behind them, spelling certain defeat for Blücher. Napoleon's handwriting was so bad, however, that d'Erlon read Wagnelée as Wagenies, a completely different village situated a mile and a half south-west of Fleurus and behind the French flank, not the Prussian. Whatever the truth of the matter, the fact is that d'Erlon and his 20,000 men spent the day of 16 June marching backwards and forwards between Quatre Bras and Ligny without firing a shot and to no avail whatsoever.

At Quatre Bras, with the arrival of the Guards Division Wellington now outnumbered Ney in every arm except cavalry. The Guards were fed into Bossu Wood as they arrived, and succeeded in driving out the French from the southern edge and in recapturing the farm of Pierrepoint, while Picton's and the Hanoverian infantry pushed back the French to Gemioncourt farm and beyond. A stubborn knot of French infantry held grimly on in a house and garden just short of the crossroads, but they were dealt with by a charge of the 92nd, the Gordon Highlanders, who were glad to move from their exposed position around the crossroads. The charge was actually led by Major General Edward Barnes, who was the adjutant general, a senior staff officer who had no business to be anywhere near the front but could not resist a taste of the action. He was slightly wounded, but the commanding officer of the Gordons was killed. As dusk approached, the French had no more to throw in, and as the Allies retook all the ground the Dutch-Belgians had been forced to give up earlier in the day, Ney accepted that he could do no more and returned to Frasnes, from where he had started.

At Ligny, where Napoleon had now committed both corps and the Imperial Guard, experience eventually told. Shredded by artillery fire from the French twelve-pounders, the Prussian line buckled and then broke. The French infantry hammered through the gap in the now pouring rain and marched up the slope, to be met by 2,000 cavalry led by Blücher in person. Again and again the hussars and the uhlans charged, and again and again they were driven back by a combination of French cavalry, artillery and musketry, but they did give the Prussian infantry, what was left of it, time to get off the field. During one of his charges Blücher's horse was killed and fell, pinning the field marshal under it. Darkness was closing in, and in the heavy rain no Frenchman noticed the half-conscious figure pinned under a horse. Only swift work by one of Blücher's ADCs and a cavalry sergeant enabled the old warrior to be rescued and carried off the field to join the broken remnants of the Prussian army as it retreated into the night. By about 2100 hours Napoleon was able to survey the field devoid of any Prussians save the dead, the dying and those too badly wounded to hobble away. Despite all the problems, the emperor had defeated one of his enemies, and now he had only the Anglo-Dutch to worry about. He and his staff retired to the Ferme d'en Haut on the outskirts of Ligny for the night.

Wellington reported the British and Hanoverian casualties at Quatre Bras as twenty-nine officers and 321 Other Ranks killed, 126 officers and 2,254 Other Ranks wounded, and four officers and 177 Other Ranks missing. He reported that the missing officers were presumed killed, while most of the missing Other Ranks had probably been taken wounded to the rear and would rejoin. The report also listed nineteen horses killed, fourteen wounded and one missing.[26] The Dutch-Belgians reported 1,500 casualties, of which around 500 were probably killed, and the Brunswick casualties were around 200 killed, including their duke. The 3rd Battalion 1st Foot, the Royal Scots, lost 200 men killed and wounded out of a strength of around 650; the 42nd and the 92nd around 300 each; the 79th over 300; and the two battalions of the 1st Foot Guards around 500 men between them. The French lost around the same. At Ligny, there were 16,000 Prussian casualties, killed, wounded and missing, and they lost twenty-one guns. French casualties were around 11,500.

On the profit-and-loss sheet of 16 June 1815, the French had prevented the Anglo-Dutch army from combining with the Prussians, but shoddy staff-work, confused orders and dilatoriness had robbed them of the overwhelming victory that should have been theirs. Wellington had been slow to recognize where the main French thrust was coming from, and only the recognition of the importance of the crossroads at Quatre Bras by the Prince of Orange and Generals Rebecque and Perponcher prevented a potential disaster on 15 June. Even then, had Ney attacked early on the morning of 16 June, much could have been achieved. Napoleon had failed to bring Lobau's VI Corps into action at all, which could have made a difference to either battle. As it was, each wing thought that the other was coming to support it, and the failure to make it clear to Ney that he was to despatch d'Erlon proved crucial. It prevented the latter from placing his corps in rear of the Prussians and forcing them to retreat towards home, rather than allowing them to act as they actually did. This was a major factor contributing to the French defeat at Waterloo that would come two days later.

As the rain bucketed down, all three armies licked their wounds and pondered their next moves.

7

THE CRISIS APPROACHES

During 16 June, while battle raged at Quatre Bras and Ligny, the weather alternated between broiling hot sun and summer thunderstorms. In the evening this had changed to an almost constant downpour, making the lives of the wounded and the retreating even more miserable than they would otherwise have been. Blücher, still half-conscious, was carried on a horse to a house in the village of Mellery, five miles north of Sombreffe. Being trapped under a dead horse in heavy rain is not conducive to the well-being of a 73-year-old,* and it says a great deal for the health-giving properties of a diet of onions, tobacco, coffee and gin that the field marshal was soon demanding to know the whereabouts of his army. The army had been scattered at Ligny, with individuals and small bodies making their way off the battlefield as best they could, but this army was staffed by Germans, and the chief of staff, Gneisenau, had sent out staff officers, ADCs and cavalrymen to every road junction, every fork in every track, and every hamlet with details of a rendezvous for every battalion, regiment and

---

* It's not conducive to well-being at any age, as this author can testify.

battery of guns to which stragglers were to make. Once reunited, units were to march north, for Wavre.

If Gneisenau had had his way, they would have headed east for Liège and home: he did not trust the British and was convinced that they would withdraw from Europe back to England if it was in their interests to do so – as indeed they probably would have done if Wellington had seen no alternative. But Blücher had made it clear that, if they were driven off the field at Ligny, the army was to keep in contact with the Anglo-Dutch, and that meant going north, not east. Had Ney or d'Erlon been able to do what Napoleon wanted them to do earlier in the day – fall on the Prussian right wing – then Blücher would have had no choice but to go east, and it was this failure of communication, in all senses, that was perhaps the key to eventual French defeat.

As yet, Wellington had no knowledge of the fate of the Prussians. The last he had heard, at about 1800 hours, was when an officer sent by Blücher reported that they were still under heavy attack but hoped to hold their ground until nightfall (when the battle would die down – night operations of any magnitude were almost never undertaken in an age before telephones, radios and accurate maps). Units of the Anglo-Dutch army were still arriving at Quatre Bras, and, although he no longer needed them there, Wellington did not rescind his instructions: to order an about-turn would not bother the British, who would merely grumble and tramp back the way they had come, but for some of the Allied contingents, whose morale was more fragile, such an order could be taken as indicative of a defeat and allow panic to spread. In any case, to try to turn around the columns of ammunition wagons, ambulances, guns, horses and marching men at night would be a recipe for chaos. As battalions and regiments arrived, they were allocated bivouac areas and did their best to sleep in the rain while doing everything they could for the wounded who had not yet been recovered to the medical aid posts and the hospital in Brussels. Desultory firing by piquets on both sides went on all night, but there was no offensive move by either.

At this stage Wellington seems to have intended to go on the offensive the next day, in combination with the Prussians, and he and his staff rode off to Genappe, about two miles north, to spend the night in the Roi d'Espagne Hotel. At first light on 17 June, a cavalry patrol accompanied by one of Wellington's ADCs, Captain and Lieutenant Colonel Alexander Gordon, 3rd Foot Guards,* rode over to Ligny and found the field littered with dead and wounded Prussians and French cavalry. Gordon returned to Wellington and his report was confirmed by a Prussian staff officer who arrived to deliver a message from Blücher to the effect that his army was reorganizing at Wavre and, while it could not undertake any offensive operations that day, would be ready to do so on the morrow.

Wellington was now very much out on a limb. If he stayed where he was, he risked being cut off from his lines of communication (and escape route to the Channel); if Blücher had withdrawn north, then so must he. There was indeed now some urgency, for if Napoleon turned on him now, or caught him in the act of withdrawing his troops, he could still suffer a defeat from which there would be no recovery. Any concern he may have felt was shortly allayed by Major General Muffling: he had fought Napoleon and assured Wellington that there would

---

* As an officer of the Guards, he was a captain when serving with his regiment, but a lieutenant colonel (and paid as such) when on ERE (extra-regimental employment), as he was as an ADC.

be no possibility of an early start for the French – they would be allowed to have their breakfast in a leisurely fashion and would be unlikely to stir much before midday. Colonel DeLancey now began to scribble orders for the withdrawal, which Wellington said was to be to Mont-Saint-Jean, a ridge four miles south of the hamlet of Waterloo, or to Waterloo itself. Meanwhile a message went off to the Prussians saying that Wellington intended to take up a position on the ridge of Mont-Saint-Jean and would fight the battle there, provided that Blücher could support him with at least two corps. If Blücher was unable to support him, Wellington intended to abandon Brussels and fight a defensive battle further back on the route to Antwerp.

The withdrawal was and is one of the most difficult phases of war, particularly if it is to be done in contact with the enemy. Unless there is a very firm grip, it can too easily develop into a rout. The secret lies in clear orders laying down exactly when each unit is to vacate its position and the precise route that it is to follow, with particular attention paid to traffic control at choke points – road junctions, bridges, villages and the like. Ideally the withdrawing formations should attempt to break clean of the enemy, but if that is not possible, there must be a dedicated rearguard whose task it is to fend off the pursuing enemy to allow the main body to get clear.

In this case, while to the individual soldiers hastening to get clear of the French the withdrawal seemed chaotic, in fact it was meticulously planned and superbly controlled by DeLancey and his staff. The wounded and baggage wagons were sent off first, at around 1000 hours, followed by units in rear of the front line, in order to give the impression to Ney that the Allied army was still in position at Quatre Bras. As newly arrived battalions approached the crossroads in accordance with the previous day's orders to concentrate there, they were fed into the front line while those units they relieved slipped away up the Brussels road. All this was going on under torrents of rain, and while the quartermasters of some battalions managed to get some food up to their men, most did not, owing to the strict traffic control that made the high road a one-way route north. Most soldiers did manage to get their ration of liquor, however – a pint of wine or a third of a pint of spirits per day, in Flanders usually gin, this being easily and cheaply procured from Holland – and as commerce does not come to a stop just because there is a war on, the 95th Rifles found a farmer to sell them a number of hams, while other regiments availed themselves of the services of purveyors of brandy who appeared by the roadside.[27] The main body began to move at around 1130 hours, battalions of infantry marching off up the high road, flanked by the cavalry in two columns. The rearguard was commanded by the cavalry corps commander, Lieutenant General the Earl of Uxbridge, and consisted of the 7th Hussars, the Royal Horse Artillery and the 95th Rifles, with the heavy cavalry of the Life Guards and the Royal Horse Guards – the 'Oxford Blues', as they were known in the army – in support. Uxbridge was instructed to remain in position as long as possible, but to avoid a serious engagement. In other words, he was to hold the French up and delay them, but to withdraw the rearguard before the French could make a serious attack upon it. This Uxbridge did brilliantly.

That the withdrawal was able to proceed so far unmolested was greatly helped by the lethargy of Ney and a misapprehension on the part of Napoleon. As far as the emperor was concerned, the Prussians had been roundly defeated – patrols had reported them streaming down the road to Namur – and they had not been able to join with Wellington, who had no doubt retreated towards Brussels, or even towards the Channel ports. It was not until mid-morning that it became clear that the traffic on the Namur road was non-essential baggage and deserters and that the main Prussian army had in fact retreated north. Grouchy was at last given permission to follow them up, but a later message from him to Napoleon identifying the area of Prussian concentration as Wavre – the Prussians had picked Wavre because in the dark the night before it was the only town that they could identify on their very basic maps – was not replied to. Had Napoleon ordered Grouchy to get in between the Prussians and the Anglo-Dutch, which he could easily have done, and stop them combining, or at least delayed them, then the result of the Battle of Waterloo – if it had been fought at all – could have been very different. As it was, Grouchy followed the Prussians north, rather than moving to the west of Wavre.

When Napoleon did send patrols down the Roman road towards Quatre Bras – or Quatre Chemins, as the French called it – he was astounded to find that there were still Allied troops there, for the patrols could not get close enough to see that the withdrawal had begun. Now there was a chance to defeat the second of his enemies, and gathering his staff about him, he made for Quatre Bras. He got to Marbais, halfway between Ligny and Quatre Bras, at around 1300 and hit the Brussels road shortly after that, to find Ney's men sitting around the roadside cooking and doing little else, with no sign of any Allied troops at the crossroads. The emperor was displeased and made this known to Ney, ordering him to throw the so far unblooded, albeit footsore, corps of d'Erlon in pursuit. According to d'Erlon's memoirs, published long after the event (and long after d'Erlon's death), Napoleon said to him:

'France has been ruined. Go, my dear general, place yourself at the head of the cavalry and pursue the rearguard vigorously.'[28] By the time d'Erlon was ready to march, Wellington had long gone, and the situation now developed into a race: could Wellington get his army back to Mont-Saint-Jean and into a defensive posture before his men were caught on the march by the French pursuit?

The weather, unpleasant though it was, helped Wellington. It had, of course, been pouring all night, and it was still raining. Infantrymen kept rags, old socks or any available piece of material wrapped around the locks of their muskets, so they would still fire, but reloading could only be done under cover, otherwise powder sprinkled into the pan was washed away or so wet that it would not ignite. The ground was such that horses sank up to their fetlocks in the mud, and anything other than a laborious trot was out of the question. Artillery could not move off the road, for if it tried to, the wheels of the guns sank into the mud and even the six-horse teams could barely shift them. This meant that pursuing French cavalry and artillery were confined to the road and so could not execute a wide flanking move, which could have cut off the withdrawing Anglo-Dutch.

As it was, the 95th Rifles were the last to withdraw. They first halted in the village of Genappe, intending to make a stand there if necessary, and soon found themselves sniping at French lancers who came clattering up the road. They executed a fighting withdrawal through the village, and as the lancers debouched from the northern end of Genappe, they were attacked by the 7th Hussars, encouraged by the commander of the cavalry, Uxbridge, himself. Against the lancers the hussars came off worse, but the situation was saved by a charge of the 1st Life Guards, who chased the French back the way they had come before continuing the withdrawal.

That was the pattern for the rest of the day: at each ridge line the Rifles would take post using whatever cover they could find, the horse artillery would unlimber and the cavalry would stand by in rear; as the French approached, the guns would open fire, the Rifles would snipe, the French were forced to try to deploy off the road, and once they had done so, the gun teams would limber up and withdraw, and the Rifles would scamper off covered by the cavalry. The Rifles were impressed by the 1st Life Guards, who supported them closely and charged anything that looked like a threat. Initially, the adjutant of the Rifles, Lieutenant John Kincaid, was concerned that, judging by the number of troopers being sent to the rear, there appeared to be an inordinate number of wounded among the Life Guards, until he discovered that it was not wounds but mud on their jackets that caused the men to be sent rearwards as 'not fit to be seen on parade'.[29] While the Life Guards had been in the Peninsula for the last year of the war, that had been their first taste of active service since the Marlborough wars: the sartorial standards of the King's Guard in London had to be maintained.

Wellington had decided that he would take up position on the ridge of Mont-Saint-Jean and that, subject to Prussian support, he would fight his battle there. All day, staff officers reconnoitred the positions that battalions and regiments were to take up when they arrived, and in some cases wooden pegs were driven into the ground to mark where their front ranks should be. The wagon-loads of wounded arrived first and were sent on to the hospitals in Brussels, while baggage and ammunition carts were sent to the hamlet of Waterloo, four miles north of Mont-Saint-Jean. After the administrative units came the cavalry and then the artillery batteries, which were ordered to take position along the ridge. Wellington has often been criticized by artillery experts for dispersing his guns, rather than concentrating them in the French fashion. But the French always had sufficient guns to produce grand batteries of them and still have enough left to support individual divisions; the British were always short of guns and had perforce to spread them out along the line. From around 1600 hours, the battalions and the regiments, the guns and the knots of staff officers were coming up the road and reaching the ridge of Mont-Saint-Jean, to be led from the road to the battle positions that Wellington had planned for them. The men were wet, tired, hungry and filthy. Some of the younger soldiers had lost their boots in the ankle-deep mud, and as they sank to the sodden ground for a brief rest before scouring the area for firewood, few had any idea that this was where they would stop and that this was where, on the morrow, they would fight the deciding battle of the campaign.

Further to the east, Marshal Grouchy – with a total of around 30,000 men in Vandamme's III Corps and Gérard's IV, Exelmans' and some of Pajol's cavalry, and a mix of foot batteries (six guns and two howitzers) and horse batteries (four guns and two howitzers), ninety-six guns in all – had made little progress. Much time had been wasted investigating the road to Namur, and by the time Grouchy got his wing moving along the route that the Prussians had actually taken towards Wavre, it was late in the day. A despatch sent off to Napoleon shows that Grouchy was unsure whether the Prussians were making for Brussels (why would they?) or whether they were intending to join with Wellington. By 1800 hours on 17 June, Grouchy had only got as far as Gembloux, eight miles from Ligny and twelve from Wavre, and it was here, despite there being three or four hours of daylight left, that he bivouacked for the night. Although it was not until 2200 hours that all his infantry arrived at Gembloux, there can be little excuse for the marshal not at least pushing his cavalry forward to harry the withdrawing Prussians. According to Captain Charles François, orderly officer to the 46-year-old Major General Marc Nicolas Louis Pécheux, commanding the 12th Division in Gérard's IV Corps, there was much argument among Grouchy's generals about what to do next.[30] Many thought progress was painfully, and unnecessarily, slow, Vandamme said that he did not trust his own chief of staff, and others thought that the emperor's position, facing the Anglo-Dutch army, was perilous.

By the morning of 17 June, the Prussian army was once more a coherent force, with brigades and corps that had fought at Ligny having gathered up their scattered men. Blücher arrived at Wavre around 0600 hours, having ridden past cheering columns of his men also heading there. There were still between 7,000 and 8,000 men missing, either deserters or stragglers whom the staff had not managed to scoop up. Blücher's reaction was that, if men did not want to fight, then he was better off without them. Ziethen's I Corps was the first to arrive at Wavre and was instructed to bivouac in the hamlet of Bierge, to the west of Wavre and north of the River Dyle.* Next to arrive was Pirch and II Corps, who were deployed north to Sainte-Anne. There was still some doubt about the whereabouts of the ammunition carts – vital if the army was to be replenished in time to fight the next day – but they eventually turned up around 1700. Now at least two corps could take the field. Thielemann's II Corps was later in arriving as there had been some delay in his getting the orders for the move to Wavre, but when

---

* A river line that would, ironically, become familiar to British soldiers 125 years later in the scramble to avoid the German onslaught in the 1940 Battle of France.

the main body of his corps did turn up at around 2000 hours, his troops were positioned around the Château de la Bawette, north of Sainte-Anne. His rearguard, positioned to ensure the French could not interfere with the withdrawal, did not come in until early the following morning.

There was some doubt about exactly where Bülow and the so far unblooded IV Corps were, but eventually Thielemann managed to establish communications with him and the orders to make for Wavre, avoiding the French on the way, were passed on. When Bülow's men started to come in during the afternoon, they were sent to Dion-le-Mont, three miles south-east of Wavre. Now the Prussian army could sort itself out and prepare for further operations. Equipment and rations were short – the French had captured many of the baggage wagons – but in general things were improving. Ziethen was ordered to keep the line of the River Dyle under continuous observation. The Dyle was a formidable obstacle at the best of times, but the heavy rain had turned its valley into a quagmire, and if the French did attack Wavre, they could only cross by the bridges, which would be stoutly defended.

By around 1800 hours on 17 June, Napoleon had accepted that he was not going to catch Wellington's army on the march. The emperor was not overly concerned; indeed, he was more worried that Wellington might slip away and rob him of another victory on the morrow. At this stage Napoleon seems to have discounted the Prussians entirely: they were a spent force, and even if they were withdrawing north instead of back to Germany as he had hoped, they could not interfere – and, if they tried to, Grouchy would soon stop them. When, towards dusk, French cavalry reported that the English seemed to be taking up position on Mont-Saint-Jean, Napoleon told Major General Milhaud, commanding IV Cavalry

Corps, to send some of his light cavalry helter-skelter straight up the road towards them. A storm of artillery fire from all along the ridge confirmed that the English were indeed present in strength. The 'sepoy general' (as Napoleon referred to Wellington) had, he thought, made a major tactical error – he had positioned his army with its back to the Forest of Soignés, which was impenetrable to guns and any wheeled vehicle. Should the English general think of retiring further, he could not, and would be pinned against the forest and defeated in the morning.

Napoleon duly ordered his army to take position on the last ridge before Mont-Saint-Jean. This lay about 1,500 yards south of it and was marked by an inn, La Belle Alliance, that stood at its centre, alongside the main Brussels road. Napoleon established his own headquarters at the farmstead of Le Caillou, 1,500 yards south of La Belle Alliance. He and his immediate staff were warm and comfortable – which could not be said for his escort, a battalion of the Imperial Guard, which trudged up covered in mud and had to make camp in the orchard, with little cover from the rain. For the rest of the French army, it was a long and unpleasant night. Strung out as they were along the only approach road, itself clogged with guns and wagons, their progress was torturously slow. Several memoirs mention how the mud clung to the tails of their greatcoats, adding even more weight to the infantrymen's loads.

When Wellington had arrived in Flanders in April to command the Anglo-Dutch army, his priority was to plan for a coordinated invasion of France with the Prussians, Austrians and Russians. However, being a soldier who neglected no eventualities, he had also considered the alternative that Napoleon might strike first, and to that end he had drawn up a number of options in cooperation with Blücher and the Prussians. Wellington had reconnoitred a number of possible defensive positions, including the ridge of Mont-Saint-Jean. He had also considered the ridge of La Belle Alliance, along which the French army was now assembling, but had rejected it as not having a reverse slope long enough to conceal the Allied army and lacking flanks that could be secured. In linear defence – and at the time defence involved finding a suitable piece of ground and lining up along it – the main risk to the defender was to his flanks, which the attacker might attempt to turn, or where he might try to get in behind the defence line or roll up the line by attacking the flanks.

In many ways, the Mont-Saint-Jean position allowed a typical Wellingtonian posture. It was a crescent-shaped ridge just over two miles long, with a reverse slope that, apart from a short distance in the centre, ran all along the ridge, and with flanks that could be anchored to prevent any turning movement by the French. Contrary to what Napoleon assumed, the Forest of Soignés was not an obstacle to withdrawal, should that become necessary; indeed, as Wellington had noted, the trees were far enough apart to allow the passage of guns through them. A minor unpaved road ran along the whole ridge; it was not much more than a track but wide enough for wheeled vehicles and, most importantly, for guns. On the left, or east, flank was the farm of Papelotte, which was built, like Gemioncourt at Quatre Bras, in an age when marauding armies or armed brigands were always to be expected and which, if properly defended, would be very difficult to take. On the right, or west, was another farm, Hougoumont, which again was easily defensible, while in the centre and about 200 yards forward, or south, of Wellington's intended front line was La Haie Sainte, yet another group of farm buildings, which could become a springboard for an attack on the centre if taken by the French and would have to be held by the Allies. At the centre of the position, the Brussels high road ran through a cutting, which meant that the minor east–west road that cut across it became a sunken road for a hundred yards or so to the west and thus provided an obstacle for cavalry.

Throughout the afternoon, evening and night of 17/18 June, as the rain still bucketed down, the British, Dutch-Belgian and Allied German troops were placed in position by staff officers and ADCs. The procedure was for an arriving division to be ordered to halt off the road and for the divisional chief of staff and brigade majors to report to one of DeLancey's staff officers, who would take them and show them the ground that the division was to occupy.* They would then return and show the commanding officers and adjutants where their men were to go and the soldiers would be marched to their battle positions. The men would then pile arms, drop their packs and, if they were not detailed for fatigues of some nature, start looking for firewood with which to cook their meal.

Despite all the evidence pointing to the main, or only, French thrust being north towards Brussels, Wellington was still concerned about a possible French outflanking move via Mons. To counter that, Hill's II Corps was stationed between Tubize, nine miles off to the west, and Halle, two miles north of Tubize. Hill's

---

* Brigades had two staff officers: the brigade major (often actually a captain) who was responsible for operational staff work, with an assistant as staff captain. Additionally there was a commissary, a civilian but with military rank to give him authority, responsible for rations and transport. The brigade commander's ADC also helped. The number of ADCs depended on the rank and the appointment of the commander – if the brigade commander was a major general, there would be one ADC.

command consisted of one ostensibly British division, of four British and five Hanoverian battalions, one Netherlands division of five regular and six militia Dutch-Belgian battalions, an 'Indian' brigade, and a total of seventeen guns (nine- and six-pounders) and five howitzers. The Indian brigade of six battalions was not, as has often been assumed, composed of Indians, but of Dutch soldiers enlisted for service in the Dutch East and West Indies, colonies in what is now Indonesia and the Dutch Antilles in the Caribbean. Those colonies had been restored to the Netherlands at the close of hostilities in 1814, but the regiments raised to garrison them had not yet been despatched overseas. Altogether, around 17,000 of Wellington's troops were positioned to deal with a threat that did not, in fact, materialize. Hill also had two regiments of Hanoverian cavalry under command, about 1,200 horsemen in all, so he could push out patrols to give advance warning of a French advance in his direction as well as maintain communications with Wellington at Mont-Saint-Jean.

If the French should attempt to turn Wellington's main position, the threat to his right flank was much greater than that to his left. Not only was the left the direction from where the Prussians would come, if they were to come, but the whole area to the French right was a network of sunken roads, some of them fifteen or twenty feet below the surrounding land, and while these could be negotiated by infantry with relative ease, cavalry might get into a track and find they could not get out, and guns would not be able to cross them. Napoleon was thus highly unlikely to attempt to manoeuvre around the Anglo-Dutch left, but to anchor it Wellington placed Saxe-Weimar's Dutch-Belgian brigade in Papelotte farm and the houses and farm buildings around it, including the château of Fichermont, which lay some 500 yards south-east of Papelotte. The brigade had fought well at Quatre Bras on 16 June, holding Bossu Wood all day, and had now received replenishment ammunition for its variety of weapons.

In support of Saxe-Weimar, Wellington placed the 4th and 6th Cavalry Brigades, commanded by Major Generals Sir John Vandeleur and Sir Hussey Vivian respectively. Vandeleur, fifty-two years old in 1815, was an Anglo-Irishman from a family that had long provided officers for the British army.* A highly experienced officer, he had initially been commissioned into the infantry but as a junior and field officer had served in both infantry and cavalry regiments. As a colonel he had commanded a regiment and then a brigade in India and was known to Wellington, who was there at the same time, and as a major general from 1811 he had commanded both an infantry and a cavalry brigade in the Peninsula. His 4th Cavalry Brigade at Waterloo consisted of three regiments of light dragoons, or around 1,300 men altogether. Vivian, one of the younger generals of the army at thirty-one, was a West Countryman who had originally been an articled clerk but abandoned a legal career to join the army as an ensign in 1793. Having moved up the ranks through both infantry and cavalry regiments, as a lieutenant colonel he commanded the 7th Light Dragoons in the retreat to Corunna, and as a colonel he commanded a cavalry brigade in the latter stages of the Peninsular War. He had been a major general since June 1814 and his brigade at Waterloo consisted of three regiments of hussars, two British and one King's German

---

* They still do. A descendant commanded the Irish Guards in the Arnhem campaign, and when this author commanded the Gurkha depot in the late 1990s, his opposite number commanding the Guards depot at Pirbright was a Vandeleur.

Legion, about 1,500 men altogether. Uniquely, Vivian managed to keep the troop of Royal Horse Artillery usually allocated to each cavalry brigade. All the other cavalry brigades had lost theirs to thicken up the artillery on the ridge, but Vivian had Gardiner's troop of five six-pounders and a howitzer.

Wellington's right flank was much more of a risk, and to guard it Wellington put a garrison into Hougoumont farm and a division in and around the village of Braine-l'Alleud, 1,000 yards north-west of Hougoumont. The farm stood 300 yards forward of the ridge and consisted of a manor house with a chapel attached, servants' quarters, barns and storerooms around a courtyard, the whole enclosed by a stout brick wall. To the east of the house was a kitchen garden and beyond that a fruit orchard, which was surrounded by a brick wall running along the south and east faces. Behind the farm was a sunken track or 'covered way' with a hedge running along it. There were two main entrances to the enclosure, one on the north side facing the ridge and one to the south. To the south of the farm was a wood, which ran more or less due south for 300 yards, although there was a cleared open strip about twenty yards wide between the south face of the farm enclosure and the orchard wall and the trees. The farm and its orchard were to be the responsibility of the light companies of the Guards Division. There were two brigades in the Guards Division, each of two battalions. Guards battalions were larger than battalions of the line, so, despite the casualties suffered at Quatre Bras on 16 June, the four companies totalled around 400 officers and men.

With immediate responsibility for the farm buildings, and overall command of the Hougoumont complex, was Captain James Macdonnell, the officer commanding the light company of 2nd

Battalion Coldstream Guards.* At thirty-five, he was relatively old for a captain (although as a Guards officer he held army rank of lieutenant colonel) and had been a lieutenant colonel in the 78th Foot before exchanging into the Coldstream as a captain and lieutenant colonel in 1809. In the farm buildings he had his own light company and the light company of 2nd Battalion 3rd Foot Guards. The defence of the orchard was delegated to the light companies of the 2nd and 3rd Battalions of the 1st Foot Guards under Captain (and Lieutenant Colonel) Alexander George Fraser, 16th Lord Saltoun of Abernathy in the Scottish peerage. He too had started life in a line regiment, being commissioned into the 35th Foot in 1802 aged seventeen, and had exchanged into the 1st Guards in 1804, before achieving the regimental rank of captain in 1813. Additionally, two German battalions, one recruited from Lüneberg and one from Nassau, and a company of Hanoverian riflemen were sent into the woods. It was well that they were sent when they were, for no sooner had the troops arrived in the Hougoumont area than they had to drive off an attempt by the French to come through the woods and seize the farm. They, too, had realized its significance. Once they arrived at the farm, the men set to, creating loopholes in the walls and the roof and erecting a platform behind the orchard wall to be used as a firing step. Straw was put down on the floor of the chapel, as it would be used as a shelter for the wounded, and ammunition and water were stockpiled.

---

* At this time the regiments that would later become the Grenadier Guards and the Scots Guards were the 1st and 3rd Regiments of Foot Guards respectively. Originally Monk's Regiment of Foot, the 2nd or Coldstream Regiment of Foot Guards had held the latter name since 1670 to commemorate their crossing of the River Tweed at Coldstream in 1660, at the beginning of the campaign that was to lead to the restoration of King Charles II.

Further to the north-west in the village of Braine-l'Alleud was placed the 3rd Netherlands Division, consisting of twelve Dutch-Belgian battalions and two batteries of Belgian artillery (twelve six-pounders and four howitzers), commanded by the fifty-year-old Lieutenant General David-Hendrik Chassé. Chassé had made his name in the army of Napoleon – he was known as *'le général bayonette'* for his aggressive character – and was distrusted by those Netherlands officers who had fought against Napoleon rather than with him. He had fought the British in the Peninsula and his division was mostly composed of militia and raw recruits who were, in British eyes, not to be wholly trusted. In the event, both Chassé and his division would fight well for their new masters when eventually deployed late in the afternoon of 18 June.

Having anchored his flanks, Wellington had to consider La Haie Sainte, forward of his centre, and there he placed the 2nd Light Battalion of the King's German Legion, about 400 men commanded by Major Georg Baring and equipped with the Baker rifle. Baring was forty-two at Waterloo and had originally been commissioned as an ensign in the Hanoverian army. He was one of the first officers of the KGL when it was formed in England and was a competent and experienced officer. On the other side of the road from La Haie, and fifty yards north, was a sand quarry into which Wellington put six companies, or about 400 men, of the 95th Rifles who would act as a further defence against an assault on the Anglo-Dutch centre.

The rest of the Allied infantry was deployed along the ridge and behind it. Wellington's left was covered by the British 5th and 6th Divisions, amalgamated under the command of Lieutenant General Sir Thomas Picton, since the commander of the 6th Division, Lieutenant General Sir Lowry Cole, had obtained leave to get married and was not present.* Picton, fifty-seven in 1815, was born in Haverfordwest in Pembrokeshire and commissioned at the age of thirteen, although he did not join for duty for two years. He made his name as a soldier in the West Indies, becoming the governor of Trinidad after its capture from the Spanish, learning the Spanish language and acquiring a mixed-race mistress half his age, with whom he had four children. On return to England he was accused of permitting in Trinidad the extraction of a confession by torture of a young woman accused of robbery. The court found that he had, as a British governor, permitted an illegal act, but that as he was administering Spanish law, which allowed torture, he had no evil intent. He commanded the 3rd Division in Wellington's army in the Peninsula and was one of his most competent generals. Wellington described him as a 'rough, foul-mouthed devil' but went on to say that no one could have discharged his duties better. Although a strict disciplinarian, Picton paid little heed to dress regulations and rarely wore uniform, frequently appearing in the field in civilian clothes or in mixed dress, a habit copied by his officers, so he and his divisional headquarters became known to the rest of the army as the 'bear and ragged staff'. He had retired to his estates at the end of the war in 1814, and when recalled he agreed to serve only if he was under command of Wellington directly and no one else. It is said that he had a premonition of his own death, and he certainly made a new will before departing England, leaving £1,000 to each of his four Trinidadian children.†

---

* No doubt the question 'What did you do in the great battle, Grandpa?' would be countered by changing the subject to the Peninsular War, where Sir Lowry had a starring role.
† A very handsome sum, equivalent to perhaps £200,000 today, and particularly handsome if you are living in a hut on a West Indian island.

As it was, he had already been hit by a musket ball at Quatre Bras and suffered several broken ribs. Although in considerable pain, he told no one save his ADC, who strapped up his chest.*

Picton's augmented division consisted of three British and two Hanoverian brigades – a total of nineteen battalions, of which eleven were British, all save the 1/27th Foot (Inniskillings) veterans of the Peninsula, and eight Hanoverian *Landwehr*. In addition, he had attached to him Bijlandt's brigade of five Dutch-Belgian battalions. Artillery support to the division was one British and one Hanoverian battery, ten nine-pounders, five six-pounders and two howitzers in all. Wellington had personally placed the brigades and had ensured that the less experienced or less reliable troops were placed where there was least risk or beside units that were known to stand come what may. Beside the crossroads, the centre of the Allied position, was Lambert's brigade of three British battalions. The brigade had only arrived at around 1030 hours on the morning of 18 June. They had marched up from Ghent having been shipped across from America, where the war of 1812 was now over, and since they had not been involved at Quatre Bras, the battalions were fully up to strength.

Wellington placed the 3rd British Infantry Division and the Guards Division on his right. Despite its name, of the three brigades of the 3rd Division only one was British, although another was King's German Legion, which was just as good. The third brigade was Hanoverian. The divisional commander was Lieutenant General Sir Charles (Karl) Alten, who had been born in Hanover and was forty-one at Waterloo. Originally commissioned

---

* There is little you can do about broken ribs, save wait for them to knit. This author, having broken most of his over the years, mostly coming off horses, would advise the avoidance of coughing, laughing or constipation.

into the Hanoverian Foot Guards, he was one of the first officers of the KGL and had extensive experience with Moore in Spain and in Wellington's Peninsular army, where he commanded the Light Division after Crauford's death in 1812. The division had thirteen battalions: four British, of which only one had been in the Peninsula; four KGL, of which two were Peninsular veterans, including the 2nd Light in La Haie Sainte; and five Hanoverian. There were two field batteries of artillery in support, one British and one KGL, totalling ten nine-pounders and two howitzers. Next to the crossroads was the KGL brigade, then the Hanoverian and then Major General Sir Colin Halkett's British.

Beyond Alten's troops was the Guards Division, of two brigades, each of two battalions, commanded by Major General Sir George Cooke.* Aged forty-seven in 1815, Cooke had been commissioned into the 1st Foot Guards in 1784 and, except for periods on the staff, had spent his entire service in that regiment. A major general in 1811, in the Peninsular War he commanded the troops in Cadiz after Graham had fallen out with the Spanish general Manuel La Peña. Guards battalions being established at 1,200 all ranks, compared to just over 800 for a line regiment, the division numbered around 4,300 officers and men, despite the casualties at Quatre Bras. Major General Maitland's brigade of the two battalions of the 1st Foot Guards was positioned to the right of Halkett's brigade, and next to Maitland were Major General Sir John Byng's 2nd Coldstream and 2/3rd Foot Guards. All four battalions were placed where they could overlook Hougoumont farm and support it if necessary. Cooke's artillery support was one

---

* Cooke's sister would become the mother of James Brudenell, Lord Cardigan of Crimean War fame.

British and one KGL battery, a total of ten nine-pounders and two howitzers.

That, then, was Wellington's front line, but there was more infantry positioned in reserve. The 2nd British Infantry Division, like Alten's 3rd Division, had one British, one KGL and one Hanoverian brigade, a total of eleven battalions: three British, all Peninsular veterans; four KGL, two of them Peninsular veterans; and four Hanoverian *Landwehr*. It was posted in rear of the Guards on the far side of the Nivelles road, along with a brigade of three British battalions (two of them Peninsular veterans) commanded by Colonel Hugh Henry Mitchell, which was attached to the 2nd Division and detached from Hill's corps at Halle. The division's commander, Lieutenant General Sir Henry Clinton, the son of a general and forty-four at Waterloo, had been commissioned into the 11th Foot in 1787, later exchanging into the 1st Foot Guards. He had extensive experience of active service in Flanders, the West Indies and India, and was with Moore on the retreat to Corunna and a divisional commander under Wellington in the Peninsula. A strict disciplinarian with a habit of rebuking wrong-doers in public, Clinton was not always popular with those whom he commanded, but was competent enough and was specifically requested by Wellington for the Waterloo campaign. The Brunswick and the German Nassau contingents, under their own commanders, Colonel Olfermann for the Brunswickers and Major General August von Kruse for the Nassauers, were placed behind the centre of Alten's 3rd Division. Like many of the Allied officers, Kruse had commanded his regiment in the Peninsular War as part of the French army, until being told by his duke to change sides, which he did in December 1813 when it was obvious that the French empire was beginning to fall apart. The total of Wellington's infantry on the ridge was around 53,000, of which about one third was British.

At Waterloo Wellington had twenty-nine regiments of cavalry, ten heavy (seven British and three Dutch-Belgian) and nineteen light (nine British, four KGL, four Dutch-Belgian and one Hanoverian). The two British heavy cavalry brigades were either side of the crossroads; the Household Brigade of the 1st and 2nd Life Guards, the Royal Horse Guards (the Blues) and the 1st Dragoon Guards were behind Colonel Ompteda's KGL brigade; and the Union Brigade – so called because it had a regiment from each country of the United Kingdom – of the 1st (Royal) Dragoons, the 2nd Royal North British Dragoons (Scots Greys) and the 6th (Inniskilling) Dragoons took post behind Picton's division. The Dutch-Belgian heavies were behind the Household Brigade and the light cavalry were either further back still or backing up Saxe-Weimar on Wellington's extreme left (two brigades of six regiments in total) or behind the Guards Division (two brigades of four British and two KGL regiments). Altogether, there were present on the ridge around 13,000 cavalrymen.

At last, at about 0300 hours in the morning of 18 June, a message arrived from Field Marshal Blücher at Wavre: he would move to support his ally with at least two corps at first light. Now Wellington knew that he could stay on the ridge and fight his battle there.

Fifteen hundred yards away to the south, down one gentle slope and up another, the French army was straggling into position. Having got on the road much later than the Anglo-Dutch on 17 June, many of the brigades and regiments would not arrive until well into the morning of 18 June. They too were directed into position by Soult's staff, in accordance with Napoleon's orders, while the emperor himself went forward as far as La Belle Alliance several times during the night, still concerned that Wellington might slip away. The thousands of camp fires on the opposite ridge reassured him, and at one stage he sent forward Major General François-Nicolas Haxo, born in France of Hungarian descent and the chief engineer of the Imperial Guard, to determine whether or not Wellington was entrenching. In fact Wellington was not – he hardly ever did, as to do so restricted his ability to move troops about from one threatened area to another. Satisfied that the Anglo-Dutch intended to make a stand on Mont-Saint-Jean, pinned, as he thought, against the Forest of Soignés at their back, and continuing to discount the Prussian army, Napoleon returned to Le Caillou to snatch a few hours' sleep, having instructed Soult that the battle would open at 0900 hours on the morning of 18 June. He was confident that he would score another victory.

On the French left flank was placed Major General Reille's II Army Corps. While Wellington's corps were ad hoc formations, cobbled together from what was available, French corps had a formal establishment and were miniature armies with their own integral artillery, engineers, medical support and administrative train. Reille had three divisions, each with six six-pounders and two howitzers, an engineer company and a detachment of the train. On the extreme left was the 6th Infantry Division, of thirteen battalions, commanded by Major General Prince Jérôme Bonaparte, the emperor's youngest brother. Jérôme was thirty-one at Waterloo and his military career had been spent in the Consular Guard until Napoleon made him an admiral and transferred him to the navy. Being totally ignorant of matters naval and disliking shipboard life, Jérôme jumped ship in America, became involved with a local beauty and married her. Napoleon was furious, and when the happy couple returned to France, he annulled the marriage and packed Jérôme's pregnant and now ex-wife back to Baltimore with a large bag of gold. Subsequently a failure as king of Westphalia and a corps commander in the Russian campaign of 1812, Jérôme was working his way down the French military hierarchy, and if one word described him, it would be 'irresponsible'. Napoleon was well aware of his brother's limitations and had appointed Major General Armand Charles Guilleminot as his second-in-command, despite the fact that divisional commanders in the French army did not have seconds-in-command. Guilleminot had enlisted as a private soldier on the outbreak of the Revolution, was commissioned in a volunteer battalion, and served in Flanders, Italy and Spain; as a major general he commanded a corps in the Russian campaign. He was regarded as sensible and prudent, and his appointment was intended to curb any rash initiatives by his nominal master.

In the centre of the corps was the 9th Infantry Division of Major General Maximilien Sébastien Foy. Forty years old and among the best generals in the French army, Foy was one of the last pre-Revolution cadets to be admitted to the artillery school at La Fère and was commissioned in 1792. He was hugely experienced, having served in northern Europe, Italy and Turkey, and as a divisional commander in Portugal and Spain. He refused, on principle, the offer of becoming an honorary ADC to Napoleon when the latter assumed the throne, and this may explain why he never became a marshal – for he was a far better soldier than most of those who did receive that honour. He had already been wounded fourteen times (he would receive his fifteenth wound at the forthcoming battle), and subsequently wrote an excellent – and remarkably unbiased – account of the Peninsular War from the French perspective. His division contained eleven battalions.

Next to Foy's division, and nearest to La Belle Alliance, was the 5th Infantry Division, commanded by the 38-year-old Major General Gilbert Désiré Joseph Bachelu. Despite a middle-class background (his father was a lawyer), Bachelu was a fervent republican and enlisted as a private in the engineers on the outbreak of the Revolution, soon being commissioned in the infantry. He commanded a battalion in Egypt, refurbished the fortifications in the French West Indies, served as chief of staff to Soult, commanded a brigade in the Russian campaign, and as a major general from June 1813 fought in the final campaigns of 1813 and 1814 in northern Europe. In his division were nine battalions.

The French right flank was covered by d'Erlon's I Army Corps of four divisions. Next to the road and just forward of the Belle Alliance estaminet was Brigadier General Joachim Quiot du Passage's 1st Division of eight battalions. Forty-year-old Quiot, originally the senior brigade commander of the division, was standing in for Major General Allix de Vaux, who had failed to turn up. Next to Quiot was the 2nd Division of nine battalions commanded by Major General François-Xavier Donzelot. At fifty-one, Donzelot was one of the oldest French divisional commanders at Waterloo, and the most devoid of recent experience. Originally commissioned into the Bourbon army in 1785, he survived the Revolution and fought in the early European battles. A major general from 1801, he arrived in Egypt just in time to surrender to the British. Further active service in northern Europe was followed by his appointment as governor of the Ionian Islands. From 1808 he was based on Corfu, where he remained, surviving the Royal Navy blockade and holding out after Napoleon's abdication in 1814 until ordered by Louis XVIII to hand the islands over to the British.

Next in line came the eight-battalion-strong 3rd Division, commanded by Major General Pierre-Louis Binet de Marcognet. Fifty years old and a major general since 1807, Marcognet was another ex-officer of the Bourbon army who had joined as an officer cadet in 1781 and been commissioned in time to fight in the last two years of the American Revolution, when the ungrateful colonists had objected to being asked to make a modest contribution towards the costs of their own defence. As a lieutenant, he supported the French Revolution and was wounded twice in the early battles before his dismissal for being of noble blood. Eighteen months later, the Directorate gone, he was rehabilitated and served in Europe, Spain and Italy.

D'Erlon's 4th Infantry Division, of eight battalions, was stationed on the extreme right, about 400 yards from Papelotte farm, and commanded by Major General Pierre François Joseph Durutte. The 48-year-old son of a well-to-do merchant, Durutte had a good education and enlisted as a private soldier in a revolutionary volunteer battalion, and was soon commissioned. He served in numerous appointments both in command of troops and, thanks to his education, as a staff officer. He was promoted to major general in 1803, but his career suffered a temporary dip in 1804 when, as a firm believer in republicanism, he refused to sign a document expressing the support of officers of the army for Napoleon's assumption of the throne. After two years in the wilderness as governor of Elba, however, he was back as a divisional commander in Italy and then in Russia. From 1814 he was governor of the fortress of Metz, which held out until the war was over. Like most of his contemporaries, he served on under the restoration, before rallying to Napoleon once again.

In reserve immediately behind La Belle Alliance and stationed either side of the road was Lobau's VI Corps, of two infantry divisions, the 19th and 20th, with two cavalry divisions, the 3rd and 5th, attached. The 19th, commanded by the 37-year-old Major General François Martin Valentin Simmer (wounded eight times, he had been promoted on Napoleon's return in April 1815), had nine battalions, while the 20th, under Major General Jean-Baptiste Jeanin (yet another born in the same year as Napoleon and Wellington, 1769) had only four.

Immediately behind VI Corps and in its customary role of last resort was the Imperial Guard headed not by its usual commander, Marshal Mortier, who was suffering from an attack of sciatica, but by his chief of staff, Major General Antoine Drouot. Drouot was forty-one in 1815, and, although of humble origins (his father was a baker), he had managed to get a first-class education by dint of passing numerous examinations for entry to the better church-run schools. Shortly after the outbreak of the Revolution, he passed the examination for the artillery school and was commissioned from there after only one month's training. He served in northern Europe and Italy and was then detailed to join the fleet of Admiral Villeneuve as the gunnery expert. Despite being prone to appalling seasickness, he survived Villeneuve's dash to the West Indies, designed to lure the Royal Navy away from the Channel. He only just missed the Battle of Trafalgar, being summoned back to join the Grande Armée just before the fleet put out from Cadiz in October 1805 – although the ship that he had been on, the forty-gun frigate *Hortense*, was one of those that managed to escape back to Cadiz. Drouot then served in Spain and in the Russian campaign, being promoted to major general in September 1813. He accompanied Napoleon to Elba and remained with him until the return to France in 1815.

The Guard had three infantry divisions: the division of the Grenadiers à Pied, with four battalions of the Old Guard and four of what was (possibly unofficially) known as the Middle Guard (the 3rd and 4th Grenadier Regiments); the division of the Chasseurs à Pied, again with four battalions of the Old Guard and four of the Middle; and the division of the Young Guard with eight battalions of light infantry. The grenadiers were commanded by Major General Louis Friant, now fifty-seven and the oldest of the French divisional commanders. A corporal in the Bourbon army, he had been elected as a lieutenant colonel in the revolutionary army and had served in northern Europe and in the Russian campaign. Commanding the chasseurs was Major General Antoine Morand, now forty-four years old. A lawyer before the Revolution, he was elected captain and then lieutenant colonel of volunteers, and he served in Flanders, the Low Countries, Egypt and Russia. A major general from 1805, he accepted a knighthood from the restored Louis XVIII before turning his coat yet again when Napoleon returned from Elba. Major General Philibert Guillaume Duhesme commanded the Young Guard Division. The 39-year-old son of a lawyer, he had raised with his own funds a battalion of revolutionary volunteers and was given command of it. The Revolution was good for him, and in 1794, aged only twenty-eight, he was promoted to major general. A thoroughly nasty piece of work, albeit a natural and courageous leader, he fought in the early battles of the revolutionary wars and then in Italy and in Spain. Accused of robbery, torture, murder, misappropriation of funds and looting in Spain, he was recalled but survived.[*]

---

[*] As just about every senior French commander in Spain was involved in looting, corruption and misappropriation of funds, and some in murder and torture, it is quite possible that these were trumped-up charges intended to get rid of a competitor.

The Guard had its own reserve artillery, of eighteen twelve-pounders – the heaviest guns at Waterloo – and six six-inch howitzers. The light cavalry division of the Guard, two regiments, one of which was armed with lances, was placed in rear of the right flank, while the heavy division, again of two regiments, was in rear of the left flank. Of the non-Guard cavalry, the 2nd Division of two light and two lancer regiments under Major General Hippolyte-Marie-Guillaume Piré was on the extreme left, next to Jérôme Bonaparte's division, while the 1st Cavalry Division, also of two light and two lancer regiments, was on the extreme right, supporting Durutte's infantry division. In support of Lobau's reserve were the cavalry divisions of Major General Jean-Simon Domon (3rd – three light regiments) and Major General Jacques Gervais Subervie (5th – one light and two lancer regiments). Otherwise Kellermann's III Reserve Cavalry Corps of two divisions with eight heavy cavalry regiments in total was stationed immediately to the rear of Reille's corps on the French left, while Milhaud's IV Reserve Cavalry Corps of two divisions, each of four regiments of heavy cavalry, was immediately behind d'Erlon's corps on the right. To begin with, every cavalry division had a battery of horse artillery, on paper six six-pounders and two 5½-inch howitzers, although, owing to the difficulty of obtaining sufficient horses, some batteries had only four six-pounders.

In total, and not counting Grouchy's detached wing of the French army, Napoleon had 103 infantry battalions at Waterloo, compared to Wellington's eighty-four (not counting those detached under Hill), but as the numbers on the strength of French battalions varied widely, a better comparison might be to say that Napoleon had around 53,000 infantry opposed to Wellington's total of around the same or slightly less. Napoleon had thirty-four regiments of cavalry to Wellington's twenty-nine, but as the number of squadrons in regiments varied, there were around 15,000 French cavalry soldiers compared to Wellington's 13,000. Napoleon had 246 guns including thirty-six twelve-pounders (eighteen with the Guard and six with each of I, II and VI Corps), the rest six-pounders and howitzers, while Wellington could field 157 guns, nine- and six-pounders, and howitzers. In total numbers, including gunners, engineers, trumpeters and the like, Napoleon had 78,000 men at Waterloo, facing around 70,000 Anglo-Dutch.[31] Considering that Wellington had no intention of going on the offensive with what he had on the morning of 18 June and that Napoleon would have to attack, in order to get the battle (and, as he thought, the war) over before overwhelming strength could be brought against him, these were not bad odds facing Wellington, and nothing like the generally accepted ratio of three attackers to one defender needed for success. Of course these odds could be tipped either way: by Grouchy moving to join Napoleon, or by the Prussians appearing in support of Wellington. As yet, only time would tell.

8

THE BATTLE FOR EUROPE

By midnight on 17/18 June, the Prussian army had reunited in and around Wavre. It had lost around 30,000 men in the fighting before Ligny, at Ligny itself and in desertions after the battle. Ziethen's I Corps had been the worst mauled and Pirch's II Corps had also taken considerable casualties. Thielemann's III Corps was already engaged as the rearguard, so Bülow's IV Corps, uninvolved in the battle at Ligny and thus up to strength and with all its equipment, was the obvious corps to lead the move towards Waterloo. Gneisenau, Blücher's chief of staff, issued orders during the night instructing Bülow to leave at first light and head for Chapelle Saint-Lambert, seven miles from Wavre. He would be supported and preceded by Colonel von Schwerin's 1st Cavalry Brigade (like all Prussian brigades, actually the size of anyone else's division). Once there, he was to deploy into battle formation and could either deploy on Wellington's left flank, or attack the French right, depending upon the situation when he got there. Next to go would be Pirch's II Corps and finally Ziethen, leaving Thielemann to ensure that there was no interference from Grouchy.

On the face of it, Bülow – despite the fact that his starting point was three miles south-east of Wavre and so he was further away from Waterloo than the other Prussian troops – should have been able to reach Chapelle Saint-Lambert in five hours, but there were all sorts of problems in his way. First, he had to get across the River Dyle, and there was only one narrow bridge. Second, he had to wind his way through Wavre, which his lead troops eventually reached at around 0700 hours and where there was traffic gridlock with ammunition wagons, ambulances, ration carts and all the other wheeled impedimenta of an army clogging up the narrow roads. It got worse, for a fire broke out in the town – whether it was caused by an ammunition wagon exploding or by Prussian cooking fires getting out of control is unknown – making progress even slower than it already was. Once out of Wavre, the country was hilly, crossed only by farm tracks and with numerous ravines and stream valleys to cross. Although the rain had stopped, the ground was boggy and slippery, making it very difficult for the horses to pull the guns uphill and impossible for them to hold them on the way down. The horses had to be unhitched and the guns attached to tow ropes and lowered downhill by soldiers. Eventually, the heaviest guns, a battery of twelve-pounders, were abandoned. All this took time, and as the only maps the Prussians had were very rough sketches produced in haste by the British Royal Engineers, navigation too was a problem. It was 1000 hours before Bülow's last formation, Major General von Ryssel's division-sized 14th Infantry Brigade, could leave Dion-le-Mont, and then he had to drop off two battalions of infantry and a regiment of hussars from Schwerin's brigade to hold off Exelmans' cavalry, which was now biting at his heels, until he got across the Dyle.

Schwerin's cavalry reached Chapelle Saint-Lambert and then pushed on through Lasne and into the Bois de Paris, from where the corps could either go north-west to join Wellington, whose left flank was about one-and-a-half miles away, or strike the French right, at about the same distance. It was here at about 1430 hours that the Prussians suffered their first casualty of the Battle of Waterloo when Colonel von Schwerin, up with his leading squadron of cavalry, skirmished with some scouting French cavalry and was killed by a shot from a horse artillery gun. Then, from around 1530 hours onwards, the units of Bülow's corps began to arrive in the Bois de Paris, while the leading elements of Pirch's corps headed towards the Anglo-Dutch left flank.

Earlier at Le Caillou, over breakfast, Napoleon had discussed the forthcoming battle with his staff and senior commanders. His original intention had been to start operations at first light, but during the night this had been put back several times, eventually to 0900 hours, and even this start time was about to be postponed. Many accounts say this was because Major General Ruty, commanding the army's artillery, supported by Drouot, the commander of the Imperial Guard and another gunner, protested that the ground was too wet to allow deployment of the guns and that, even if they could by much effort and sweat of man and horse be deployed, the round shot would bury itself in the soft ground at the first strike, instead of skipping along the surface and taking out file after file of enemy soldiers. This is most unlikely. Napoleon, himself a gunner, did not need anyone else to tell him the effect of wet ground on artillery. The real reason was surely that his army was not ready, and in some cases not even present by 0900 hours, and he could not begin the battle until it was. The French battalions were still struggling up the only road, and, although it was no longer raining, the going was still very heavy and on arrival men needed to dry their weapons and equipment and snatch a hurried meal.

As it was, at around 1100 hours Napoleon issued his final battle orders, which were to the effect that, after an initial softening up by the artillery of the Grand Battery, d'Erlon's infantry would attack the Allied left centre, followed by Lobau's corps and the Imperial Guard, which would punch a hole through Wellington's line, knock this Anglo-Dutch rabble out of the way and march on to Brussels. The attack was to begin on a signal given by Marshal Soult, the chief of staff, and d'Erlon's attack was to be preceded by a diversionary attack on Hougoumont. This latter was a perfectly sound plan: if Wellington's right were threatened, the duke would have to reinforce it, and he could only do that, so the Napoleonic logic went, by moving troops from his centre, thus weakening it for d'Erlon's attack. But warnings by Soult, Ney, Reille and others who had fought Wellington in the Peninsula that it was unwise to attack British troops in a defensive position head-on were swept aside – they had all been beaten by Wellington and so were afraid of him, whereas Wellington was a bad general and the English were bad troops. The whole affair, claimed the emperor, would be no more difficult than eating one's breakfast.

The artillery of the Grand Battery, positioned in front of Quiot's and Donzelot's divisions, consisted of the Imperial Guard's artillery reserve of eighteen twelve-pounders, d'Erlon's six twelve-pounders, the forty six-pounders from the cavalry divisions, and the divisional artillery of Quiot and Donzelot, another twelve six-pounders. There is some debate about exactly how these guns were drawn up. To be effective as a battery, the guns needed to be reasonably close together, but they could not be positioned wheel to wheel or there would be no room for the infantry and cavalry to move through them. Assuming twelve feet wheel to wheel between guns, eighty guns would take up a frontage of 475 yards, so it is possible that the guns were positioned in two ranks in which the rear gun line was made up of the twelve-pounders placed along the track that ran along the French front (and eventually to Papelotte farm), with the lighter six-pounders further down the hill in front. Overhead fire was not normally practised (although the British had used it at the siege of San Sebastián in Spain), but this may have been the only way to make the battery manageable without restricting the movement of the infantry and cavalry. In whatever formation the battery was deployed, however, the number of men, horses (480 just to pull the guns, never mind officers' chargers, horses to pull wagons, farriers' forges and the like), limbers and wagons of extra ammunition would have caused an enormous problem in traffic control, and it seems likely that the limbers and the horses were positioned behind d'Erlon's infantry on the reverse slope.

Contemporary accounts of Waterloo give widely differing times for the start of the action. Partly this is because many participants would have known only what was happening on their immediate front – and there was much unharvested maize and rye to restrict vision until it was eventually trampled down – and also because watches were expensive and only officers had them, and then only those who could afford such a luxury. There were, of course, no BBC pips to set the watch by and owners checked with the sun – it was 1200 hours when the sun was at its highest, although views on when the sun was actually highest in the sky could vary by two hours or more either way. Strangely, perhaps, there seems to have been no attempt to synchronize watches, as would be done today. We do know that Napoleon's final battle orders were timed by Soult at 1100 hours. Given that it would take around two hours for them to be promulgated to all units and for

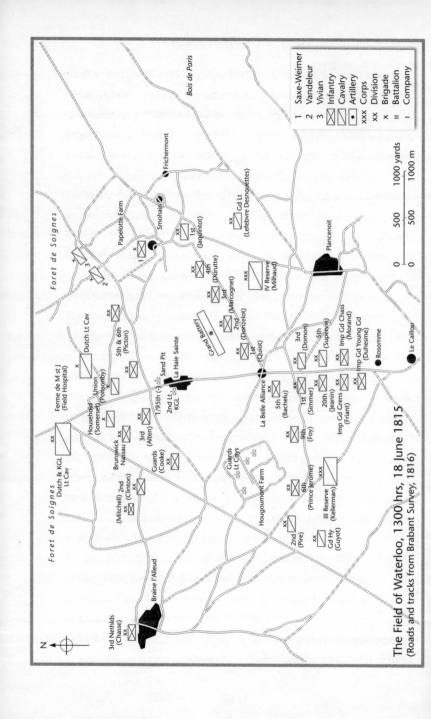

The Field of Waterloo, 1300 hrs, 18 June 1815
(Roads and tracks from Brabant Survey, 1816)

Legend:
1 Saxe-Weimar
2 Vandeleur
3 Vivian
Infantry
Cavalry
Artillery
xxx Corps
xx Division
x Brigade
== Battalion
I Company

N

Foret de Soignes
Bois de Paris
Braine l'Alleud
Frichermont
Smohain
Papelotte Farm
Foret de Soignes
Ferme de M st (Field Hospital)
Dutch Lt Cav
5th & 6th (Picton)
Household Union (Somerset) (Ponsonby)
Sand Pit
La Haie Sainte
2nd Lt KGL
1/95th (2)
3rd (Alten)
Brunswick Nassau
Guards (Cooke)
Dutch & KGL Lt Cav
(Mitchell) 2nd (Clinton)
3rd Nethlds (Chasse)
Guards Lt Coys
Hougoumont Farm
La Belle Alliance
5th (Bachelu)
1st (Simmer)
20th (Jeanin)
Imp Gd Grens (Friant)
9th (Foy)
6th (Prince Jerome)
2nd (Pire)
Gd Hy (Guyot)
III Reserve (Kellerman)
Grand Battery
1st (Quiot)
2nd (Donzelot)
3rd (Marcognet)
4th (Durutte)
1st (Jacquinot)
IV Reserve (Milhaud)
3rd (Domon)
5th (Subervie)
Imp Gd Chass (Morand)
Imp Gd Young Gd (Duhesme)
Rosomme
Le Caillou
Plancenoit
Gd Lt (Lefebvre Desnouettes)

0   500   1000 yards
0   500   1000 m

any final dispositions to be sorted out, and that Napoleon then inspected his army drawn up on the forward slope, it would seem very unlikely that anything happened much before 1300 hours and it was probably later – although there was some scrapping between Durutte's skirmishers and those of Saxe-Weimar on the French extreme right, almost certainly much earlier than that.

When the emperor had taken up his position of observation on the high ground just south-east of the Belle Alliance estaminet, the French artillery began its preliminary bombardment. As Wellington's infantry was on the reverse slope, there was little for the gunners to aim at, but they did not need a specific target: as long as their shot and shell landed just over the Anglo-Dutch ridge, they were bound to hit something. On the Allied left, a frontage of 1,800 yards, stood six brigades totalling just over 14,000 men. Allowing for officers and supernumeraries, that gives around eight men per yard of front, which means that battalions of infantry would almost certainly be deployed in close column of companies. A British battalion so formed would have nine companies of eighty men each in line of two ranks, the companies positioned behind each other with thirty yards between them. The tenth company, the light company, would, initially at least, have been forward of the ridge in skirmish order. Dutch-Belgian battalions had a different establishment to that of the British, but the principle was the same. The point is that there were a great many people spread out to a considerable depth behind the ridge: very roughly, there was an area 1,800 yards long by 270 yards deep that was occupied by men, and, although all were ordered to lie down, it would have been difficult for the French artillery not to do some damage as long as its shots hit somewhere in that rectangle. The mathematics for the Allied right flank with its six brigades shows six men per yard of front, so the occupied rectangle was shallower, but there was still a very large area for the French gunners to drop their shots into.

As it happened, the achievements of the artillery bombardment seem to have been mixed. Some battalions suffered considerably, whereas others seem to have escaped unscathed. According to a soldier of the 71st Foot, in Adam's brigade behind the Guards and across the Nivelles road, the bombardment went on for an hour and a half and cost the battalion sixty men.[32] Lieutenant John Kincaid, adjutant of the 95th Rifles, himself behind the ridge near the crossroads, with three of his companies forward in the sand quarry, says that a cannon-ball 'from lord knows where for it was not fired at us' took the head off his right-hand man, but does not mention the bombardment further.[33] Many contemporary accounts do not mention it at all. The bombardment appears, however, to have gone on for about half an hour – although to those under it, like that soldier of the 71st, it would obviously have seemed much longer – and overall does not seem to have had much effect. This is perhaps surprising, given the extensive target area, but may have been due to the decline in the standards of French artillery. Charles de Gaulle, in an historical résumé of the French army, pointed out that many guns had been left behind in Russia, and others had been lost in the battles of 1813 and 1814.[34] Furthermore, by 1815 the armaments industry was poorly paid and inefficient, leading to substandard workmanship. Other contributory factors would have included the use of unseasoned wood in the manufacture of trails and gun carriages and the difficulty of getting enough skilled gunners and suitable horses, particularly for the twelve-pounders. As well as the decline in capability and equipment, the Allied troops' positions on the reverse slopes, the height of the crops, at least before they were trampled down, and the dense clouds of smoke that would have hung about on that windless day would have made it difficult for the battery commanders to correct their aim based on fall of shot – which they could not see. Many of the rounds expended must therefore have fallen on the forward slope or, as an officer in Picton's division remarked, have gone over the heads of the troops, who, apart from the mounted officers, were lying down.

With the artillery bombardment underway, the diversionary attack on Hougoumont farm could now begin, while d'Erlon's infantry readied themselves for an attack on the Allied left centre once Wellington had weakened it by a transfer of troops to the right flank. The diversion was entrusted to the extreme left-hand French division, that of Prince Jérôme, who despatched Brigadier General Pierre-François Bauduin's 1st Brigade of seven battalions of light infantry, who were to advance due north through the wood and attack the orchard and garden wall and the south gate. Aged forty-seven at Waterloo, Bauduin had joined the revolutionary army as a lieutenant in 1792 and was promoted to major and given command of a battalion on the field of the Battle of Marengo in 1800, where he was wounded. After two years in ships under Admiral Villeneuve, he returned to the land service before the Battle of Trafalgar, became a colonel in 1809, served in the Russian campaign and was promoted to brigadier general in 1813, before taking part in the battles in northern Europe in 1813 and 1814. Decorated by Louis XVIII, he nevertheless returned to his old allegiance on Napoleon's return from Elba.

Four thousand men, led by Bauduin, tramped down the slope and into the woods. They had little trouble in chasing out the Lüneberg and Nassauer skirmishers, who were there more as an early-warning trip wire than as a serious defence line. Twenty yards from the south gate of Hougoumont farm, the trees abruptly ended in flat open ground. This was a killing ground for the guardsmen and the Germans in the farm and the orchard – at that range even the notoriously inaccurate smooth-bore musket could not miss, and from every window and every loophole in the walls and roof, and from the firing platform behind the orchard wall, there came a hail of fire. Behind every firer were two or three men loading muskets and passing them forward, and the first rush of French soldiers from the tree line got nowhere, the dead and the wounded littering the open ground between the farm and the trees. Very soon a dense cloud of black smoke obscured both objective and target, but all the defenders had to do was to fire into the smoke and they were almost bound to hit someone. Not only was there an unceasing rattle of musketry for the French to cope with, but also Major Robert Bull's Royal Horse Artillery battery of six howitzers on the ridge was dropping its shells in the woods: to run forward meant death by musket ball, to retreat risked death by shell. Showing great courage but perhaps little intelligence, the French kept coming on and kept running into a storm of lead from the defenders. A few lucky men who managed to get as far as the wall were bayoneted trying to climb over it, and when Bauduin himself was killed, the attack petered out. A painting in a Waterloo museum shows the gallant general emerging from the wood line, mounted on his horse and his sword drawn. While we do not know for certain, it is very unlikely that Bauduin would have ridden through the wood, and far more likely that he would have come through on foot, with his horse led by an orderly somewhere behind him. Withal, the result was the same, and to this day there is a plaque on the orchard wall commemorating the first general to die at Waterloo.

The first brigade having failed, Prince Jérôme now launched his second brigade, another six battalions of 3,500 men under Brigadier General Jean-Louis Soye, who, scooping up the survivors of Bauduin's brigade on the way, showed a little more finesse this time by going west, outflanking the farm and assaulting the northern gate, which was open. Leaving the gate open was not as daft as it sounds, as the avenue to the farm's main entrance – which this was – constituted the route by which resupplies of ammunition could be delivered and the wounded removed. There was, apparently, a wagon driver – he may have been named Brewer or Brewster,* and he may have been a soldier of the Royal Wagon Train (the 'Newgate Blues'†) or a civilian under contract to the commissariat – who most courageously drove a wagon up and down from the crest to the farm, in through the northern gate; here he would hurl casks of musket ammunition out of his wagon, take on board wounded, and gallop, or more probably fast-trot, back up the hill.

Fighting on the west side of the farm was severe, with the remnants of Bauduin's 1st Légère (light infantry) trying to get to the open gate. The regimental commander, Colonel Amédée Louis Despans-Cubières, who had assumed command of the brigade when Bauduin was killed, was well to the fore, still on his horse and slashing at the red-coated guardsmen with his sabre. Cubières, at twenty-nine one of the younger regimental commanders, was an aristocrat who survived the Revolution (his father was a marquis and had been imprisoned for a time). He enlisted as a private in

---

* The 3rd Foot Guards thought it was a Private Joseph Brewer and later allowed him to transfer to their regiment, but sources are vague.
† They were not highly thought of, somewhat unfairly, and by Waterloo had scarlet tunics rather than blue.

1802, was commissioned in 1804, and made rapid progress upwards, helped by having three horses killed under him in Russia, after which he went from captain to colonel in one year, 1813. Eventually he slashed at one man too many, the sergeant major of the 2/3rd Guards, Ralph Fraser, a native of Glasgow who had enlisted in 1799. Fraser unhorsed Cubières, seized his horse and dragged it into the farmyard. Cubières, who went on to become a major general under the July monarchy and died in 1853, always claimed that Fraser had spared his life out of human decency. The truth almost certainly is that bagging a good French horse was of far more interest to Fraser than killing its rider.

On this occasion, some of Soye's men did manage to get into the yard of the farm through the open gate. Their leader was a second lieutenant of pioneers whose name is given as Legros, although whether this really was his name or a nickname (by all accounts he was a giant of a man) we do not know. He is also referred to as *L'Enfonçeur*, 'the enforcer', which undoubtedly is a nickname and he was armed with a pioneer's axe. Storming into the yard swinging his axe and followed by French infantry, he might have made a difference had he been able to keep the gate open long enough for enough men to tip the balance to enter, but the situation was saved by Captain Macdonnell, who spotted the danger and with two other officers and a handful of NCOs forced the gate closed. Now it was a bar-room brawl, with fists, musket butts, bayonets and belts, until all the forty or so Frenchmen who had penetrated the courtyard were dead or dying. Only one survived: a drummer boy whom the guardsmen thought too young to kill and who spent the rest of the day sitting in a corner weeping – not because of the blood and mayhem all around him, but because a guardsman had put his boot through his drum.

Instead of being the diversion that it was supposed to be, the attack on Hougoumont now became an end in itself that sucked in more and more French troops to no avail. Occasionally a particularly vigorous assault might get some men into the orchard, whereupon one or two companies from the garrison's parent battalions on the ridge would be sent down to chase them out and restore the situation; if the French ever did look likely to take the whole complex, then troops from the nearest brigades were sent down and recalled when the danger had passed. At one stage the farm was set on fire, a dangerous situation for the defenders and one that prompted Wellington to send a message to Macdonnell. Written in pencil on donkey skin,[*] it said:

> I see that the fire has communicated from the Hay Stack to the roof
> of the Chateau. You must however keep your Men in those parts to
> which the fire does not reach. Take care that no Men are lost by the
> falling in of the Roof or floors. After they will have fallen in occupy
> the Ruined walls inside of the Garden; particularly if it should be
> possible for the enemy to fire though the Timbers in the Inside of the
> house.[†]

Legible, perfectly punctuated even down to the use of the semicolon, and, apart from the proliferation of capital letters, grammatically accurate, the memo shows Wellington's extraordinary ability to remain calm and focused when all around him was noise and confusion.

Most sources suppose that the fire was started by a French

---

[*] Commanders and their ADCs carried prepared strips on which messages could be written and then rubbed out by the recipient so that a reply could be written.
[†] One of the very few messages that survive, this one is in the British Museum.

shell, although it is perhaps more likely that it was caused by one of Major Bull's shells dropping short or simply by burning musket wads falling on the straw or hay that littered any farmyard. There was a haystack opposite the south gate and the fire seems to have started there and then spread into the outbuildings and the château. It was particularly unfortunate for some of the wounded, who had been put in the chapel to await casualty evacuation, when the straw on which they were lying caught fire, burning some of them to death. As it also burned the legs of the life-size wooden crucifix on the wall of the chapel,* it was obviously a serious conflagration, but was eventually brought under control.

The battle for Hougoumont went on all day, eventually drawing in Reille's other two divisions, those of Major Generals Bachelu and Foy, and all to no avail, for the French never did capture the farm. Wellington said later that Hougoumont was the key to the Battle of Waterloo, but even if the French had captured it, that alone would not have allowed them to roll up Wellington's right flank, for they would have been overlooked by the infantry and artillery on the ridge. Any attempt by the French to exploit the capture of Hougoumont by extending to their left would have run up against the troops in Braine-l'Alleud and Hill's corps to the west and beyond. Perhaps what Wellington meant was that Hougoumont occupied one third of Napoleon's infantry all day, infantry that might otherwise have been available to punch through the Anglo-Dutch centre later in the battle. What is extraordinary is the continuation of the battle for Hougoumont when it was obvious that Wellington was not going to – and did not need to –

---

* The crucifix was stolen, probably to order, in 2011. There are some very sick people about.

reinforce it by weakening his centre. Once that became apparent, Napoleon should have called off the attack on the farm, leaving perhaps a couple of battalions to occupy the garrison and prevent the farm being used as a jumping-off point for an attack on the French left. That Wellington had no intention of launching any such attacks was, of course, not known to the French.

The answer to why the French persisted at Hougoumont lies in a failure by Soult and his subordinate staff officers to get a grip of the battle and to know what was happening. From Napoleon's observation post and tactical headquarters above and behind the Belle Alliance estaminet, it was almost certainly not possible to see Hougoumont,* but a proper system of command, control and communication should have kept the emperor informed of what was happening there. Such a system did not exist, or where it did exist did not function properly, and Reille, instead of querying the need to send more and more troops against an objective that was so well defended, just went on and on fighting a pointless battle. On a tactical level, it is hard to understand why on the initial assault by Bauduin's brigade from the south a single cannon was not brought through the woods and used to blow in the gate. Even where the trees were too close together to permit the passage of a gun, pioneers could have cleared a route, and one or two round shot fired from the edge of the tree line at a range of twenty yards would have blown the wooden gate to matchwood; a few more could have demolished the orchard wall. Perhaps Bauduin thought that the capture of the farm would be a simple matter and did not

---

* An intersection diagram on a modern map shows that, if contours remained unchanged and trees were removed, it would be just possible, but on the day it would have been unlikely, even without the clouds of black smoke.

want to wait for a gun.

Although the attack on Hougoumont had not caused Wellington to weaken his centre, the attack by French infantry on the Anglo-Dutch centre and left was to happen anyway. It began about half an hour or an hour after the beginning of the initial assault on Hougoumont and was entrusted to d'Erlon's I Corps, supported on the left by the heavy cavalry of Brigadier General Dubois' brigade of cuirassiers from the 13th Cavalry Division and on the right by Major General Jacquinot's light cavalry. The objectives were the capture of La Haie Sainte and the smashing of Wellington's left. The artillery of the Grand Battery would cover the advance by bombarding the ridge.

Sometime at around 1400 hours the French guns increased to rapid fire, shooting as fast as the gunners could load, fire, drag the guns back into position, sponge out, load and fire again. It was at this point that Grouchy's men, still making a relatively stately progress towards Wavre and the Prussians, or where they thought the Prussians were, heard the increased tempo of the artillery fire, and once again there were doubts about what they should do. According to Captain Charles François, with Gérard's corps, Grouchy's infantry left Gembloux at about 1000 hours on the morning of 18 June and reached Walhain, five miles north, at 1300 hours, when they heard the increased cannonade from the direction of Mont-Saint-Jean on their left.[*] François, who was at the head of the column with the lead battalion of the 30th Line, says that Grouchy called a halt and seemed anxious, not knowing whether to cross the River Dyle or to march to the sound of the

---

[*] It was probably nearer 1400 hours, but, as explained, timings in contemporary accounts vary widely.

guns to support the emperor. According to François, Grouchy called a council of war (and as orderly officer of the day to Major General Pécheux, commanding the 12th Division of Gérard's IV Corps, François would have been present) at which commanders were asked to consider the options of marching immediately to Mont-Saint-Jean to reinforce the emperor, or attacking Wavre. Gérard and II Cavalry Corps' commander Exelmans were all for joining Napoleon at best speed, while Vandamme of III Corps thought that they should follow Napoleon's orders to attack the Prussians. The various messages telling Grouchy to move over to Mont-Saint-Jean had not, of course, got through, thanks to faulty staff work and the sending of despatches by only one galloper. François describes Grouchy as saying that, while he agreed that the emperor was now engaged fully with the English (as the French always refer to the Anglo-Dutch army), were he to move to join Napoleon and Blücher then attacked him in flank, his army would be destroyed. The decision was to continue towards Wavre.[35]

On the field of Waterloo, d'Erlon's infantry readied themselves for the advance on Wellington's line. First they had to move through the gun line, which they did by battalions, moving in file led by their commanding officers. Given that no one could see very much through the banks of smoke and the various bits and pieces of artillery equipment to be negotiated, this would have taken some time. Once the troops were level with them, the guns stopped firing while the battalions, brigades and divisions sorted themselves out into their formations for the advance. Divisions were to attack in echelon from the left – that is, there would be a series of blows as successive divisions hit the Allied line one after another, beginning with Quiot's 1st Infantry Division. As the troops on the left had farther to go than those on the right, Quiot's men would be hitting the Allied line as the extreme right-hand French division, Durutte's 4th, was leaving its start line. Divisions moved in column of divisions – that is, each battalion in line of three ranks, battalions behind each other with an interval of five yards between them. A company from each battalion was deployed forward as *voltigeurs* (skirmishers). An observer of a division of four regiments totalling eight battalions, each of 400 men (the light company being detached), would see a cloud of around 1,600 *voltigeurs* preceding a rectangle of men, 130 yards wide and 75 yards deep, containing around 3,000 soldiers and four eagles.* As maintaining this formation was critical for control, the advance could not be swift, probably no more than 50 yards a minute on rough ground.

Once the divisions were through the gun line and in their columns, they could start to move down the slope, drummer boys beating time and officers on horseback. When they were clear of the guns, the artillery could open up again, firing over the heads of the infantry. As with the initial bombardment, the effect was scrappy, and, although there undoubtedly were casualties to the Allied infantry lying down on the reverse slope, they were not significant. There is considerable disagreement among historians about the precise position of Bijlandt's brigade at this point, the third brigade along from the crossroads included in Picton's division. It is alleged that this brigade, unlike any of the others, was positioned on the forward slope and thus suffered heavily, before eventually running away. This is variously

---

* Some regiments had three battalions, occasionally four, and battalion strengths varied, but the principle is the same, with only the senior battalion of the regiment, the 1st, having the eagle.

explained, ranging from Wellington having forgotten them to his deliberately placing them on the forward slope to draw the enemy's fire, with all sorts of unlikely theories in between. This is, of course, nonsense: Wellington had an incredible eye for detail and would never have overlooked a whole brigade, far less deliberately exposed them to fire. The more prosaic truth is that, while they may have been on the forward slope early in the morning, bringing in their piquets and sentries, they would have been moved back, if not by Wellington, then by their divisional commander Perponcher or by the Dutch chief of staff Constant Rebecque. It is inconceivable that they could still have been forward when d'Erlon's infantry began their advance, and reports that say otherwise are surely products of the tricks that memory can play later when the brain attempts to make some sense out of a whole series of confusing and traumatic events.

While Wellington's infantry were lying down on the reverse slope out of sight of d'Erlon's men and the gunners of the Grand Battery, the skirmishers and the Allied artillery were not. The technology to allow indirect fire – that is, firing at targets that the gunners could not see – did not exist, and would not for nearly a century, so the horse and foot artillery batteries were positioned on or just forward of the crest line. This did mean that they were vulnerable to French artillery fire, but it also allowed them to open up on d'Erlon's approaching infantry. The best opportunity to do this came as the French battalions threaded their way through their own gun line and formed up in front of it, and lasted until the divisional columns had moved sufficiently down the slope to allow the Grand Battery to begin firing over their heads. The Allied guns, nine- and six-pounders, were firing at extreme range, and in the soft ground round shot hitting a divisional column would probably only kill two or three men. Shells fired from howitzers would be more effective, as would shrapnel, provided the fuse was cut correctly, but like the guns they were at their extreme range of 900 yards. Of course, once the French guns could recommence firing, the Allied artillery again became vulnerable. But as ever the soft ground meant that a round shot would actually have to score a direct hit to be effective, and the French guns too were at maximum range and would remain so, whereas the advancing French infantry were marching into the ideal beaten zone of the Allied artillery. From 400 yards or so, the Allied guns could switch to firing canister, a devastating weapon against close-packed infantry, and all guns and howitzers could continue firing until the French closed to within musket range (100 or 150 yards); then the crews would abandon their positions and scuttle off behind the infantry, usually taking a wheel with them to prevent the enemy taking the gun away.

Given that it would have taken the leading French division twenty minutes to get from the start line in front of the Grand Battery to within musket range of Wellington's men, it might be wondered that, with the round shot, shell, shrapnel and canister aimed at them, they ever got there at all. But there were not, in fact, very many guns and howitzers on the Allied left – one British and two Hanoverian batteries of five guns and a howitzer each, and two Dutch-Belgian batteries of four guns each – and despite the target-rich environment presented to them, twenty-three guns and three howitzers were just not enough to stop, or even significantly slow down, the 18,000 or so approaching infantrymen. It was, though, not only the artillery that the French had to withstand as they tramped down into the valley and then began to move up the slope towards the Allies, but also the three companies of the 95th Rifles in and around the sand pit on the other side of the road from La Haie Sainte, and the King's German Legion men in La Haie itself. Both these units, armed with Baker rifles, were able to snipe at the French long before the latter got within range to fire back. From the time the French reached the bottom of the valley onwards, the riflemen would have been picking off officers, *porte-aigles* (eagle-bearers), *porte-fanions* (flag-bearers) and drummers. But despite their sterling work, the mass of men came on, seemingly unstoppable, Marshal Ney and General d'Erlon on horseback in front of Marcognet's 3rd Division. Once the French were within musket range, the 95th evacuated the sand pit and scurried back to the ridge – their job was to harry and snipe, not to exchange volleys at short range. The skirmish line of the light companies of the infantry battalions were able to cause some damage before they too retired, forming up as the rear company of their battalion in column, preparatory to becoming the left-hand company when in line. Most of the skirmishers' musketry was directed against the French skirmish line, which also retired as their main body approached the crest.

The leading French division, that of Quiot, now split. The left-hand brigade of four battalions commanded by Colonel Claude Charlet moved to attack La Haie Sainte, supported by Dubois' cuirassiers, while the second brigade, another four battalions under the command of Brigadier General Charles-François Bourgeois, carried on towards the ridge line. Aware of the risk to La Haie, Wellington sent a battalion from Major General Kilmannsegge's 1st Hanoverian Brigade to reinforce the garrison, but it was scattered by the French cuirassiers and now the French infantry were through the orchard on the south side of the farm buildings and milling around the walls. The men of Bourgeois' brigade and those of Donzelot's division, behind and to the right of Bourgeois, could see the hedge in front of them but not much else, and Bourgeois and his men actually got to the hedge and began to force a way through it. So far, despite casualties during the advance, the advantage seemed to be with the French.

And then the balance began to shift. Lieutenant General Picton was ordering his men to stand up and move forward, and the forward battalions of the brigades of Kempt – next to the crossroads – and Pack came from column into a two-deep line, each covering a frontage of around 400 yards. In between was Bijlandt's brigade, covering perhaps 200 yards. It was Donzelot's leading battalion who hit the hedge, crossed it and advanced on the Dutch-Belgians, who fired one or possibly two volleys and then, with the exception of a Dutch battalion that stood its ground, began to fall back, despite the urgings of most of their officers. To be fair, they had been heavily pounded at Quatre Bras, many were recent veterans of the French army, many were raw recruits, and as for the rest, their hearts just weren't in it. That said, their withdrawal of labour did create a dangerous gap in the Allied line, which Donzelot was only prevented from capitalizing on by the British battalions to left and right of the gap, the 1/28th and 3/1st Foot, beginning to fire what Wellington called 'clockwork volleys' of coordinated musketry. This stopped Donzelot for a time, while further to the west Bourgeois had halted his brigade to change formation from column into line. He was thus caught in mid-manoeuvre by the 32nd and the 79th, whose volleys at a range of fifty yards could hardly miss. It was probably about this time that Picton's premonition was fulfilled. Mounted on his hairy-heeled cob, wearing a stovepipe hat and armed with an umbrella, he was cheering on his men when he was hit in the head by a musket ball and fell to the ground dead. His body was carried to the rear.[*] Meanwhile, with the action on the Allied centre left now in full swing, the infantry on the right centre, realizing the threat from Dubois' 700 cuirassiers, moved into square.

The fighting around La Haie Sainte was fierce. Baring's men, assisted by the 95th Rifles, had built a road block across the Brussels road and had loopholed the roof and the walls, but while the cuirassiers were in the area, sending infantry reinforcements down was not a sensible option. Nevertheless, the French advance had been stopped and thrown into some confusion: now it was time for them to be thrown back. Major General Lord Edward Somerset, commanding the Household Brigade stationed behind the infantry to the west of the Brussels road, had posted one subaltern from each of his four regiments on the crest, to keep him informed of what was going on. Somerset, born in 1776, the fourth surviving son of the fifth duke of Beaufort, had become a cornet in 1793 aged seventeen and progressed rapidly through the ranks, becoming a lieutenant colonel in 1800 at the earliest possible time after the regulation seven years' service. He served in the Peninsula, being present at all the major battles from Talavera in 1809 to the end of the war at Toulouse in 1814 as a lieutenant colonel, a colonel and, from 1813, a major general commanding a cavalry brigade. An experienced and highly competent officer, for most of the morning

---

[*] Some accounts claim that the bearers were two Highland grenadiers of the Black Watch, the 42nd, who stole the general's gold-rimmed spectacles. This has to be a disgraceful calumny on a fine regiment, for the 42nd were in Pack's brigade, a good 500 yards away, and if any Highlanders did steal the spectacles, they could only have been from the 79th, the Cameron Highlanders, who were in Kempt's brigade and only a few yards from where Picton fell.

Somerset had his men dismounted with girths slackened, but now, knowing what was happening on the other side of the ridge, he had the 1,200 men of his brigade mounted and formed in two lines ready to go.

On the other side of the road, Major General Sir William Ponsonby could see what was happening to his front and he too ordered his men to tighten girths and surcingles and to mount up. Ponsonby, who was forty-three at Waterloo, had had a more chequered career than his fellow heavy cavalry brigade commander. He was commissioned as an ensign in 1793 and had moved through three different infantry regiments as a lieutenant and captain, followed by a stint as a major in the Irish Fencibles, before transferring to the cavalry as a lieutenant colonel in 1800. He too served in the Peninsula, where he had initially commanded his regiment in Le Marchant's heavy cavalry brigade, before taking over the brigade after Le Marchant's death at the Battle of Salamanca in 1812 and, as a major general from 1813, commanding it until the end of the war.

There is dispute over who ordered the British heavy cavalry to charge. Lord Uxbridge insisted it was done entirely on his initiative, without any prompting from Wellington. Although Wellington had given Uxbridge overall command of the cavalry, the duke did not by nature delegate, and it seems unlikely that such a critical decision was left to others. Who gave the order is immaterial: the point is that the two heavy cavalry brigades were ordered to charge to take advantage of the – probably temporary – disorganized state of the French infantry.

To the west the Household Brigade moved through the gaps in the infantry squares, negotiated the sunken road around the crossroads, and charged the French cuirassiers. 'Charge' is hardly the most apt word as it was delivered at a trot, the ground being heavy and the distance short, but the brigade's 1,200 men hit the French's 700, and after a short scrap in which the British advantage of the high ground was countered by the protection of the French cuirasses (British heavy cavalry did not wear armour) and which involved much clanging of sword against sword and sword against armour, numbers told and the French were seen off.* Without cavalry support, the infantry of Charlet's brigade around La Haie were desperately exposed and Somerset's men swept through them, scattering them and cutting down those who could not find cover or run fast enough. They then swung left across the road and into the flanks of Bourgeois' brigade. To the east of the Brussels road, the British infantry closed up to allow the Union Brigade to pass through and force the hedge, and with the brigade commander in the lead, they too hit the French of Donzelot's division, which was already in some confusion caused by the infantry volleys.

With no time to form square to receive cavalry and under fire from the British infantry to their front, d'Erlon's attack dissolved into a desperate attempt by scattered individuals to avoid the slashing heavy straight swords of the cavalry who now had their blood up. The best protection for a soldier who could not evade a cavalryman coming at him was to lie down – a trooper armed with a sword could not reach a man lying on the ground and would

---

* The Household Cavalry were equipped with armour shortly after Waterloo, along with a helmet copied from the French. It is that uniform that is worn by the Household Cavalry on ceremonial occasions today.

go off in search of an easier target.* It took a brave and confident soldier to take that course, however, and most simply ran. Against a pursuing cavalryman the running soldier was reasonably well protected. His shako protected his head, the thick high collar of his tunic his neck, his epaulettes his shoulders and his haversack his back,† so the experienced cavalryman did not waste time and effort in slashing at the fleeing infantryman from behind, rather he overtook him and backhanded his sword, hitting the unprotected face and splitting the man's head.

Once the British heavy cavalry were into the French infantry, the carnage was considerable: their heavy sword was not particularly well balanced, but it was long – and heavy – and it created fearful wounds. There was no question of the French infantry standing, and as individuals or as small groups in companies and half-companies they fled back whence they

---

* This statement has been disputed: one otherwise thoroughly reliable historian has said that, as a sword is the same length as a polo mallet, with which it is possible to hit a ball running along the ground, then stabbing a prone man would be no problem. It would appear that the writer has never ridden a horse, handled a sword or played polo. From personal experiment, using dummies, this author has found that it is possible to reach a man lying down with one's sword if one is fit and supple, but not when the horse is carrying all the impedimenta issued to the cavalryman. Strapped to various parts of the saddle, among other bits and pieces, were piquet ropes and pegs, a spare set of horseshoes, a hay net (full, if possible), rations for the soldier and the horse, the soldier's haversack with his personal kit, and the issue carbine in its leather bucket plus ammunition for it. All of this restricted the rider's movement considerably, and leaning over and stretching down far enough to stab a prone opponent would not have been possible.
† Today we would drop our large packs before attacking; then to do so meant that they would be stolen – if not by the enemy, then by your own, albeit from a different regiment. The soldier carried all he had with him as the only sure way of retaining his meagre possessions.

came. Had the cavalry now rallied and held hard, they would have rendered a significant service. While not all of d'Erlon's men had been scattered – Durutte's division had only just left their start line and were untouched, and much of Marcognet's division were able to withdraw in good order – they had nevertheless received a bloody nose; La Haie had been saved and the Allied centre left flank was intact. Unfortunately, the British cavalry rather tended to be a 'fire and forget' weapon, delivering a magnificent charge and then disappearing over the horizon in search of loot or glory or both and not returning until the battle was over. On this occasion, despite the efforts of the two brigade commanders to curb their enthusiasm, and the trumpeters blowing the recall over and over again, most took absolutely no notice and pursued the French infantry down the hill, and when they had overtaken them, they spotted the French Grand Battery and decided to charge that too. One soldier reported afterwards that he was passed by an officer with sword in the air shouting, 'On to Paris!' In the Union Brigade, the Royal North British Dragoons, or Scots Greys,* who were ordered to form the second line, refused to be left out of the fun and moved up to be level with the leading squadrons, capturing the eagle of the 45th Line of Marcognet's division. Most did in fact reach the gun line and were having a jolly time whacking the

---

* So called because they rode grey horses, and continued to do so. In the First World War their horses were dyed brown or black with vegetable dye to make them less conspicuous. In 1815 camouflage was not a consideration. The well-known painting *Scotland Forever* by Lady Butler (née Thompson) was done in 1886 when her husband commanded at Aldershot. A trench was dug for her to sit in with her easel while a regiment of cavalry galloped past her. A wonderful painting, certainly, but it is a lot more glorious-looking than the real thing.

gunners when the inevitable reprisal struck. Napoleon saw what was happening and ordered a counter-attack by two regiments of lancers and one of hussars from Jacquinot's light cavalry, on the French extreme right flank, and four regiments of cuirassiers from Milhaud's reserve cavalry corps, stationed behind the French centre right.

The French had first come across the lance when experiencing it in the hands of Polish and Russian soldiers, and while there were Polish lancers in the French army (chiefly in the Imperial Guard), most lancer regiments were now composed of Frenchmen, albeit dressed in the Polish manner. The lance was nine feet long with a steel spike and a wooden shaft, and as it could only be effective in a charge when held by men in the front rank, only about one third of soldiers in lancer regiments actually had a lance, the others having carbines and light cavalry sabres. Although the sight of a line of galloping lancers, lances couched and levelled and pennants fluttering in the wind, would indeed have been terrifying to the inexperienced, they were not as fearsome as they looked. If a defending cavalryman could evade the first thrust and get inside the point, then all the lancer had to parry the other's sabre was the unwieldy wooden shaft; and while a lancer could of course reach an infantryman lying on the ground, he had to come to a halt or at least a walk before spearing him, as to do so at the canter or gallop would propel the lancer off his horse. Similarly, if a lancer did manage to skewer an opposing horseman, it required considerable skill to extract the lance and remain mounted.

Lancers were trained to couch the lance under the arm but in practice the best way to use it was to hold it by the point of balance and allow the momentum to do the damage, the rider then twisting his body and head round while extracting the lance.

Above left: Le Caillou. The building in which Napoleon and his staff spent the night before Waterloo, and where he gave his final orders for the battle on the morning of 18 June. It is now a museum.

Above right: Wellington's Headquarters. At the time of the battle, Waterloo was an insignificant hamlet on a dirt road some two miles north of the battlefield. The inn where Wellington spent the night after the battle, and where he penned the Waterloo Despatch, is now a museum in the main street of a sizeable town, which, due to ribbon development, is fast becoming a suburb of Brussels.

The Battle of Waterloo – the Life Guards charging the French Imperial Guard. There are lies, damned lies, and artists' impressions. Both regiments of the Life Guards, seriously under-strength, were at Waterloo and they charged D'Erlon's infantry and the French gun line as part of the Household Brigade, suffering considerable casualties as a result. It is unlikely that they ever charged the Imperial Guard, although they were charged by French lancers, which is probably what this picture actually represents, the title having been corrupted over the years. (Franz Josef Manskirch, 1815)

The Farm of Mont-Saint-Jean. Located a few hundred yards behind Wellington's line it was the Allies' main field hospital and also a stores depot. Piling large stocks of spare ammunition next to operating tables would probably be regarded as unwise today.

The Battle of Waterloo. Sometime near the close of the battle, Wellington is seen in the centre foreground with La Haie Sainte on the left. It would be some time before photographic evidence could show artists that horses do not canter or gallop as shown here, with both forelegs extended. It was fashionable at the time to show horses with small Arab-type heads and arched necks, which in reality few military chargers had. (Aleksander Sauerveid, 1819)

The Old Guard at Waterloo. The elite of the elite of the French army, the Guard were usually held back to pluck victory from defeat or to add a crushing blow to a battle already won. At Waterloo they were played as Napoleon's final card, and failed, but fought a gallant rear-guard action to allow the Emperor to escape the field, thus creating a legend of French military valour that endures to this day. (Hippolyte Bellangé, 1869)

The End of the Glorious Battle of La Belle Alliance. Waterloo was La Belle Alliance to the Prussians. Here Prussian cavalry (identified by the initials 'FW' for Frederick William on the pistol holster of the mounted officer in the foreground) is seen chasing French infantry, including some bearskin-cap-wearing members of the Imperial Guard, away from Plancenoit, where the village church can be seen in the background. While the Prussian blue was much darker than that of the French, at a distance it was easy to mistake the two. (Fredrich Campe, 1821)

The Meeting of Wellington and Blücher. Most sources agree that the two commanders met at La Belle Alliance at the close of the battle. It is unclear what the mobile garden sheds in the foreground are – they may be intended to be French ambulances, but they had a sprung suspension, clearly lacking here. (Charles Turner Warren, 1818)

Napoleon takes Flight from the Battle of La Belle Alliance. A somewhat fanciful depiction of the Emperor and his immediate staff escaping from the battlefield. He left the area on horseback and then transferred to a coach for the journey to Paris, and an attempt to remain in control of the nation. (Friedrich Campe, 1821)

The Pursuit by the Prussians by Moonlight. With the French in full flight, it was vital to prevent them from consolidating and reorganising to the extent where they could force another battle. The pursuit, with the aim of giving the French no opportunity to halt and regroup, was undertaken by the Prussian cavalry, which was fresher than that of the Anglo-Dutch. All through the night the Prussians followed, harrying and keeping the French on the move. (Charles Turner Warren, 1818)

The Morning after the Battle. While perhaps not quite as closely crowded with wounded as is shown, the field next morning did present a ghastly sight. It took several days to bring in all the wounded, by which time many had been murdered after resisting being looted by local peasants. Looking at the carnage, Wellington is reported as remarking that next to a battle lost, nothing could be half so melancholy as a battle won. (John Heaviside Clark, 1817)

The Château of Hougoumont. Denis Dighton (1791–1827) was one of the few contemporary artists who painted realistic depictions of the aftermath of battle. He arrived at Waterloo a few days after the battle and painted what he saw. Here bodies of soldiers, stripped naked so that uniforms can be reissued, are being tipped into a grave-pit opposite Hougoumont Farm, while two Prussian officers look on.

The Execution of the Sentence on Marshal Ney. Most of the officers who had risen to prominence under Napoleon happily turned their coats on the Emperor's first abdication, and turned them again when he returned in 1815, and most got away with it. One who didn't was Marshal Ney. Due to a failure to understand the law by the officer members of the first court to try him (had they found him guilty and given him a lenient sentence of imprisonment or exile, he would have been rehabilitated after a few years), he ended up being tried by the royalists of the Chamber of Peers, and the end was inevitable. He faced death bravely, refused to wear a blindfold and insisted on giving the orders to the firing squad himself. (Innocent-Louis Goubaud, 1816)

Failure to 'follow the point' meant that the butt of the lance would hit the lancer on the back of the head, putting him on the deck.[*] Against an infantryman standing up, the lancer had a longer reach than the musket and bayonet but, as when cavalry were attacked by lancers, if the infantryman could evade the first thrust, he could bayonet the lancer or his horse. Against fleeing cavalry on less fit horses, however, the lance was deadly, and in this case the lancers were able to come up behind the British on their already exhausted horses and poke their lance points into their opponents' backs.

Attacked by 2,500 fresh French horsemen, the British cavalry, disorganized and with horses blown, had no alternative but to try to return to their own lines as fast as they could. Unfortunately, that was not very fast. In their flight back whence they had come, one brigade commander, Ponsonby, was killed; the other, Somerset, escaped unscathed, but his brigade major, Smith, was killed, as were three of the seven commanding officers of regiments, while two others were wounded. Had Ponsonby been mounted on his main charger, he might well have survived, but precisely at the wrong moment its groom had taken it for a walk and Ponsonby had to charge on the inferior hack that he had been riding during the morning. Coming back up the hill in the mud, he had no chance against a lancer. Altogether, only about half the men of the two brigades returned with their horses and capable of duty. The others were taken prisoner, wounded, dead or without their horses, and there is nothing more useless than a heavy cavalryman without his horse, or a heavy cavalry horse without its rider.

It was while all this was happening that Grouchy launched his attack at Wavre. Vandamme hurled the infantry of his III

---

* As this author discovered the first time he tried tent-pegging.

Corps at the bridges defended by Thielemann's Prussians, but this was a totally pointless operation, which contributed not a jot to Napoleon's strategic situation, for it had no effect whatsoever on the activities of the three Prussian corps on their way to Waterloo. Captain François says the attack on Wavre began at about three o'clock, and it was at around this time that, despite the problems of moving large number of troops across difficult country, the advance guard of Prussian infantry and cavalry was in the Bois de Paris and throwing out a skirmish line to ensure that they were not interfered with by the French cavalry on the emperor's right wing. But those cavalrymen were far too interested in what was going on to their front to notice what was happening in the woods, and it was probably the sight of Prussian troops on the heights of Chapelle Saint-Lambert, about four miles away to the north-east, that alerted Napoleon to the imminent arrival of the Prussians. From the emperor's point of view this was serious, but not critical – he could still defeat the English and their lackeys long before the Prussians could possibly intervene.

9

THE DECISION

By around 1530 hours, it was obvious to Napoleon that the Prussians were appearing off to his right and that, despite increasingly urgent summonses, which never got though, Grouchy was nowhere to be seen. For the ordinary soldier who might have peered through the smoke over his right shoulder, Prussian black was not easy to distinguish from French blue at a range of almost two miles, and any who had the temerity to ask were told that the troops in the far distance were those of Grouchy, come to reinforce. As Reille's infantry was still wholly occupied by Hougoumont farm and that of d'Erlon was still recovering from its repulse by Picton's division and the British heavy cavalry – a recovery that they managed remarkably quickly, despite the casualties incurred – the only French infantry so far uncommitted were those of Lobau's VI Corps, stationed on either side of the Brussels road south of La Belle Alliance, and the Imperial Guard, further back still. Unwilling to deploy the Guard until absolutely necessary, Napoleon ordered

'Mr Sheep', as Lobau was unofficially known,* to deal with the Prussian approach.

One of the kinder plays on Lobau's name was made by Napoleon, who on one occasion remarked, '*Mon mouton est un lion*.' In this campaign, however, Lobau was anything but lion-like. He had been slow and cautious during the advance to the River Sambre on 15 June and now, instead of advancing into the Bois de Paris, where so far there was only Prussian cavalry and vanguard infantry with a thin skirmish line, he deployed his two infantry divisions, Simmer's 19th and Jeanin's 20th, in a static blocking position between the village of Plancenoit and the edge of the Bois. Had Lobau been a little more adventurous, he would have used his two cavalry divisions, those of Domon and Subervie, to sweep the late Colonel von Schwerin's hussars and uhlans out of the way (Lobau had over 3,000 men against 1,200) and drive into the Bois, where he could have caught Bülow on the line of march and pushed him back, perhaps as far as the valley of the River Lasne, a tributary of the Dyle. In any event, he might have bought valuable time, but as it was his deployment did nothing to prevent the Prussian build-up in and in front of the Bois de Paris.

Elsewhere on the battlefield, skirmishing between Saxe-Weimar's troops in and around Papelotte farm and Durutte's division on the Allied right flank continued. Durutte had been virtually unscathed during the repulse of d'Erlon's corps, but Saxe-Weimar conducted a skilful defence, abandoning outlying

---

* His name was Georges Mouton but he was officially known by his ennobled title, Comte de Lobau, which he had acquired after performing well in the 1809 campaign against the Austrians (Lobau is an island in the River Danube).

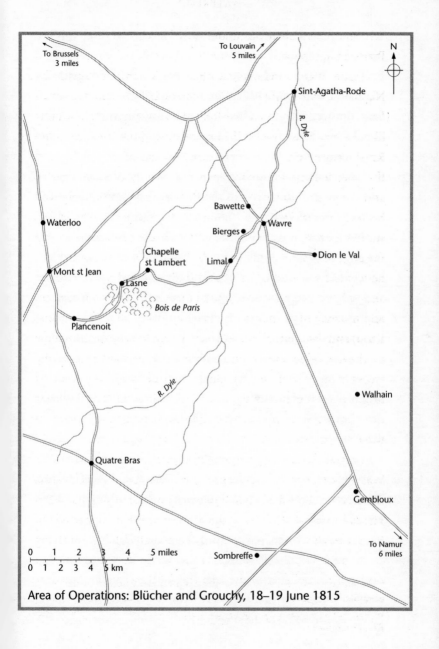

To Brussels
3 miles

To Louvain
5 miles

N

Sint-Agatha-Rode

R. Dyle

Bawette ●

Waterloo ●

Bierges ●

Wavre

Dion le Val ●

Chapelle
st Lambert

Limal ●

Mont st Jean ●

Lasne ●

Bois de Paris

Plancenoit ●

R. Dyle

Walhain ●

Quatre Bras ●

Gembloux ●

0   1   2   3   4   5 miles
0 1 2 3 4 5 km

To Namur
6 miles

Sombreffe ●

Area of Operations: Blücher and Grouchy, 18–19 June 1815

farms and hamlets when there was no point in hanging on to them, but preserving his position in Papelotte itself, supported by the two brigades of Allied cavalry to his rear. At Hougoumont the battle went on, with Allied reinforcements moving down from the crest when required and back up again when not, while attacks by elements of d'Erlon's corps against La Haie Sainte were almost continuous, so far without success.

It was around mid-afternoon that Napoleon is said to have felt ill and went to recover in the farm of Rosomme, just behind his tactical observation post and where the Victor Hugo memorial is now. Clearly, it would not have done for the troops to see the emperor in a state of discomfort, although there is some doubt about what was so wrong that he had to go and lie down. True, he was short of sleep and had covered many miles of rough roads in badly sprung vehicles or in the saddle, and as he knew full well that this was his last chance to recover his former eminence, the mental stress would have been considerable. Still, he was only forty-six, the same age as the Duke of Wellington, and while he had not taken the same care of his body as his adversary had, he should nevertheless have been able to withstand the strain. One authority, after an exhaustive examination of post-mortem reports, has suggested that Napoleon suffered from gonorrhoea and syphilis, and symptoms of the latter include lightning pains and temporary loss of balance. One account says that Napoleon slipped on the muddy ground and had to be helped up, but a momentary loss of balance could have happened to anyone, regardless of his state of health. Whatever the cause of Napoleon's temporary incapacity, it left Marshal Ney, nominal commander of the left wing of the army at Waterloo, without the supervision of his emperor, which would lead to yet another misreading of the situation, with serious consequences.

*

It is perhaps apposite at this point of the battle to compare the command styles of the two main protagonists. Wellington is constantly moving about the battlefield, personally checking that his orders are being carried out, seeing and being seen by his subordinate commanders and, perhaps even more important, by the non-British elements of his troops. He is alert, aware of what is happening in every corner of the field, full of energy in directing the defence: completely on top of his task and seen to be so. Napoleon, on the other hand, seems content to let the battle run its course without intervention from him. He makes little effort to find out what is happening, those orders that he does issue are unclear, and except when he goes to the rear to rest, he remains at his command post, unable to influence the course of the day by his presence. Whether his lethargy was physical, mental or a combination of both, he is an old man, overweight, unfit and seemingly unable to muster that tactical acumen that won him a score of battles and conquered the whole of Europe. The old magic that inspired thousands of men to march willingly to their deaths for him has somehow gone.

As it was, although d'Erlon's attack had been repelled, it had not been without cost to the Allies, and, although their artillery had been far less effective than the French had hoped, it too had caused casualties. Although the infantry on the reverse slope of the ridge occupied by Wellington were out of his view, Ney could see horse-drawn vehicles on the ridge itself and the tops of regimental colours moving away, and, excitable fellow that he was, he assumed that this was the Allies retreating. In fact, what he was observing were wheeled ambulances taking wounded back to the main field hospital, ammunition carts going back to be replenished, and columns of prisoners and colours going to the rear.

A British battalion had two colours:* the king's colour, which was the union flag with a crown and the regimental number in the middle, surrounded by the 'union wreath', a wreath of shamrocks, roses and thistles; and the regimental colour, which consisted of the regimental facing colour (blue, buff, green, black, white, grey or yellow) with the union flag in the top left-hand corner. Each colour was six feet square and made of heavy, double-sided silk and was carried on a pole ten feet long. Originally intended as a rallying point in battle, as the years went by, the colours acquired a mystical significance, representing the spirit of the regiment, and were even consecrated before presentation to the battalion. It was regarded as a frightful disgrace to have one's colours captured,† and in this case commanding officers, sensing that things were going to hot up, had very sensibly told their colour parties to get out of the danger area.‡

Having convinced himself that the Allied right was retiring, Ney sent an ADC to the nearest cavalry brigade, that of Brigadier

---

* The Guards had colonel's, lieutenant colonel's and major's colours as well as company colours, while rifle regiments (the 95th and the 60th) had no colours at all.

† Until very recently the only British regiment still on the army order of battle to have its colours exhibited as captured trophies of war was the Royal Scots, whose fourth battalion lost theirs at the Battle of Bergen op Zoom in 1814. They can now be seen in the museum of Les Invalides in Paris. The Royal Scots have since been subsumed into the Royal Regiment of Scotland.

‡ Colours were last carried into battle in 1881, during the first Boer War, and are now only carried on ceremonial occasions. They are still highly regarded, however, are still consecrated, and are saluted by all ranks. They are now only 3 feet 6 inches by 3 feet in size and carried on a pole that is 8 feet 7 inches in length, which makes them a lot easier to carry. On a battalion giving a general or royal salute, the regimental colour is lowered, but the king's or queen's colour is lowered only to the reigning monarch, his or her consort, and the heir to the throne.

General Pierre Joseph Farine du Creux, who was forty-five, had enlisted as a volunteer in 1791 and had been elected lieutenant three years later. Coming to a halt in front of Farine, the ADC shouted that Marshal Ney wished him to advance his two regiments of cuirassiers and seize the plateau – that is, the ridge on the Allied right. Farine was reluctant – he had fought the British in Spain and been captured and sent to England as a prisoner of war, from where he had escaped back to France – but faced with orders coming from a marshal of France, he began to move his squadrons forward. Farine's divisional commander, Major General Jacques Antoine Adrien Delort, who was forty-three and whose military career had begun when he enlisted as a national guardsman in 1789, saw what was happening, spurred his horse forward and told Farine to stand still. To protests from Ney's ADC, Delort pointed out that Farine took orders only from his divisional commander – him – and that *he* took orders only from his corps commander, the 39-year-old Major General Édouard Jean-Baptiste Milhaud. A hard-bitten cynic, Milhaud was not one to blindly obey the orders of Ney, even if he was a marshal, particularly when those orders were delivered second-hand and to one of his subordinates rather than through him.

Ney himself, increasingly agitated at the lack of action despite his orders transmitted through an ADC, now appeared and ordered Milhaud to take the whole corps, not just Farine's brigade, and capture the ridge from which the English were retiring. Milhaud demurred: attacking British troops head-on when they were on a position of their choosing and making use of a reverse slope was unwise; time and again in the Peninsula such an approach had failed, and it could well fail here. Ney, despite his own experiences in Spain, would have none of it, and Milhaud, finally and reluctantly, accepted that he had no alternative but to do as he was told.* The two divisions of IV Reserve Cavalry Corps began to move forward down the hill to form up in the valley. The corps consisted of four regiments of cuirassiers, three with four squadrons and one of three, a total of around 3,000 horsemen, allowing for the casualties incurred by Watier's division in supporting d'Erlon's attack. Behind Milhaud's regiments was the light cavalry division of the Imperial Guard, commanded by Major General Lefebvre-Desnouettes, late resident of Cheltenham and breaker of parole. Unable to resist the opportunity to take part, Lefebvre, without orders, followed with his division of the Chasseurs à Cheval and the 'Red Lancers',† each of five squadrons, or around 2,500 officers and men altogether.

The valley where the cavalry would form up prior to advancing and through which the attack would take place was the gap between Hougoumont farm and La Haie Sainte, a distance of 900 yards. Although both those locations were under attack and would continue to be so, allowing for leaving a musket shot's distance from each, the cavalry had a frontage of around 700 yards available to them, although this would widen out once past those two farms. This would give a frontage of just over 100 yards for each of the seven regiments. A horseman needs an absolute minimum of a yard of space, and, although squadron sizes varied from sixty-five men in the 6th Cuirassiers to 230

---

* The suggestion that Napoleon was not present on the field is reinforced by Milhaud's acceptance of Ney's orders without appealing to the emperor.

† Whose No 1 Squadron was entirely Polish and wore blue, but it is such inconsistencies that delight the observer of *la vie militaire*.

in the Chasseurs à Cheval of the Imperial Guard, the frontage would only allow regiments to form up in double column of squadrons, each squadron in two ranks. A typical regiment such as the 1st Cuirassiers would have its first and second squadrons abreast, in two ranks, in the first line, and its third and fourth squadrons, also abreast and in two ranks, in the second line. The regiment's frontage would be 120 yards. The Chasseurs à Cheval, by contrast, drawn up in the same formation but with its fifth squadron forming a third line, would cover 230 yards. The point is that there was not very much room to get 5,500 men lined up to deliver what Ney hoped would be the blow to win the battle. Indeed, some French sources claim that the men were packed so tightly together that, when they moved off, some horses and men were lifted into the air by the press of those on either side – ridiculous, of course, but it makes the point.

To a young Allied soldier looking at the flower of the French cavalry forming their regiments and squadrons in the valley 400 yards below him, the sight would have been both magnificent and terrifying. The polished, albeit by now mud-spattered, cuirasses and helmets flashing in the sun, the lance points glistening, the guidons and pennants fluttering in the slight breeze, the gorgeously caparisoned officers in front lining up their men – all gave the impression of an unstoppable juggernaut that only had to charge up the hill to put all in its path to flight. Only a few Allied soldiers could see all this, however: skirmishers of the infantry light companies, those defenders of Hougoumont and La Haie Sainte who were not otherwise engaged, and the gunners on the ridge. To the gunners, it must have seemed that all their Christmases and birthdays had come at once, for, although the French Grand Battery bombarded the Allied gun line over the heads of the cavalrymen, it took a very accurate (and lucky) shot to do any damage to the Allied guns at a range of nearly a mile, whereas these latter were firing at a distance of only 400 yards or so. Wellington had always considered his right flank to be the one most at risk and had concentrated his artillery there. There were eleven British and German batteries on the right flank, and with one battery covering La Haie Sainte, there were ten batteries, or sixty six-pounder and nine-pounder guns and howitzers, to take on the cavalry. And take them on they did.

Once the French cavalry regiments were lined up in their regimental columns, Marshal Ney took post in the front centre and the order was given to draw swords. Thousands of blades glinted in the sun and the whole mass moved forward. Tactical advice for a 'normal' cavalry charge dictated that the men should walk their horses for the first quarter-mile, trot for the second, canter for the third and gallop for the last quarter-mile. There is, however, rarely any such thing as a 'normal' situation in battle, and this one was far from normal: the heavy going (and the bottom of the valley was little better than a bog) and the still untrampled rye restricted the horses to little more than a walk, escalating into a slow trot as they moved up the slope. A horse trots at about eight miles per hour on level ground but in these conditions would hardly manage six, so would take two minutes to reach the crest, giving the Allied artillery time to get off three or four rounds per gun. At that range round shot would plough through the column, taking out as many as four troopers before hitting the ground and sinking in the mud; canister would do even more damage, as would common shell and shrapnel. Even allowing for the degradation caused by firing downhill, the artillery would have caused considerable damage to the French cavalry well before they reached the crest. Once the cavalry reached within carbine shot of the guns, the gunners withdrew, leaving their guns where they were and retiring to the protection of the infantry behind them, as usual taking a gun wheel with them.[*]

The Allied infantry had ample warning of what was to come: although the men and the junior officers could not see over the crest, the senior, mounted, officers could and the battalions were ordered to form square, a process that from column took about a minute. In a ten-company battalion a square was actually an oblong, with men packed shoulder to shoulder in four ranks. The long sides of the oblong each had six half-companies, while the short sides each had two companies. The light company which would be out in front in the skirmish line – and horribly vulnerable to cavalry – was the last company to come in when the battalion formed square and was the outer two ranks for one of the short sides. Whether a short or a long side faced the cavalry threat depended on the ground, the position of other battalions, and the formation that the battalion was in prior to the order 'Prepare to receive cavalry'. At Waterloo some battalions presented a short side to the French cavalry, others a long side. In a battalion that was up to strength, the short sides would be twenty-seven yards in length (two feet per man) and the long sides eighty yards. The front rank knelt, with muskets at an angle of forty-five degrees, the butts on the ground and

* Except for the men of Mercer's troop, who took cover under their guns. Mercer thought that the nearest infantry square, that of Brunswick, was unsteady and might panic if they saw the gunners running towards them. Despite the continual passage of French cavalry, his men remained unscathed, emerging to service the guns when an opportunity arose.

bayonets fixed. This front rank did not normally fire, except in dire emergency; rather, their task was to present an impenetrable hedge of bayonets. The firing was done by the second and third ranks, with the fourth filling gaps in the other three caused by men killed or wounded. The short sides would fire by rank, meaning a pause of fifteen seconds between each volley, or by file, while the longer sides would fire by half-companies with an interval of ten seconds. In the centre of the square would be the commanding officer, the adjutant, the sergeant major, the colour party if not already despatched rearwards, the drummers, gunners from the nearest gun, and a few spare men as stretcher-bearers to pull the wounded or the dead into the centre and out of the way. Company officers and NCOs were behind their companies, company commanders remaining mounted so that they could see over the heads of their men in front.

The skill required of the company officers and NCOs commanding half-companies was in knowing when to give the order to open fire. Firing at too great a distance was ineffective, whereas waiting for the cavalry to get too close meant that a dead or dying horse might crash into the square, creating a gap through which other cavalrymen could enter. If that happened, as it did on one occasion in 1812 to a French square at Garcia Hernandez in Spain, then the square was doomed. Experienced officers and sergeants – and most of the British officers and sergeants were experienced – would give the order to fire when the cavalry were thirty yards away, and men were told to fire low so as to hit the larger target of the horse rather than the smaller one of the rider.

By the time the cavalry breasted the hill, the gunners had retreated to the squares and the skirmishers had rejoined their battalions. As the French rode through the Allied gun line, they were faced with twenty-seven battalion squares to the west of the Brussels road, and the 1/27th just to the east of the crossroads but also in square. The squares were laid out like pieces on a draughts board, in a chequered fashion, so that the soldiers could fire without hitting their neighbours. The French, still only at a trot, came on, and at a distance of thirty yards the faces of the squares began to belch flame and smoke. At that range the carnage among the horses was considerable. Down they went, dead, dying or badly wounded, creating an obstacle to be negotiated by those behind. No horse will charge at something that it cannot jump over,* and, however the riders may have dug in their spurs, the horses would not approach the line of bayonets. Instead, they swerved off left and right, with their impotent riders able to do little but ride round and round the squares waving their swords. Even the lancers could achieve little, and while the riders in some cavalry squadrons, their horses refusing to go forward, discharged their carbines at the infantry, this did little damage, as apart from the inherent inaccuracy of the short-barrelled smooth-bore carbine, firing from a moving horse was very much a hit-and-miss business – mainly miss. Horses wounded but not brought down were quite likely either to dump their rider or to whip round and try to get back whence they came, causing confusion and adding to the difficulties of movement for the remainder. The heavy ground did at least prevent the horses from bolting – galloping off out of control. The types of bit in use in 1815 with their very long curbs

---

* Readers who hunt (most, I fondly hope) will know that it is pointless to gallop at a hedge that the horse decides he cannot jump. The rider may well clear the obstacle, but without his horse.

would stop a charging elephant, although if fitted today – along with the razor-sharp spurs then in common use – they would spark instant prosecution by the RSPCA.*

The private soldier standing or kneeling in square would have seen little after the first volley was fired. After that he could only listen to the commands of his officer or sergeant as he reloaded his musket and waited for the command to fire into the smoke. Packed shoulder to shoulder and unable to move except to handle his weapon, he would have to urinate and defecate where he stood. The inside of a square was not a pleasant place to be: the horrific noise of screaming horses, the firing of one's own and one's comrades' weapons, the rotten-egg smell of discharged gunpowder, the moans of the wounded dragged into the centre of the square, the bellowing of the sergeants – all just had to be endured. Many of the British soldiers had done it all before, and for those who had not there were plenty of old campaigners to reassure them that as long as they stood, as long as they followed the drill movements that had been hammered into them in training, as long as they fired low, then nothing could harm them. The desperate thirst brought on by the saltpetre content of the bitten cartridge, the bruised and painful shoulder caused by the mule-like kick of the musket, the skinned knuckles caused by ramming down if bayonets were still fixed: all could be ignored and overcome as long as the mechanical movements of loading, firing and reloading were followed. For soldiers in some of the foreign contingents who

---

* For the benefit of readers who are not British, the Royal Society for the Prevention of Cruelty to Animals is an organization that does a great deal of good work to ensure that animals are treated properly; it also has a tendency to spend large amounts of its supporters' money engaging in class warfare against packs of foxhounds.

had never experienced the excitement and the terror of standing still with huge horses coming at them, the temptation to break and run must have been almost overwhelming, and it says much for the faith that their officers had in Wellington that the men kept to their duties and did not quit the field.

All nations' tactical manuals recognized that steady infantry in square were completely impervious to the actions of cavalry. The way for cavalry to deal with infantry was to charge at them to force them to form square, and then to peel off, allowing the horse artillery that should be following close up to tear great holes in the square – holes that could then be exploited by the infantry that should also be following close up. What Ney should have done, therefore, was to ensure that the cavalry divisional commanders had their attached batteries of horse artillery close behind them and to send infantry behind the artillery. Artillery did go forward with the cavalry, but the operation was mishandled: in some cases a division's own battery had been taken away to form part of the Grand Battery, and so that division had either to take a battery not known to its officers or to go without. In any event, instead of the cavalry peeling off once the first assault had obviously failed, and thus allowing the artillery a clear field of fire, they continued to ride round and between the squares, preventing their own artillery that did get to the ridge from being able to fire. On the rare occasions when the French horse artillery did get a chance to open fire, they did do considerable damage. One of the 1st Foot Guards squares had a gap torn in its side, and had the commanding officer not reacted swiftly by pushing rear-rank men into it, the hovering lancers, waiting for just such an opportunity, would have been in.[36]

The French cavalry who did manage to pass between the squares without injury were counter-attacked by the Allied cavalry in rear. The remnants of the Household and Union heavy cavalry brigades – along with the British and KGL light cavalry of Generals Grant, Dornberg and Arenschildt, as well as that of de Collaert's Dutch-Belgians – seemed to have learned the lesson of pursuing too far: instead, they made short, controlled charges to stop the now disordered attackers advancing any further. Only one of the Allied cavalry regiments failed to do its duty, and that was the Duke of Cumberland's Hussars, an essentially amateur regiment of wealthy Hanoverian gentlemen who provided their own horses and equipment. Ordered forward to take on French cavalry by Dornberg, they would not budge, broke and began to filter to the rear. Despite appeals from both Dornberg and Arenschildt, the Cumberlands' commanding officer, Lieutenant Colonel Georg von Hake, refused to rally his men, who made off as fast as their expensive mounts would carry them in the direction of Brussels, where they spread a certain amount of alarm and despondency by assuring all who would listen that the battle was lost. Hake was later removed from command and brought before a court martial in Hanover, which ordered him to be reduced to the ranks and cashiered, while his second-in-command, Major Mellzing, was severely reprimanded for failing to prevent the defection of the regiment.

As for Ney, not only did the marshal fail to coordinate the movement of the cavalry and artillery, but he also failed to support them with any infantry. Most seriously of all, at no stage did the French cavalry attempt to spike the Allied guns. A spike was essentially a six-inch nail that was driven into the touch-hole of a gun, rendering it useless. If a spike was well hammered home, it could not be removed in the field and the gun had to be taken back to workshops to have the metal around the touch-hole drilled out and a cone of metal with a new touch-hole inserted from inside the barrel. Cavalrymen usually carried spikes and mallets for this very purpose, but either the French had not issued them or in the heat of the action their cavalry neglected to use them. Either way, the failure to spike the guns when there was ample opportunity to do so exposed the cavalry to even more death and destruction, for each time the regiments pulled back to re-form and charge again, the Allied gunners ran out and gave them one or two more rounds. How many times the French cavalrymen pulled back and came on again is disputed, but what is not is that each time they retired, the Grand Battery was able to reopen its bombardment of the Allied gun line. And yet despite the ever more frantic urgings of their officers – who all Allied accounts say were extraordinarily brave – to urge them on, Milhaud and Lefebvre's men could make no headway, and Ney, reinforcing failure, next added Kellermann's III Reserve Cavalry Corps to the mix. Another eight regiments of heavy cavalry – two of dragoons, four of cuirassiers and two of carabiniers (cavalry men who carried a rather better carbine than the rest of the cavalry), about 3,500 men in all – plunged down the hill into the valley and up the slope towards the ridge. Kellermann, sensibly, had told the commander of the carabiniers to stay back near Hougoumont as a reserve, but Ney would have none of it and so the carabiniers too joined the rush. The marshal had already had several horses killed under him and was rapidly running through his stable of chargers; he was also dashing about excitedly and ignoring the chain of command by barking orders directly to regimental and even squadron commanders. It was no way to direct a battle.

Around 9,000 men in total were now committed to no avail – virtually all of the French cavalry, save the heavy cavalry of the Imperial Guard, two divisions with Lobau over at the Bois de Paris and Piré's division of two regiments of lancers and two of *chasseurs à cheval* attached to Reille's corps, which hovered on Wellington's extreme right flank but took no part in this action. While there were significant Allied casualties, mainly from the French horse artillery, not a single square broke. When some battalions had taken so many casualties that they could not sustain a square of their own, they amalgamated with another battalion to form a square with it, while in contrast the 52nd Light Infantry formed two squares. Napoleon, returning from Rosomme, was aghast: how could cavalry be sent against infantry without supporting infantry of its own? By the time some infantry had been found to send forward, it was too late. The French cavalry, that magnificent instrument, was broken, and the trampled ground in front of and around the infantry squares was littered with dead and dying horses, with dead and dismounted cavalrymen, the latter being rounded up and sent to the rear as prisoners.

By now it was around five o'clock in the afternoon, and over in the Bois de Paris Bülow had two brigades (effectively divisions) present, those of 53-year-old Major General Michael Heinrich von Losthin and 43-year-old Colonel Johann August Friedrich Hiller von Gartringen. Each brigade had nine battalions of infantry, an attached cavalry squadron and a field artillery battery. Also present were the two regiments of the late Colonel Schwerin's cavalry. Still to come were two brigades of infantry, two cavalry brigades and the artillery reserve. Bülow had originally intended to wait for the rest of his corps to arrive before moving against the French, but seeing the mass cavalry charges through his telescope and realizing the precarious situation that Wellington was in – and despite the carnage handed out to the French cavalry, Wellington's situation was, if not perilous, then at least dangerous, with more and more of his reserves being moved forward – he decided to move with what he had got. Two battalions were sent off to link up with Saxe-Weimar and reinforce his position around Papelotte, while the remainder, preceded by a cavalry screen, moved out of the woods and started to advance on the village of Plancenoit, whose church spire could be seen and was an obvious point of reference.

Plancenoit, behind the French right flank, was one of those villages built for defence during the wars of religion, with stout, thick-walled buildings clustered around the church. Napoleon, ever the optimist, had not ordered it to be prepared for defence, but it would nevertheless be a veritable fortress and a tough nut to crack if properly manned. Bülow's leading brigade soon brushed Lobau's men away from their forward position, so Mr Sheep, perfectly sensibly, pulled back, anchoring his right flank in Plancenoit and taking up a position to cover Napoleon's right. The slogging battle for Plancenoit was about to begin. Also at about this time, the leading elements of Ziethen's corps began to appear on Wellington's extreme left flank. At first there was some confusion, with Prussian black mistaken for French blue, but Major General Muffling had been sent over by Wellington to coordinate the Prussian arrival and a serious friendly fire incident – or what the modern army calls a 'blue on blue' – was averted.* From Napoleon's perspective, the arrival of the Prussians in force was serious, but

---

* Until the First World War British maps always showed the position of friendly troops in red (British soldiers had worn red coats for much of their history) and enemy troops in blue (the enemy had usually been the French). French maps, with the same logic, used the reverse system – enemy in red, friendly in blue. When the First World War broke out, it was obvious that for the two now allied armies to retain their existing map-marking conventions could be confusing (to put it mildly), and so the British changed to the French system. Hence 'blue on blue' means friendly forces firing on each other.

not yet a deciding factor. There was still time to beat the English before the Prussian intervention swung the balance, and soon it looked as if that might indeed happen.

La Haie Sainte had been under almost continual attack all day. Time and time again the French had come forward, and time and time again they had been beaten off by the riflemen of the 2nd Light Battalion of the KGL. During the night of 17/18 June Baring's men had done their best to put the farm into a state of defence, but their efforts had been hampered by the withdrawal of their pioneers to work on Hougoumont farm. Nevertheless, they had managed to loophole the walls and build a roadblock on the Brussels road. What they had not managed to do was compensate for the missing gate leading into the farmyard on the west side. Whether this had always been missing or whether it had been used for firewood by the soldiers during the night is not known, but it was a weakness of the defence and would remain so.

From the French position, the La Haie Sainte complex consisted of an orchard thirty yards across and forty deep running along the road, then a barn and a wall, then the farmyard, then the house, and finally a garden to the rear. Baring's initial deployment was to put three companies in the orchard, two in the buildings and one in the rear garden as a reserve. During the initial French assault by Charlet's brigade of d'Erlon's corps, the defenders of the orchard were driven back into the farmyard, and in subsequent attacks the French infantry concentrated on trying to force their way through the gateless entrance on the west side. This was defended fiercely, to such an extent that the bodies of seventeen dead Frenchmen were piled up as a barricade across the gateway. Baring's men were taking heavy casualties, however, mostly outside the farm in the orchard or by the west gate, and on two occasions reinforcements were sent down to him, once of a KGL light company and once of a detachment of Nassau infantry. On occasions the French got so close that they attempted to wrest the rifles from soldiers firing from loopholes. At one point the thatched roof of the barn was set alight, whether deliberately by the French or by the burning wads of the battalion's rifles we do not know, and the cooking pots carried by the Nassau soldiers were pressed into service to carry water from the pond in the yard to douse the flames.

In the constant fighting for La Haie Sainte, Baring's men were beginning to run out of ammunition, despite beginning the day with sixty rounds a man. An officer was sent up to the crossroads to ask that more should be sent down, but none came. As the afternoon wore on, increasingly frantic messages were sent, but to no avail: no ammunition appeared. Finally, when Baring's men were down to three or four rounds a man, a messenger was again sent back up to the ridge to say that without an instant resupply of ammunition he would not be able to withstand another attack. Ammunition still did not come, but French infantry supported by cavalry did. Despite desperate work with the bayonet, once the French got onto the roof of the barn and forced their way into the courtyard via the palisade of their own dead countrymen, the Germans were forced to withdraw into the farmhouse itself, after which that bloodiest sort of warfare – close and in built-up areas – was soon over. French infantry cleared the house room by room and gave no quarter – and to be fair to them, when the enemy is but a bayonet's length away, it is too late to surrender. The survivors of the garrison could do no more than try to extricate themselves by the back door and retreat to the relative safety of the ridge.

It was while this final, hopeless defence of La Haie Sainte was in progress that a further disaster befell the infantry. Seeing that the farmhouse was about to fall, Colonel Christian Ompteda, commanding the 2nd KGL Brigade (Baring's parent formation), stationed to the immediate west of the crossroads, was ordered to counter-attack. There is some doubt about who ordered the counter-attack – some say it was the Prince of Orange himself – but in any event Ompteda personally led the 5th Line Battalion, recruited from the Lüneberg area, down the slope towards La Haie. With the large number of French cuirassiers milling about, the sensible formation for this move would have been to do it in square. Advancing in square was not easy but it could be done, albeit not as swiftly as moving in column or in line, but Ompteda deployed the battalion into line. Again, it has been suggested that Ompteda was ordered to advance in line by the Prince of Orange, thus repeating his error of Quatre Bras two days before, or that the order was given by his divisional commander, Lieutenant General Sir Charles (Karl) Alten, who assuredly should have known better. The result was entirely predictable and the end was swift. Ompteda was killed, his battalion routed and La Haie Sainte abandoned. Of the total of around 500 men who had defended the farmhouse – Baring's own battalion plus the reinforcements sent to him – only forty or fifty men were still there at the last, unwounded and capable of carrying on.[37]

There have been a number of explanations offered for the failure to resupply Baring with ammunition – and if he had been resupplied, he could almost certainly have held on – ranging from administrative incompetence on the part of his battalion rear echelon and quartermaster or by his parent brigade, to a report of an ammunition wagon of the KGL overturning on its way up to the battlefield. Of course, rifle ammunition was in much shorter supply than that for the larger-calibre musket, with which the majority of the troops were armed, but the 1/95th Rifles, who were also armed with the Baker rifle, were less than a hundred yards away on the other side of the road and had no problems with ammunition. It does seem extraordinary that the KGL could not obtain ammunition from them – perhaps Baring's emissaries came up against a quartermaster who refused to issue anything to anybody not of his own regiment, whatever the situation. Such military jobsworths were and are few, but they did and do exist.

It was during this last attempt to hold La Haie Sainte that rockets were used for the first and only time in the campaign. Earlier in the year there were several rocket batteries in the British contingent, but Wellington had ordered that those batteries were to hand in their rockets and draw guns instead. Wellington had seen rockets in the Peninsula and, although by no means a technophobe, he was not impressed: they were too inaccurate, had a nasty habit of circling round and coming whizzing back at their firers and, in the duke's opinion, did little but frighten the horses. Only Captain Edward Charles Whinyates, a 33-year-old commander of a horse artillery battery, managed to retain a rocket section, as well as five six-pounders. When Wellington heard that Whinyates had kept his rockets and that it would break his heart to abandon them, the commander of the forces is said to have replied, 'Damn his heart, tell him to draw guns.' It took a brave man to disobey a Wellingtonian order, but at the height of the struggle for La Haie Sainte Whinyates and his men came forward to the crossroads on foot, laid their rockets on and through the roadblock on the Brussels road, lit the blue touch-paper and retired. The rockets had no effect on the outcome, but their firing would have given great pleasure to Whinyates and his rocketeers. His disobedience was not held against him and he was later knighted and eventually became a full general.

With the constant attacks on La Haie Sainte and the increasing effectiveness of the French artillery as the ground dried out, Allied casualties were mounting. In the main field hospital, in the farm of Mont-Saint-Jean, the piles of amputated arms and legs were growing as the queues of wounded waited for attention. The standards of military medicine had improved hugely since 1793, when medical officers were required to purchase their commissions and pay for their own instruments. Then no formal qualifications were required and surgeons learned on the job, usually by killing most of their patients. Properly qualified medical men had no interest in joining the army when they could earn far more in civilian private practice. It was the Duke of York, as commander-in-chief, who insisted that matters must be improved. Henceforth, medical officers would be commissioned free of purchase, their equipment would be provided, and they would be required to have graduated from a recognized medical school (in the event, mostly from Edinburgh).

Most battle wounds were caused by bullets, blast or edged weapons. The ball from a smooth-bore musket, being of relatively low velocity, was unlikely to kill unless it hit a vital organ. Medical officers were skilled in probing for the ball and extracting it; the trick was to remove the detritus that the ball drove into the wound – bits of jacket and shirt and general muck. If this was not removed, then the wound would turn gangrenous, leading to amputation if in a limb, and death if in the trunk. It was for this reason that one sees so many letters home from officers asking that white linen shirts should be sent to them: a clean shirt put on before a battle reduced the risk of infection. The survival rate of officers wounded was better than that of Other Ranks, not because they received priority – casualties were treated in strict order of arrival at the hospital, regardless of rank – but simply because the private soldier was issued with two shirts: one he had sold for drink and the other had not been washed for a very long time, hence there was a far higher risk of infection.

Medical men of the time were largely ignorant about sepsis, but they did know about shock, where the blood pressure drops swiftly, leading to vital organs ceasing to function, so if amputation was required, it had to be done swiftly. Surgeons were supposed to be able to amputate a leg in under a minute – some claimed they could do it in twenty seconds. The wounded man would be held down by sturdy surgeon's assistants, given a slug of rum in lieu of anaesthetic and a stirrup leather to bite on. The flesh would be cut through by a tool shaped like a small sickle, the bone sawn through, the arteries sewn up, a flap of skin sewn over the stump and the whole cauterized by tar. The amazing thing is that in around 60 per cent of amputations of legs at the thigh patients survived, and for amputations below the thigh the survival rate was 75 per cent.[38]

Some medical procedures were primitive, though, and had no scientific basis whatsoever. During the advance by d'Erlon's corps, Lieutenant George Simmons of the 95th Rifles was in the skirmish line and turned to give an order to his men when he was hit in the back by a French musket ball. It broke two of his ribs, went through his liver and lodged in his lower breast. Unconscious, he lay there until the French infantry had retreated, when his sergeant found him, got him on a loose horse and took him to Mont-Saint-Jean hospital. There Assistant Surgeon James Robson cut under his right breast and removed the ball. He then took a quart of blood from his arm. The next day Simmons was bled again, and again daily, until by 3 July, long after the battle, he was vomiting and in great pain with a swelling where the surgeon's knife had cut. The swelling was lanced, more bleeding carried out and leeches (he says twenty-five) applied to his sides. Extraordinarily, after several weeks of this barbarous treatment, Simmons recovered and was able to return to duty, although ever afterwards he had to wear stays, and he died in 1858 aged seventy-two.[39]

Now, around 1830 hours, came the crisis of the battle. More and more of Wellington's reserves had been called forward to plug the gap in the centre, and Marshal Ney had ordered artillery forward to La Haie Sainte and sent an ADC back up the hill to Napoleon asking for the immediate despatch of infantry: here was the chance to burst through the Anglo-Dutch centre, roll up the line, and win the battle before the Prussians could interfere. But Napoleon had more pressing problems to attend to, for the Prussians were posing a far greater threat than anything Wellington might do. Bülow had been ordered to attack the village of Plancenoit, partly to draw Napoleon's troops away from Wellington and partly to procure a jumping-off area for an attack on the French right rear. He deployed Hiller's brigade of nine battalions to the left (south) of the road leading from the Bois de Paris to Plancenoit, and Losthin's brigade – now of seven battalions, two having been sent off to reinforce Saxe-Weimar at Papelotte – to the north, on the right of the road. Each brigade was preceded by its own integral cavalry squadron and had its divisional artillery battery of six six-pounders and two howitzers close up. The River Lasne, to the south of the village, ran through a deep ravine, so a head-on attack was the only option. At about 500 yards from Plancenoit, both divisional artillery batteries moved forward, unlimbered and began a bombardment of the village, which lasted around ten minutes. Then six of Hiller's battalions, in battalion columns, attacked the village, while Losthin watched his fellow general's right flank and engaged Lobau's second brigade, which was astride the road facing east.

Although the village of Plancenoit had not been prepared for defence, it was immensely strong, and the high walls of the cemetery around the church gave the French excellent cover and the Prussian infantry a severe obstacle to get over. French artillery was in the village and opened up with canister, and the fighting in the cellars and the rooms of the stone cottages was bloody and brutal, with bayonet and musket butt more effective than powder and shot at close quarters. Eventually, after thirty or forty minutes' fighting the Prussians of Hiller's brigade forced their way into Plancenoit and Lobau's surviving defenders withdrew, with his other brigade withdrawing to avoid exposing their right flank. Prussian round shot that had gone over Plancenoit bounced behind the French centre, on the Brussels road along which the Imperial Guard were waiting, as yet unblooded in this battle, and the realization that the next Prussian move would be to attack the French rear made it imperative to retake Plancenoit. Major General Philibert Duhesme was ordered to take his Young Guard Division, of eight battalions of elite light infantry, to restore the situation. Duhesme, despite his recall from Spain in disgrace, was remembered more for his capture of Barcelona by a ruse.* He fought in the 1814 battles in northern Europe and became inspector general of infantry during the brief Bourbon restoration, before joining Napoleon once again and being given command of the Young Guard.

The Guard, with the remnants of Lobau's division, attacked

---

* He had persuaded the Spanish governor to permit the entry of a column of French sick and wounded. Once within the fortifications the sick and wounded leapt from their stretchers, produced concealed muskets and overpowered the garrison.

Plancenoit from the west, and again fighting around the church was particularly severe, with Duhesme being wounded in the head (he died in Genappe a few days later). At last the Guard managed to push the Prussians out of the village, only for them to reorganize and come on again. Plancenoit could not be lost – it was critical to the French ability to remain on the Belle Alliance ridge – so the emperor sent another two battalions, from the Old Guard this time, to reinforce. The first battalion of the 1st Chasseurs à Pied and the first battalion of the Grenadiers à Pied swung off the Brussels road and along to Plancenoit. For the moment, the French could hold.

Meanwhile, Marshal Grouchy was fighting his battle at Wavre, eight miles away. There the French were still trying unsuccessfully to storm the bridge into the town. In the greater scheme of things, they were achieving absolutely nothing – Thielemann's Prussians had only to keep Grouchy occupied and prevent him moving off to join Napoleon, which most of his senior commanders wanted to do (or so they said, in the blaming and counter-blaming that followed the campaign). There was now not the slightest possibility that Grouchy could affect the outcome of the battle in any way.

But now, at La Belle Alliance, came Ney's urgent, hysterical demand for infantry to exploit the capture of La Haie Sainte. 'Infantry, where am I to get it? Does he expect me to make it?' was, supposedly, Napoleon's reply to the wretched ADC bringing the message. And in truth the emperor had very little infantry left. Reille's corps was still battering ineffectually at the walls of Hougoumont farm, d'Erlon's men had captured La Haie Sainte, while his right wing was engaging Saxe-Weimar and the increasing numbers of Ziethen's Prussians. Lobau's corps, the Young Guard and two battalions of the Old Guard were tied up in the struggle for Plancenoit, and all that was left were twelve battalions of the Old and 'Middle' Guard, between 5,000 and 6,000 men altogether. That, though, was what the Guard was for – to pluck victory from the jaws of defeat; and with them Napoleon might – just might – be able to finally turn the tide of battle, if he could only beat Wellington before the Prussians enveloped his rear. It was the last throw, a desperate gamble, but it was all that was left, the last chance for a Bonapartist Europe.

One of these battalions was still at Le Caillou, the overnight billet, and two were left at La Belle Alliance as a rearguard. The remaining nine battalions formed on the French ridge and began to move down the slope in two columns, led by Napoleon in person.* The firing from off to the right, from the direction of Papelotte and Plancenoit, was announced to the men as heralding the arrival of Grouchy, and there can be little doubt that the sight of the emperor in person, at the head of his Guard, lifted French spirits – just one more push, and victory would be theirs. The Guard reached the valley, and at a cottage, which is still there, argument broke out between the emperor and his staff. Napoleon, who had little regard for his own life (or for anyone else's), seems to have genuinely intended to lead this last attack in person, an attack that would save France, but he was persuaded that he *was* France and that, if he died, the imperial ideal would die with him. He handed over to Marshal Ney.

One of the great mysteries surrounding this final assault by

---

* There is considerable disagreement among historians (French, British and German) about exactly how many and which battalions of the Guard were involved in this final effort, and what formation they were in. What follows seems to this author to be most likely, but he would not regard it as a resigning issue if he was wrong.

the Guard is why they did not attack straight up at the crossroads, at the centre of the Allied line. That was Wellington's weakest point (although Ziethen's arrival on the left flank did allow some Allied troops to be moved across to fill in the gaps) and it was on the shortest route from La Haie Sainte, now in French hands. As it was, the Guard moved diagonally across the valley to their left and up the slope, emerging on the crest in front of the British Guards Division and Halkett's Hanoverian Brigade. It may be that the roadblock had not been demolished and the columns were attempting to bypass it and went too far off course; it may be that sniping from the 95th Rifles forced them to edge over to their left; or it may be that Ney thought the afternoon-long cavalry attacks and the fighting at Hougoumont had seriously weakened that part of the Anglo-Dutch front. But in any event it was the wrong decision – if decision it was.*

Despite the failure of the French army to make any great impression on the Anglo-Dutch so far, the guardsmen tramping up the slope would have been confident that once again they would triumph and secure victory for their emperor. They had waited

---

* Some years ago this author carried out an experiment on the field of Waterloo using a platoon of his own soldiers, there taking part in an exercise with the French army. The Gurkhas were formed into a column (albeit one much smaller than the French) and briefed to advance on the Allied centre keeping to the left (west) of the Brussels road. They were then told to tie their camouflage face veils over their eyes, thus restricting their vision and so replicating the clouds of black smoke hanging over the battlefield on 18 June 1815. The order to advance at a steady pace was given, and the men emerged very much as the real Guard had done, for if an aiming point to head for cannot be seen, the shape of the ground pushes walkers over to the west.

well behind the French front line until called for, and had thus been sheltered from the effects of the battle so far. Impressive in their greatcoats and bearskin caps (although without their full dress tunics and plumes, which were rolled up inside their packs to be worn for the victory parade in Brussels), muskets at the shoulder and with their band playing behind them, they would have seen little, for, although the rye grass and the maize had been trampled down by the mass cavalry attacks, only the muzzles of the Allied artillery were visible – and even those were masked by the gouts of yet more black smoke that belched forth as round shot and then canister tore great holes in the French columns, before the gunners abandoned their pieces and retired to the rear. But the Guard could withstand punishment and still they came on, until as the columns breasted the ridge, they were greeted by a scene of utter devastation: dead horses, dying horses, wounded cavalrymen, ploughed-up ground and all the detritus of the afternoon's fighting, and beyond that, the lines of red-coated British and Hanoverian infantrymen climbing to their feet.

Wellington, with that extraordinary knack of his of always (or nearly always) being present at the critical juncture, had been sitting on his charger behind the Guards Division, whose soldiers had been lying down. 'Now, Maitland, now's your chance,' said the duke, and Maitland's two battalions, followed by Byng's two, began to fire volleys at a range of no more than fifty yards and probably less. Although British military legend has it that the Imperial Guard were seen off by the British Guards alone (with a little help from the 52nd Light Infantry), there was much more to it than that. The right-hand French column at least managed to penetrate some way over the ridge, for von Kruse's three-battalion Nassau brigade, mainly of soldiers without experience but led by officers with plenty, also found themselves firing defensive volleys, while the 33rd Foot of Major General Sir Colin Halkett's brigade recovered whatever reputation they may have lost at Quatre Bras.

By now Adam's brigade, initially in reserve, had been moved forward to the right of the British Guards. Of three battalions and two companies of the 3rd Battalion 95th Rifles, it contained what was probably numerically the strongest battalion in Wellington's army, the 1st 52nd Light Infantry, commanded by Colonel Sir John Colborne.* While the purchase system generally worked well and, by 1815, British brigade and divisional commanders were competent and experienced men, it did not work well for Colborne, at least not initially. Colborne's father, a Hampshire landowner, had lost most of his money speculating on the stock exchange, and while there was enough left to get John, a younger son, through Winchester, there was none to purchase him a commission. Fortunately the Earl of Warwick was a friend of the family and secured the sixteen-year-old John a free commission as an ensign in 1794. Almost immediately on active service, he obtained promotion to lieutenant as a result of battle casualties and a captaincy in 1800 aged twenty-two, both without purchase. He had to wait eight years before promotion to major without purchase as military secretary to Sir John Moore. He accompanied Moore to Spain, served in the retreat to Corunna and was again promoted, to lieutenant colonel free of purchase, in accordance with Moore's deathbed recommendations. He served with considerable distinction in the Peninsula and, although only a lieutenant colonel, successfully commanded a

---

* It had not been involved at Quatre Bras and mustered around 1,000 all ranks.

brigade on several occasions. At the end of hostilities in 1814, he was promoted to colonel and knighted in January 1815. It was Colborne's misfortune that from lieutenant colonel upwards promotion was by seniority, and not enough generals were being killed (although not for want of their trying) for the available vacancies to reach as far down as Colborne. Had he been able to purchase, he could well have been a lieutenant colonel early enough to have been a general by 1810 or 1811, as some officers of his age were. Colborne would unquestionably have been an excellent general, in command of a brigade or a division, but as it was he did not become a major general until 1825, although he did become a field marshal and a peer eventually.

Colborne saw what was happening to his left front, and on his own initiative swung his battalion around ninety degrees, put them into line and ordered volley-fire into the flank of the left-hand Imperial Guard column. This was not without risk: the 52nd's right flank was exposed; there was French cavalry milling about Hougoumont that might charge it; and the French Guard did momentarily halt and reply with at least one volley, which killed Ensign Nettles, who was carrying the king's colour, thought lost until it was found under his body after the battle. In the regiment's account, published in 1860 and whose editor had interviewed the 85-year-old Colborne (then Lord Seaton), it is claimed that the 52nd drove the Imperial Guard back as far as the Brussels high road, where the French ran 'like a mob in Hyde Park', and then formed into column and advanced southwards along the road, passing the French Grand Battery and halting in face of the French rearguard drawn up at La Belle Alliance. It was some time later that other 'red regiments' came up to support the 52nd.[40]

There are, of course, lies, damned lies and regimental

histories. The accounts by those who were there (not only that of the commanding officer) are not deliberate untruths but what participants thought had happened, and in the gathering dusk and the clouds of smoke they no doubt did think that it was the 52nd that won the Battle of Waterloo. Any account of a battle can only be a balance of probabilities, but with the Imperial Guard under fire from artillery as it came up the slope, then finding itself under close-range fire from four battalions of British Guards, two battalions of Adam's brigade and three of Nassauers, and then coming under fire from the flank as well, it is hardly surprising that it broke. The watchers at La Belle Alliance, peering anxiously at their last possible chance of salvaging something as Plancenoit behind them once more fell to Bülow's Prussians, with those of Pirch pressing on in support, could see little. But then guardsmen began to emerge from the smoke stumbling back down the hill – individuals at first and then little groups, and then whole companies. '*La Garde recule!*' was the cry. The immortals, the elite of the elite, the crème de la crème of the French army, were beaten, something that no French soldier on that field had seen before. The French army was brittle and now it broke, amazingly quickly. The Guard was scattered, the units that they had been told were Grouchy's were firing on them: treason was the cry, followed by '*Sauve qui peut!*' At La Belle Alliance what was left of the Imperial Guard formed three squares, with two guns and a handful of cavalry in support, to allow the emperor to get away – back to Rosomme on his horse, and then transferring to a coach in which he hastened for Paris.

On the ridge of Mont-Saint-Jean the Duke of Wellington raised his hat and ordered a general advance. The great battle was over.

10

THE END

The Battle of Waterloo was over, but the war was not. The Anglo-Dutch battalions, severely depleted though they were, advanced down from their ridge and up towards La Belle Alliance, where the last squares of the Imperial Guard were retiring, pausing to fire the occasional volley before they too disappeared into the dusk. The very last square, that of the two-battalion 1st Regiment of Chasseurs à Pied, was commanded by Brigadier General Jacques Pierre Étienne Cambronne, a hard-drinking, hard-swearing ex-ranker, and the legend arose that, when called upon to surrender, the heroic Cambronne answered from the square: '*La Garde meurt, mais elle ne se rend pas*' ('The Guard dies but it does not surrender'). Other versions say that he replied '*Merde*' ('shit'), a much more likely tale. Alas, neither is true, for Cambronne, on foot, had by this time been captured by the mounted Colonel Hugh Halkett, commander of the 3rd Hanoverian Brigade, who had seized the unfortunate general by his aiguilettes.

It was now around nine thirty or ten o'clock, and as the Allied army breasted the rise, they came upon a scene of utter chaos: overturned ammunition wagons, loose horses, gunners trying to get their guns away, infantrymen running hither and thither desperate to escape, and the occasional foolish but brave French subaltern, sword drawn, defying the foe and swiftly bayoneted or shot. What was important now was to prevent the French from halting and reorganizing – they must be kept on the move and not allowed time to rest and recuperate. A fleeing mob could be dealt with; a reconstituted army might still pose a danger. Wellington's army was exhausted, short on ammunition, hungry and thirsty, in no condition to pursue, so that task was left to the Prussians, who came swinging up from Plancenoit, regimental bands playing, and marched off after the French, who were streaming down the road in front of them. Most of the French infantry could safely be ignored and bypassed or sent back as prisoners, but there was still enough horse-drawn artillery and cavalry to form the nucleus of a fighting force if they were given the opportunity, so the Prussian cavalry was sent after them with orders to keep harrying any French bodies of men and prevent them halting to sort themselves out. The leading Prussian cavalry squadrons borrowed infantry drummers, tied them on horses and took them along. At any sign of the French halting, the drummers would sound and the French, thinking that Prussian infantry was upon them, would move on. It was somewhere on the Brussels road, possibly near La Belle Alliance, that Wellington and Blücher met, where they no doubt congratulated each other and discussed what to do next. Both generals were on horseback, and Wellington later related how Blücher threw his arms about him, kissed him and exclaimed: '*Mein lieber Kamerad – quelle affaire!*'

On the erstwhile battlefield, the tasks of feeding the army, finding somewhere to sleep, and counting the butcher's bill could begin. Sentries were posted at intervals to keep away local civilians, who flocked to the field once the firing stopped, hoping to profit by plundering the dead and the wounded. Silver buttons from officers' uniforms could fetch a tidy sum, and as most soldiers carried with them everything they owned, money hidden inside shakos or sewn into the lining of tunics was there for the taking. There are accounts of wounded men who tried to resist the theft of their belongings having their throats slit.

It took three days to collect the dead and wounded; bodies on the battlefield were collected by fatigue parties, identified where possible, stripped and buried in mass graves. Altogether there were 1,419 British dead at Waterloo, perhaps not many in comparison to future wars, but considerable for the time and more than the largest death toll for a one-day battle in the whole of the Peninsula War – 917 at Albuhera on 16 May 1811. In total, 28 per cent of the British contingent became casualties and 6 per cent were killed. The figures for the KGL were similar (27 and 6 per cent), and these two had the highest percentage of dead and wounded of any of the Allies in the Anglo-Dutch army. Of the others, the Prussians at Waterloo suffered 13.5 per cent casualties with 2.5 per cent killed; the Hanoverians 18 and 3 per cent; the Brunswick contingent 11 and 3 per cent; the Nassau brigade 13.5 and 9 per cent; and the Dutch-Belgians 24 and 3 per cent. All these percentages are approximate: they include missing, many of whom would have turned up again days later, and the figures for deaths do not include those who died of wounds days or even weeks after the battle. Nevertheless, in round figures the Anglo-Dutch had 3,000 and the Prussians 1,200 killed at Waterloo.

The Prince of Orange was hit in the shoulder by a musket ball during the final attack by the Imperial Guard, and of the 840 British officers present, over half became casualties. In the 1st

British (Guards) Division, the divisional commander and two of four battalion commanders were wounded. In the 2nd Division, of the three brigade commanders one was killed and one wounded, and of the twelve battalion commanders two were killed and three wounded. In the 3rd Division, one of the three brigade commanders was killed and the other two wounded, and of the thirteen battalion commanders one was killed and six wounded. In the 5th, the divisional commander (Picton) was killed and two of the three brigade commanders were wounded, and of the twelve battalion commanders one was killed and seven wounded. In the British cavalry, the figures were similar: in the Household Brigade, two commanding officers of regiments were killed and the third wounded; and in the Union Brigade, the brigade commander was killed, and of the three commanding officers one was killed and one wounded. In both the 3rd and 4th Cavalry Brigades, two of three regimental commanders were wounded; and in the 5th, the brigade commander and two of the three regimental commanders were wounded; in the 6th, one out of three regimental commanders was wounded; and in the 7th, out of three one was killed and one wounded. The battalion hardest hit was the 27th (Inniskillings), part of Major General Lambert's brigade, which was stationed just to the east of the crossroads on the Anglo-Dutch centre. Although arriving on the field late in the morning, they were subject to constant harassing fire from French skirmishers and, without a reverse slope to which they could retire, spent much of the battle in square and suffered excessively from artillery fire. At the end of the day, out of 740 all ranks who had arrived on the field, 105 had been killed and 373 were wounded or missing.

Of the senior British staff officers, Lord Uxbridge had his leg taken off by a round shot; the Quartermaster General (chief of staff) DeLancey was hit, also probably by a round shot, from which he later died; the adjutant general, Major General Sir Edward Barnes, had been wounded at Quatre Bras; and the military secretary, Fitzroy Somerset (later Field Marshal Lord Raglan and commander-in-chief in the Crimea), lost an arm. As evidence that an ADC was not the cocktail party ornament that he is today, of Wellington's eight ADCs, two were killed: Captain and Lieutenant Colonel Sir Alexander Gordon, 3rd Foot Guards, of a failed leg amputation, and Captain and Lieutenant Colonel Charles Fox Canning, also 3rd Foot Guards, hit by a musket ball in the stomach. Of the other six, only one, Major the Hon Henry Percy, escaped unscathed. Once again, though, fortune smiled on Wellington, as the nearest he got to being wounded was when he got off his horse in the evening and slapped the animal affectionately on the quarters, to be answered by a double-barrelled kick that only just missed his head.

The French, having suffered a catastrophic defeat, had little time or inclination to record accurate casualty figures, but the best guess is that they had between 25,000 and 30,000 casualties, dead, wounded and taken prisoner, or around 30 per cent of their strength. Of the five infantry corps commanders, one, Lobau, was wounded; of the twelve divisional commanders, one was killed and seven wounded; and of the twenty-eight brigade and equivalent commanders, three were killed and eight wounded. In the French cavalry, six of the ten divisional commanders were wounded, and of the twenty cavalry brigade commanders, one was killed and ten were wounded.

Wellington rode back to his headquarters at Waterloo village and sat down to pen his despatch, reporting on the battle and its result. Addressed to Earl Bathurst, Secretary of State for War and the Colonies, but intended to be read by a wider audience including the prime minister and the Prince Regent, it is a straightforward, unemotional report devoid of hyperbole. It contains a number of errors of timing and location, but given that the writer had had little sleep for the past three days and had responsibilities that few British commanders have had before or since, it is hardly surprising that minor errors crept in as the duke tried to provide a coherent account of a three-day campaign, which had included two ferocious battles. As only one of Wellington's ADCs was alive and unwounded, it was to Major Percy that the despatch was entrusted. Percy left Brussels at midday on 19 June with the despatch and two captured eagles – that of the 45th Ligne, taken by the Scots Greys, and that of the 195th Ligne, taken by the 1st Royal Dragoons, both acquired in the charge of the Union Brigade against d'Erlon's infantry – and boarded a fast sloop of the Royal Navy at Ostend. Just off the Kent coast the wind dropped and Percy was put ashore in the ship's longboat at mid-afternoon on 21 June. From Broadstairs he found a fast coach and headed for London, getting there just after dark at about ten o'clock. He reported to the prime minister, Lord Liverpool, and the cabinet and to the Prince Regent, laying the eagles at the prince's feet, and found himself promoted instantly to lieutenant colonel.

It has long been rumoured that Nathan Rothschild, of the banking family, who had made loans totalling nearly £800,000 to the British government to fund the campaign,* had discovered the result of the battle on the 19th, two days before the government and the public knew of it, either by using a relay of men on fast

---

* Perhaps £12 million today – cheap at the price to avoid our having to speak French and eat snails.

horses to get to the Channel and a fast boat, or by carrier pigeon. He is then accused of selling heavily and ensuring that he was seen to be doing so. Thinking that the international banker knew something that they did not, other investors sold too, depressing the share price. Rothschild then turned buyer and scooped up a huge portfolio of depressed shares, which rose sharply when the news of the victory arrived, thereby netting a profit of a million pounds. The tale is denied in the most recent, authoritative history of the Rothschilds, and it may have been simply wishful thinking or an anti-Semitic slur.[41]

As it was, while the left wing of Napoleon's Army of the North had been scattered at Waterloo, Grouchy's right wing was still very much in being. Grouchy's approach to Wavre on 18 June had been cautious, and Thielemann at one stage considered leaving only four battalions to defend the river line and sending the rest to join Ziethen, who was arriving on the Anglo-Dutch left. Fortunately, the arrival of the French at around 1600 hours prevented this, and Vandamme, whose corps arrived at the Dyle line first, attacked towards the Wavre bridge, driving back those Prussian vedettes posted south of the river. The bridge, however, was barricaded and covered by Prussian artillery and by snipers lined along the north bank, and despite furious charges the French infantry could not cross. Engineers might have been able to blow the barricade, probably at the cost of their own lives, but sufficient powder to do so was not available. At around 1730 hours, a message from Napoleon, which had been written some four hours earlier, finally arrived. It told Grouchy that Prussians had been sighted at Chapelle Saint-Lambert and that he should move across to Waterloo and join the emperor's right flank, catching Bülow on the line of march on the way. Grouchy did consider sending Gérard's corps across, but it was too late, as that corps had now come up and was also engaged.

Unable to force the bridge at Wavre, Grouchy ordered Gérard to force a crossing at the mill at Bierges, a mile to the south-west, but there too the bridge was barricaded and stoutly defended, so Pajol's cavalry was sent further along the river to find a way across. Finally, at Limal, two-and-a-half miles from Wavre, Pajol found a bridge that was unbarricaded and defended by three battalions of infantry and a regiment of cavalry. A regiment of French hussars galloped across four abreast, scattering the nearest Prussian infantry, and Teste's division, the infantry attached to Pajol's cavalry corps, crossed and formed up on the north side. It was now dark but the French were across the Dyle, and Thielemann pulled his right flank back to cover Bierges. The battle descended into confused scrapping as darkness fell and finally petered out at around midnight.

As the noise of the firing at Waterloo had now stopped, Grouchy obviously knew that the battle there was over, but he made no attempt to send someone to find out what was happening. It seems that he assumed that Napoleon had won the battle and was on his way to Brussels, and during the night he issued orders for a renewal of the attack on Wavre the following morning, after which he would march on Brussels and join the emperor. Thielemann, who did know that Napoleon had been beaten, assumed that Grouchy would withdraw during the night and began to thin out. Somewhat to the Prussians' surprise, Grouchy was still there as dawn broke, and around eight o'clock on 19 June he began a furious attack on Bierges, with his right flank on the River Dyle. Thielemann withdrew steadily, and at around 1000 hours he very sensibly decided to evacuate Wavre altogether, pulling back to the north-east. Grouchy's men erupted into the town and, thinking they had secured a victory, pressed on after the retreating Prussians. Thielemann pulled his men back five miles north to Sint-Agatha-Rode, where he took up a defensive position, and Grouchy followed on and had reached Bawette, a mile and a half from Wavre, when at around 1030 hours a French staff officer from Waterloo finally caught up with him. The emperor had been beaten and the left wing of the army was in full retreat.

Grouchy was now in somewhat of a quandary. He could continue to attack Thielemann, who, he thought, was fleeing from him – but then what? Even if he defeated Thielemann's corps, there was still the rest of the Prussian army, to say nothing of the Anglo-Dutch somewhere in the vicinity. Vandamme, rough old soldier that he was, suggested vigorously that the army should march on Brussels, release the French prisoners there and then retire to Lille. This proposal was swiftly rejected and Grouchy briefly considered attacking Blücher's rear, but if he did that, then Thielemann would very likely attack *his* rear, so he decided to retreat in the direction of Namur. He had suffered around 2,000 casualties in the fight for Wavre, but he still had around 30,000 men left, and while he knew little of the overall situation, he might still be able to achieve something – although quite what he was unsure. Thielemann had done a superb job: he had held Grouchy off for a day and a half, had prevented him from blocking Bülow and Pirch's route to Waterloo and Ziethen's to Papelotte, and had ensured that Grouchy had contributed nothing to the fight at Waterloo. He had taken casualties – probably around the same number as Grouchy – but the Prussians could afford them, whereas the French could not.

Off to the south-west, the Prussians had followed the French on the evening of the battle as far as Genappe. There, they bivouacked for the night, before continuing the pursuit at first light the next morning, with the infantry moving as fast as they could after the cavalry. Once Blücher knew from Thielemann that Grouchy had started to move off along the Namur road, he pushed out three regiments of cavalry to watch the French marshal and to give warning should there be any attempt to take Blücher's pursuing forces in flank. There was not, and at around midnight on 19 June Exelmans' cavalry had reached Namur and secured the bridges over the Rivers Sambre and Meuse, just evading Pirch, whose corps had been sent off to block him. Grouchy's army bivouacked at Namur for the night, and on the morning of the 20th set off towards Paris.

It had been on 18 June, while the Waterloo battle was in full swing, that news of Ligny had arrived in Paris. The guns at Les Invalides had fired salutes in celebration and all who would listen had been assured that the war was now won. Then, on 21 June, Napoleon arrived at the Élysée Palace and so did the news of Waterloo. Napoleon set about trying to form a new army, for the military situation, although bad, was by no means hopeless. Grouchy still had 30,000 men; the Austrians and the Russians were moving more slowly than had been expected, so General Rapp and his army of 23,000 at Strasbourg could be recalled; the Spaniards were still in the process of trying to mobilize south of the Pyrenees, so Generals Clausel and Decaen with their 14,000 could move north to Paris; and Davout had 20,000 in the Paris garrison. If Napoleon gathered these together, cut short the training of the 100,000 conscripts recently enrolled, embodied the National Guard and included the remnants of the Armée du Nord, he could field an army that would at least equal the combined forces of Blücher and Wellington.

The Advance to Paris, 18 June – 3 July 1815

Further north, Blücher was heading for Paris via Charleroi, Avesnes, Guise and Saint-Quentin. Grouchy fought delaying actions at Compeigne, Senlis and Villers-Cotterêts, with Wellington moving further north through Nivelles and Maubeurge about two days' march behind. The garrisons of Cambrai and Péronne held out, and in each place Wellington was obliged to halt and prepare to besiege the citadels, although in both cases they surrendered before an assault on them became necessary. Wellington moved more slowly than Blücher, partly because he wanted to keep his army together and prevent them running amok, as was happening on the Prussian line of advance. There revenge was being exacted. Looting was widespread and those peasants who would not say where their valuables were hidden were likely to be shot out of hand. Blücher and his commanders turned a blind eye – the French had plundered their country, and now they would do it to them.

While speculation is pointless, it is nevertheless great fun, and the question continues to be asked: could Napoleon have won the Battle of Waterloo? Perhaps if he had hurled the Imperial Guard straight up the Brussels road first thing in the morning, might they not have broken Wellington's line and allowed the cavalry to get behind the Anglo-Dutch, dispersing the polyglot army long before the Prussians came anywhere near the field? But the Imperial Guard, along with much of the rest of the French army, were still struggling up the road from Quatre Bras first thing in the morning and were not available. Had Reille's corps not spent most of the day in a fruitless attempt to take Hougoumont farm and been available to attack from La Haie Sainte when Ney asked for more infantry… had field guns been dragged through the woods to blow in the south gate of Hougoumont and demolish the orchard wall… had infantry and artillery followed up the cavalry attack… had Grouchy got in between the Prussians and Waterloo instead of attacking Wavre… the possibilities are almost endless, but bad staff work and multiple failures in the chain of command ensured that none of those things happened.

As for whether Wellington could have won the Battle of Waterloo without the Prussians, it is the wrong question: he would never have fought the battle had he not known that the Prussians were moving across to join him, and their arrival at just the right place and just in time was critical. In many ways Wellington and Blücher did not win the Battle of Waterloo – Napoleon lost it. Indeed, one might argue that by issuing confusing and conflicting orders to d'Erlon on 16 June, when he did not come into action at either Quatre Bras or Ligny, where his presence behind the Prussians could have prevented their withdrawal to Wavre, and then by not being able to catch Wellington on the line of march on the 17th, Napoleon had already lost the campaign.

At no stage of the battle did Wellington have to direct manoeuvres of any sophistication, nor was his tactical acumen put to any great test: he simply had to stick on that ridge and hold the French off until the Prussians could arrive in their rear. There were many other British generals who could have done that just as competently as Wellington, but Wellington was known and trusted by all the Allied heads of state and commanders. There was a strong personal rapport between the duke and Blücher, and no other commander would have had the confidence of the king of the Netherlands or such faith invested in him by the minor German states. The Anglo-Dutch army might well have disintegrated at the first sign of trouble if commanded by someone other than Wellington, and it is doubtful whether the Prussians would have stayed in Flanders for anyone but him. His presence was crucial. Indeed, there is little to criticize in Wellington's conduct of the campaign: true, he was slow to realize that the main French thrust was indeed towards Brussels, and he perhaps overestimated the threat to his wide right flank, thus denying himself the services of the four reliable British battalions in Hill's corps in the Halle and Tubize area. Admittedly only one of those battalions, the 2nd 59th Foot, had been in the Peninsula, but the others would have stood their ground and would have been useful in the latter stages of the battle. Otherwise the duke did nothing to detract from his already high reputation in the Allied capitals.

But if Napoleon *had* won the battle, could he have won the war? He had always hoped that, if he could defeat the British, then the coalition would collapse and the war would be over, but this is surely false. The British, not for the first time nor the last, might well have evacuated their army from Europe, but they would have remained in the war, and British money would still have been forthcoming to subsidize the Russians, Prussians, Austrians, Dutch and others to continue the struggle. The massive Russian and Austrian armies would eventually have descended on Paris and ended the Bonaparte dream. The only significant difference would have been a much diminished British influence at the Congress of Vienna, for instead of being the victor, and the most consistent opponent of French ambitions, Britain would have been reduced to the role of a mere paymaster.

As the Allies got nearer to Paris, their lines of communication got longer and longer and had to be guarded from sneak attacks by bands of French soldiers and the depredations of peasants. Fortified towns reduced had to have garrisons placed in them to prevent their reoccupation and soon the whole of Pirch's corps was employed in guarding Prussian communications back to Belgium and manning captured citadels. The same dilution was taking place in Wellington's forces, and if the Allies were going to have to fight another major battle – to capture Paris this time – then Blücher was down to 66,000 men while Wellington had 50,000.

Whatever Napoleon's optimistic claims about raising a new army, the French bureaucracy and politicians – with whom perforce he had agreed to share power on his return from Elba – had different views. While the emperor was giving them victories, or looked as if he might, there was general support for him, but once the tide of war turned against him, that support began to evaporate very quickly. For over twenty years France had been at war; the most recent intakes to the army had known nothing else and many in the populace had had enough. The Senate and the Chamber of Deputies – the French parliament and until now firmly under the control of Bonapartists – were openly hostile; Marshal Davout advised Napoleon to dissolve the body, or at least prorogue it, but the emperor dithered, and when the parliament declared itself in permanent session, it was too late. There was now pressure on Napoleon to abdicate, and the message from the politicians was that, if he did not do so, then parliament would proclaim it. Napoleon briefly considered using force – the Paris mob was broadly in his favour, unlike the rest of the country – but then, on 23 June, he signed a document of abdication in favour of his four-year-old son and retired to Malmaison.*

A provisional French government was formed under the very dubious Joseph Fouché. Fouché, born in 1759, had been an

---

* The son, known to French historians as Napoleon II, was technically emperor for a week, before he too was declared to have abdicated.

ardent republican from his early days and voted for the execution of Louis XVI, but, always with an eye to his own advantage, he became an inveterate intriguer with the ability to trim his sails to the prevailing political wind, whatever direction that might blow. When the Terror was in the ascendancy in 1793 and 1794, he put down a royalist revolt in Lyon by means which even the Committee of Public Safety thought were extreme; he made sure he was on the right side when Robespierre and his satraps were overthrown; when the Directorate seemed shaky, he supported the coup that led to Napoleon becoming First Consul and then emperor; when Napoleon appeared to be losing, he opened negotiations with the Allies; when the Bourbons returned in 1814, he took service under them, but kept in contact with the exiled Napoleon and became minister of police (for the third time) on the emperor's return, while secretly negotiating with the Austrian chancellor Metternich. Now he saw that the empire could not survive and opened up channels of communication with the advancing Allies. On 26 June Wellington received from Blücher a letter coming from the 'French Commissioners' – Fouché's representatives – suggesting a suspension of hostilities. Wellington replied:

> Since the 15th instant… the field marshal [Wellington] has considered his sovereign and those parties whose armies he commands, in a state of war with the Government of France; and he does not consider the abdication of Napoleon Buonaparte [sic] of his usurped authority… as the attainment of the object held out in the declarations and treaties of the Allies…[42]

As far as Wellington and Blücher were concerned, the war was not over just because Napoleon had abdicated: there were still numerous French armed bodies about, fortresses and fortified towns were still manned, Louis XVIII was still in Holland and nothing had been said about his restoration, and it was becoming clear that what Fouché wanted to do was to establish a republic with himself at the head. Wellington went on to say that, while he regretted the necessity to spill yet more blood, the war would go on. While unconditional surrender was not mentioned, that is what he meant. So the Allied armies continued their advance, Wellington intending to re-establish 'legitimacy' – the return of the Bourbon monarch – and Blücher, with some justification, determined to sequester and send to Berlin everything valuable that his army could lay hands on. For his part, Wellington insisted that anything that his army took must be paid for and that civilian rights and property must be respected. He had seen the results of misbehaviour by an invading army in Spain and was determined not to provoke a guerrilla resistance movement in France.

Meanwhile, in Malmaison, the erstwhile emperor was still issuing orders to the marshals. He accepted that he was no longer emperor, but he was still a general: put him at the head of a reconstituted army and the war could still be won. But the provisional government would have none of it. They would continue to resist the Allied advance, to extract the greatest possible concessions at the inevitable peace negotiations, but they would not have Napoleon in command. Some of Napoleon's staff and supporters urged that he should put himself at the head of the army, declare martial law, arrest the provisional government and, with the troops already in Paris and its environs, go on the offensive. The erstwhile emperor vacillated, and by the time that he decided to resist the temptation on the grounds that he would not be the cause of civil war, it was too late anyway. On 28 June the Chamber of Deputies declared Paris to be in a state of siege.

They called up all retired old soldiers and summoned to Paris six battalions that had been keeping order in the pro-royalist Vendée. On 29 June Grouchy arrived in Paris with his own 30,000 men and another 20,000 that he had picked up along the way. Considering that he had now done all that he could, and no doubt with an eye on the inevitable reckoning that was to come, Grouchy resigned his command, which was taken over by Vandamme, who hastened to fortify the city and place garrisons on the bridges over the Seine.

On the same day, 29 June, Napoleon left Malmaison for the port of Rochefort on the coast of the Bay of Biscay. Fouché had said that, if he did not do so, then the government would arrest him, but he did agree to provide two frigates, and Napoleon's intention, at that stage, was to sail to America, where the United States would give him sanctuary. On 30 June, Prussian cavalry was in Versailles, Prussian infantry had seized the bridge over the Seine at Saint-Denis, and Wellington's leading units had moved up to join with Blücher. By 2 July both Allied armies were in position around the city. The French provisional government requested a ceasefire, which was refused, and realizing that not only could the combined armies of Blücher and Wellington assault Paris but also that, if they had to, they would, on 3 July, after a final sally by Vandamme, it agreed to surrender Paris and to evacuate all troops to south of the River Loire.

It took Napoleon, disguised as a secretary, and his entourage four days to reach Rochefort, and there they waited, hoping for a recall from Paris. On 8 July, with no summons likely and orders from the provisional government that he must leave French soil immediately, Napoleon boarded the frigate *Saale*, but only got as far as the Île-d'Aix, a small island two miles offshore, where he disembarked to await a favourable wind and consider his options

– options that were decreasing by the day. The Royal Navy was already blockading the estuary of the River Garonne, and once they knew that Napoleon was in the area – from information probably supplied by Fouché – the number of ships increased and the blockade tightened. Soon it was clear that sailing across the Atlantic would not be permitted. Although there were still some who advocated fighting on – and there was still support for Napoleon, particularly in the army but among some of the population too – it was becoming increasingly clear that giving himself up was the only option left.

On the day that Napoleon boarded the *Saale*, Louis XVIII entered Paris and was receiving the homage of the provisional government at Saint-Denis. The Bourbons were back, accepted by Fouché when it became clear that he himself could not be head of state, and their control was tightening. If the Bourbons had got their hands on Napoleon, they would have humiliated him, and possibly executed him, while the Prussians had said and were saying openly that they would hang him. The Russians would not exact the supreme penalty, but Napoleon could not surrender to them – he had talked down to the Tsar at Tilsit and then invaded Russia in 1812. And while the Austrians would not execute him either, he felt a strong personal animosity to the emperor Francis, who had prevented his wife, Marie-Louise, and his son from joining him on Elba and had intercepted letters to and from them while he was there.

That only left the British, and on 13 July Napoleon wrote to the Prince Regent, asking to be allowed to throw himself on the hospitality of the English people and describing the prince as 'the most powerful, the most constant and the most generous of my enemies'. The letter was never answered, but no doubt hoping it would be, at 0700 hours on the morning of 15 July Napoleon gave himself up to Captain Frederick Maitland RN, captain of HMS *Bellerophon*, a seventy-four-gun ship of the line laid down in 1786. Along with the ex-emperor were three generals, two counts with their countesses and four children, ten army officers of various ranks, a doctor, two cooks, twenty-six servants, the imperial dinner service and silver plate, and several boatloads of luggage.[43]

In France, although Paris had surrendered and the king had returned, the war still dragged on. The tiny Army of the Jura fought off the Austrians until 11 July; Suchet, based in Lyon, held them off until 12 July; and Marshal Brune held out in the great naval arsenal of Toulon until 31 July. Having surrendered the citadel, Brune was ordered to report to Paris and on the way halted in Avignon to change horses. Chased by the mob, who thought he was another revolutionary soldier who had been involved in a massacre in 1795, and cornered in the Royal Hotel, he was shot, stabbed and for good measure thrown into the River Rhône. The appearance of the Russians on the eastern border led to a brief upsurge of resistance – memories of the behaviour of the Cossacks in 1814 after Napoleon's first abdication and France's surrender were still fresh – but as news of the defeat at Waterloo and the departure of the emperor percolated through, the heart went out of the armies as desertions increased to unstoppable proportions and officers began to consider what the restored regime might mean for them. With the threat of severe retaliation for any disobedience of orders from the restored government, by August resistance had petered out and the decisions of the Congress of Vienna, which had remained in session during the 'Hundred Days', as the recent campaign became known, could be implemented.

After a smooth voyage, during which Napoleon was properly

treated by the ship's officers – although he irritated them by bolting his food and then leaving the table – the *Bellerophon* arrived at Torquay at 0800 hours on 24 July, and received orders that she was to anchor and remain where she was until further notice, with no one permitted to leave her or to board her except her own crew. The British government was now in somewhat of a quandary over what to do with their distinguished prisoner. Was he a prisoner? He had given himself up voluntarily to Captain Maitland, so was hardly a prisoner of war; he had not committed any crimes for which he could be tried under the laws of England; and while the restored regime in Paris would no doubt consider him a rebel, to hand him over to them could cause more problems than it would solve. In any case, the Treaty of Fontainebleau in 1814 had given Napoleon the sovereignty of Elba; he was therefore not a subject of Louis XVIII but an independent monarch in his own right.* Two days later, Captain Maitland was instructed to sail for Plymouth, a sheltered anchorage, which was a major naval base and the headquarters of the Channel Fleet and from where any attempted rescue or escape would be more difficult. In Torbay sightseers had crowded the docks and hired boats to try to spot the now caged ogre, and in Plymouth the crowds were even greater. Napoleon seemed to enjoy the attention and bowed and waved to his onlookers, although cutters crewed by sailors with cutlasses prevented any from getting too close.

In London the government was now becoming agitated by the attention that the ex-emperor was getting, and discussions about what to do with him were bedevilled by legal niceties: all were agreed that he could not again be allowed to 'disturb the peace of Europe' but were undecided about exactly what to do with him, and

---

* Britain had not signed the treaty, but Bourbon France had.

under what legal framework they could hold him. Already there were letters to the newspapers asking that very question, mainly orchestrated by one Capel Lofft. Lofft, who was sixty-four in 1815, had been educated at Eton and Peterhouse, and, although called to the bar at Lincoln's Inn, he had not actually practised as a barrister. A comfortably off Whig, he would have described himself as a radical: anti-slavery, in favour of parliamentary reform, against the death penalty, in favour of universal suffrage (but only for males), a religious dissenter, a vehement opponent of the younger Pitt's war and taxation policies, an admirer of Napoleon and an inveterate writer of letters to the papers. It was he who raised the threat of a writ of *habeas corpus*. Dating from 1305, *habeas corpus* – literally, 'May you have the body' – is a procedural device that requires a person under arrest to be brought before a court or a judge to determine whether the detention is legal. With the force of a writ, it was suspended during hostilities and had just been reinstated. Issued by a judge or a magistrate on request, it had to be served on the custodian of the prisoner – in this case Admiral Keith, commander-in-chief of the Channel Fleet – and could have led to considerable embarrassment for the government, which could find no sure legal grounds for detaining Napoleon. If a writ were served, the only alternatives would be a trial – and on what charges? – or release.

Eventually, after considering Scotland, the Tower of London, Malta and the Cape of Good Hope, it was decided to send Napoleon to St Helena, a rocky outcrop in the Atlantic and the British territory considered to be farthest away from civilization and prospects of rescue (or, indeed, assassination). To avoid any legal complexities consequent on the serving of a writ, it was necessary to get Napoleon and his entourage well out of coastal waters, and so Captain Maitland was ordered to weigh anchor and make his way out to sea. As his own ship was considered unfit to brave the Atlantic storms, he would then transfer his detainee to HMS *Northumberland*, another seventy-four-gun vessel but rather younger, having been launched in 1798. The newspapers had already speculated that St Helena might be the ultimate destination, and to compound fears that Lofft might succeed in obtaining a writ of *habeas corpus*, there now appeared in Plymouth one Anthony Mackenrot, who attempted to serve a subpoena on Napoleon requiring him to appear as a witness in a trial. There is some doubt whether Mackenrot was actually a lawyer, or a West Indies merchant, but he did have a writ and it was now imperative that he was not able to serve it. Admiral Keith spent most of 3 August being rowed from ship to ship, pursued by Mackenrot waving his writ, and when Mackenrot finally gave up and left a note in Keith's office requesting a meeting, Keith put to sea himself, rendezvousing with the *Bellerophon* and the *Northumberland* with their two guard frigates off Torbay.

On 6 August 1815 Napoleon was transferred from the *Bellerophon* to the *Northumberland* while the marine sentries presented arms and the drummers gave three riffs – the correct salute for a general. With him were two generals, one general's wife, a marquis and wife, a chamberlain and son, three valets, one assistant valet, three footmen, a Mameluke bodyguard, a cook, a pantryman, a lamplighter and an Irish doctor who had volunteered to go when Napoleon's French doctor decided that loyalty was all very well but exile to the middle of the Atlantic was quite another matter. Napoleon's protests that he had given himself up willingly, and that, if he was to be detained, he was entitled to due process of law, were ignored. After an incipient mutiny by her crew, most of whom had no wish to head off into the South Atlantic, had been quelled, the *Northumberland* set sail, and on 16 October she and her accompanying troopships, carrying a brigade of infantry and four batteries of artillery, hove to off the extinct volcano of black basalt that was St Helena. There Napoleon would spend the last years of his life dictating his memoirs, alternating between raging at fate and a resigned acceptance of his condition, while suffering the slights and unpleasantness of his chief jailer, Major General Sir Hudson Lowe, governor of St Helena and the man whom Wellington had sacked as chief of staff prior to the Waterloo campaign. In his account of Waterloo, Napoleon criticized Wellington for giving battle at Mont-Saint-Jean, which he says was not a suitable position, insisted that the battle was won by 1800 hours and that the Allies were only saved by the arrival of Bülow and his corps, and blamed his misfortune on Ney and Grouchy for being slow and hesitant.

At 1750 hours on 6 May 1821, Napoleon Bonaparte died, aged fifty-two. In his will he said that he 'died prematurely, assassinated by the English oligarchy and its tool', and in a codicil to the will, dated two weeks before his death, he left 10,000 francs (£400 at the time) to Second Lieutenant Marie André Nicolas Cantillon, who had attempted to assassinate the Duke of Wellington as he was returning by carriage to his residence in Paris on the night of 11/12 February 1819, by firing a pistol at him.* Much debate still surrounds the cause of Napoleon's death, ranging from murder by the English or a French royalist, to arsenic poisoning from the wallpaper and stomach cancer. The most likely cause seems, to this

---

* Cantillon missed and was charged with attempted murder in a French court, whose jury unsurprisingly found him not guilty.

author at least, to have been stomach cancer, to which there was a propensity in his family, possibly aggravated by tertiary syphilis. It has also been alleged that Napoleon suffered from haemorrhoids, but no mention of this is made in any of the autopsies performed on his body. Although attributed to his brother Jérôme, this claim may simply be propaganda intended to lessen the great man's reputation – piles are apparently very painful, but everyone without them thinks they are a suitable subject for humour.

Meanwhile, the Congress of Vienna had operated under a number of declared principles. They included a wish to grant no great rewards and exact no great punishments. France, represented by the ubiquitous Talleyrand – erstwhile servant of Bourbon, Bonaparte, Bourbon again, Bonaparte again and now once more Bourbon – was to be included in the discussions and care was to be taken not to foster revanchism. As far as possible, Europe would be returned to the status quo ante bellum, with a restoration of expelled monarchies and a return to the frontiers of 1793. While France would be kindly treated, she would nevertheless be required to return all looted artworks and pay an indemnity of 700 million francs (£28 million), and an Allied army of occupation, commanded by the Duke of Wellington and paid for by France, would stay for five years until the indemnity was paid. Inevitably, too, there were some exchanges of territory. Britain retained Malta, Heligoland, the Ionian Islands, Mauritius, Tobago and St Lucia from France, Ceylon and the Cape of Good Hope from Holland, and Trinidad from Spain, all of which she had captured or otherwise obtained during the war and was already occupying; at the same time she returned Martinique and the Isle de Bourbon (now Réunion) to France. Prussia got half of Saxony, the grand duchy of Berg, part of Westphalia, the left bank of the

Rhine from Elken to Coblenz and regained the parts of Poland lost during the war, along with Danzig, Posen and Thorn. The German Confederation, to replace the Holy Roman Empire, was established under the presidency of Austria, while Hanover, previously an electorate, became a kingdom with George III as its king. Austria made gains in Italy, retained Eastern Galicia in Poland, and got the Tyrol and Salzburg. To Russia went the rest of Poland, Finland and, from Turkey, Bessarabia. The neutrality of Switzerland was guaranteed and Sweden retained Norway, which she had obtained from Denmark in 1814. In addition to recovering Martinique and the Isle de Bourbon from Britain, France got Guadeloupe from Sweden and Portuguese Guiana.* Finally, the Congress condemned the slave trade, which the French interpreted as a manoeuvre by the British to destroy the economies of their colonies.

France now underwent a White Terror as royalists exacted revenge on revolutionaries and Bonapartists, many of whom were lynched or shot out of hand. A royal ordinance was promulgated, listing over fifty names of wanted persons who were to be tried and if found guilty – a foregone conclusion – executed. The most exalted scalp was that of Marshal Ney, who, instead of fleeing to his birthplace in Germany, stayed in Paris hoping for the best. On 3 August, he was arrested and put on trial by court martial accused of treason. The prosecutor was Major General Bourmont, the same man who had deserted to the Prussians at the start of the Hundred Days campaign; the president of the court was Marshal Jourdan (the first choice had been Marshal Moncey, who refused); and the members were Marshals Augereau, Masséna and Mortier and

---

* Which seems rather unfair, given that Portugal, with Britain, was the only consistent enemy of France during the war.

three major generals. The members of the court were, of course, in an almost impossible position: apart from Augereau, who had been struck off the list of marshals by Napoleon on his return from Elba, the marshals were all as guilty as Ney, in that they too had returned to their old Napoleonic allegiance in 1815. Eventually the court adopted what its members presumably thought would give them an escape from having to find a fellow marshal guilty and declared itself, by five votes to two, unable to try the case. This was a mistake – if the members were afraid to find Ney not guilty, they could have found him guilty with extenuating circumstances, which would have attracted a penalty of exile or imprisonment, probably followed in a short time by an amnesty. The trial was now shifted to the Chamber of Peers, recently packed with royalists and returning émigrés, many of whose relatives had been guillotined in the Revolution. With only one dissenting vote, Ney was found guilty and sentenced to death. On 7 December, in the Gardens of Luxembourg in Paris, Marshal Michel Ney was shot by firing squad. He refused to wear a blindfold and gave the orders to the firing squad himself.

A slightly lesser trophy was the life of Brigadier General Labédoyère, Napoleon's ADC at Waterloo, who was also tried for treason and shot. Others on the proscribed list were more fortunate. Marshal Grouchy and Major General Vandamme got away to America; Major General Lobau had been captured at Waterloo and was safely in England as a prisoner of war; Marshal Soult was exiled; Major General Bachelu was imprisoned for a time and then reprieved; Major General Reille evaded capture until amnestied in 1818; Major General Drouot, commander of the Imperial Guard at Waterloo, was put on trial, defended himself and got off; Brigadier General Cambronne also got off, thanks to an excellent defence counsel; and d'Erlon and others managed to get away to Germany, Switzerland or Sweden. Of Napoleon's other senior officers, many turned their coats yet again and carried on serving the Bourbons.

The White Terror lasted about a year. Allied disapproval was a factor in its ending, as was the belated realization that persecuting so many army officers and ex-imperial officials could well precipitate another revolution – and in any case, whatever their sympathies in the past, the regime needed men of ability, and most men of ability had been Bonapartists. Even those on the proscribed list were eventually pardoned and most were restored to their old ranks. Soult, pardoned in 1819, became at various times minister for war, foreign minister and ambassador to London, and in the last of these posts he even attended Wellington's annual Waterloo dinner. Even Prince Jérôme, Napoleon's youngest brother, got away almost scot-free and was appointed governor of Les Invalides, a sort of combined retirement home for old soldiers and arsenal established in Paris by Louis XIV in 1670.

Of the Allies, Field Marshal Blücher visited London, where he was greeted with acclaim and remarked that it would be a wonderful city to loot. He retired to Krieblowitz in Silesia (now Poland) and died there in 1819 aged seventy-six. In 1945, when the Red Army overran the area, Russian soldiers broke open his tomb and scattered his remains, which were later rescued by a priest and reburied. Gneisenau initially retired and wrote a biography of his erstwhile chief, but soon returned to service as governor of Berlin. A field marshal in 1825, he died in 1831 in command of an army on the Russian frontier. The Prince of Orange briefly became engaged to Princess Charlotte of Wales, daughter of the Prince Regent and his estranged queen, Caroline of Brunswick, but the engagement was broken off when his sexual proclivities came to light (homosexuality was then a serious crime).* He then married, in 1816, the sister of the Tsar, survived attempts to blackmail him and became King William II on the abdication of his father in 1840. He managed to sire five children and proved a surprisingly enlightened and indeed popular monarch, who avoided the consequences of the revolutions of 1848 by introducing a liberal constitution before dying in 1849.

Although the Allied army of occupation was intended to stay in France for five years, in fact it left after only three, by which time France had already paid off the indemnity. This was very largely due to the Duke of Wellington, who persuaded the money markets to lend to the French government at a reasonable rate of interest. He was concerned that the longer the army stayed in France, the more likely it would be that French public opinion would turn against it. He had to exercise considerable tact to curb the Prussian army's propensities for looting – he had only with great difficulty dissuaded Blücher, who still wanted to blow up the Pont de Jena across the Seine in Paris, and had to put a complete company of British soldiers there to guard it.

Wellington was, of course, feted throughout Britain and the continent. He was voted yet another monetary grant by the House of Commons to enable him to buy a London residence†

---

* Caroline then married Leopold of Saxe-Coburg, later king of the Belgians, and died in childbirth in 1817 (her child, a son, was still-born). Had she survived, she would have become queen regnant instead of William IV, and Queen Victoria would not have come to the throne.
† Apsley House, which he bought from his brother Richard (by anonymous bid) for £40,000 in 1817. It was gifted to the nation in 1947, and the family retain living accommodation there.

and a country estate commensurate with his status.* His sincerely expressed hope that he would never have to fight another battle was fulfilled – not least because, thanks largely to him, there was now peace in Europe and never any requirement to fight that battle. He insisted that a medal for Waterloo should be issued to all and not, as had been the custom in the past, only to officers. It was duly issued in 1816 and 1817 to all who had been present at any of the battles of the campaign and to the next of kin of those who had been killed or died. Altogether, about 39,000 were issued with the recipient's name engraved around the edge. The next medal to be awarded to all ranks was the General Service Medal with a bar for each battle of the Peninsular War, but as it was not issued until 1848, many of those entitled to it were dead.

There were also cash awards to the families of those killed in action in the Hundred Days, and survivors were granted an extra two years' seniority to count for pay and pension. Bounties ranging from £61,000 for the commander-in-chief (of which he returned £40,000 to the Treasury), £90.06 for a captain and £2.55 for a private were disbursed. Within two weeks of the battle, all generals not already knights were made so, most lieutenant colonels and many majors were awarded the CB (Companion of the Order of the Bath), and there was a flurry of promotions without purchase.

For the soldiers of the losers, there were no bounties, no bonuses and no thanks. The Imperial Guard was disbanded and most of the army discharged and scattered all over France. Many of the senior officers retained their pensions or had them restored, but for the rank and file, many of whom knew no other trade, there was nothing but memories of the glory days, when

---

* Stratfield Saye in Hampshire, still lived in by the family.

the seemingly unstoppable little man in his grey overcoat had led them all over Europe. For Napoleon, as we have seen, the Hundred Days campaign was always a gamble – and it was a gamble that he lost. Withal, he remains a hero in France to this day, his victories and achievements celebrated and his defeats forgotten or explained away. In truth he was a very great man, both as a soldier and as a head of state, possessing abilities and a vision that were greater by far than those of the Bourbons whom foreign arms put in his place. France would see no more of those great victories, for there was little glory in her colonial campaigns and little pride in victory in the Crimea. She was humiliated by Prussia in 1870, found herself on the winning side in 1918 only at great and irrecoverable cost, and suffered abject defeat in 1940. It is hardly surprising, then, that French men and women look back to an age when the eagles were carried to the very boundaries of the earth and glory seemed to be unending.

EPILOGUE

On the face of it, despite over twenty years of fighting, the expenditure of perhaps £600 million and the loss of around 70,000 lives, the British gained little from the French Revolutionary and Napoleonic Wars that culminated in the campaign of Waterloo. They could have stripped France of her empire and added it to their own, and they could have demanded the lion's share of the indemnity. They did neither of these things, although few would have blamed them if they had. Instead, wise heads in cabinet, particularly those of Castlereagh and Liverpool, realized that, if France was to be restored to the family of nations, then she must not be totally humiliated, otherwise the age-old enmity between the two nations would only break out yet again. What the British did get was a balance of power in Europe as a result of the Congress of Vienna, and a system that, although paying little heed to ideas of liberalism and democracy that had been encouraged by the French Revolution, did keep the peace in Europe for a century, or at least ensured that those European wars that did break out – in the Crimea and the wars of German unification – did not spread.

While it is this author's opinion that, even if Napoleon had won the Battle of Waterloo, he would have still lost the war, it might be argued that a Napoleonic victory would not, on the face of it, have necessarily been a bad thing. There would have been a European Union 150 years earlier, a common language (French), a common currency (the franc) and a system of government that would, probably, have developed into one that was reasonably liberal, for Napoleon, though he could be ruthless at times, was not an absolute autocrat. In such a framework, Germany would not have become one nation and we would have been spared two world wars. The first Russian Revolution might well have occurred but not the second, the so-called 'October Revolution' (actually November, as the Russians were still on the old calendar) that swept away the potentially liberal government of Kerensky and replaced it with Bolshevism. Such a united European bloc would have developed into the largest and richest economy in the world and would have had enough muscle, industrial, financial and military, to impose its will upon the rest of the world. But 'on the face of it' is all that such a scenario can be, for Napoleon would almost certainly still have died in 1821 when his son was far too young to replace him (and in any case that son died of tuberculosis aged twenty-one and left no heirs), none of his brothers had anything like his abilities or his powers of leadership, and it is far more likely that infighting among the marshals as they struggled for power would have caused the whole edifice to collapse.

For all that he went down in defeat and exile and suffered a lonely death, Napoleon was the greatest Frenchman of his age and perhaps of any age. Initially buried on St Helena, with a bare stone slab over his grave,* in 1840 the British acceded to a French request that his remains be returned to France. On 15 December, in the presence

---

* Napoleon's staff insisted that he was the Emperor Napoleon, Hudson Lowe that he was General Bonaparte. As they could not agree, no wording was placed on the stone.

of King Louis Philippe (the last king, although not the last monarch, of France), the remains of Napoleon Bonaparte were taken to Les Invalides in solemn procession on a bier drawn by sixteen black horses, followed by those ageing members of his Imperial Guard who had dragged out their now threadbare uniforms and their medals for one last parade for their emperor. Exactly one hundred years later, on 15 December 1940, in a Paris occupied by the descendants of Blücher's Prussians, the coffin of Napoleon's son, the king of Rome and briefly Napoleon II, was also interred at Les Invalides. It had been brought from Vienna, where the boy had lived and died, as a gift from the German chancellor to the people of France – from Hitler to Pétain. Meanwhile, in 1860 Napoleon I's body, originally interred in the chapel, had been translated in the presence of his nephew, Emperor Napoleon III, into a magnificent tomb of red quartzite placed on a green granite base, beneath a great dome and surrounded by bas reliefs of his battles and his civil and legal achievements. Also under the dome are the graves of Napoleon's brothers Joseph and Jérôme, and those of distinguished French soldiers before him (Turenne and Vauban), with him (Jourdan and Lobau), and after him (Foch, Le Clerc and de Lattre de Tassigny). It is a place of pilgrimage for French soldiers to this day.

Waterloo made Britain a world power – indeed, the only world power for nearly a hundred years. Many French historians consider that it was not Napoleon who lost France's last chance to be that power; rather, they aver that he was let down and betrayed by treasonous officials and incompetent generals. But it was Napoleon who had selected those men, Napoleon who had promoted them, and Napoleon who had appointed them, and it is Napoleon who must accept responsibility for their actions, or inactions, when the moment of crisis came.

Wellington became the most famous general in Europe. Created a field marshal in seven armies, showered with honours and gifts by grateful sovereigns, he continued to devote himself to public service until the end of his days. Commander-in-chief of the British army, Master General of the Ordnance, Constable of the Tower of London, a Knight of the Garter, a privy councillor, prime minister, foreign secretary, chancellor of Oxford, lord lieutenant of Hampshire, warden of the Cinque Ports, fellow of the Royal Society, confidant of politicians and monarchs and godfather to Queen Victoria's third son (named Arthur after the duke*) – Wellington was an indefatigable worker, although he occasionally complained that, while a costermonger's donkey was entitled to an occasional rest, he was not. Although a reluctant prime minister from 1828 to 1830, and the architect of Catholic emancipation, he was neither comfortable nor successful as a politician. Soldiers are, by and large, honest and operate by briefings and orders. They have no constituencies to satisfy and no interests to placate. Politicians do not regard integrity as paramount and operate by compromise. Wellington once said with some asperity about his cabinet: 'I told them what to do and they wanted to stay and discuss it!' Although in his long absence from England he had perhaps failed to appreciate that the old balance between landed and commercial interests had shifted, and that there was now a rising middle class and an industrial working class with an appetite for parliamentary reform, he was astute enough to give way when, as he put it, it became obvious that it would be better to give what would otherwise be taken in blood. And he did propose a settlement for Ireland that

---

* Later the Duke of Connaught, a competent soldier and governor general of Canada, and the last of Victoria's sons to die, in 1942.

might well have prevented a great deal of anguish and bloodshed over the next century and a half.* When out of office as leader of the opposition in the House of Lords, he insisted that the good of country must always take precedence over party advantage, and he always tried to remain apolitical.

It is a great pity that Wellington did not become commander-in-chief of the British army on his return with the army of occupation in 1818, when he had the vigour and the influence to force through the reforms that he knew were needed, but that post was still held by the Duke of York, who could not be peremptorily swept aside. He did briefly become commander-in-chief on two occasions in 1827 and 1828, but by the time he assumed that appointment permanently in 1842, taking over from Rowland Hill, he was seventy-six years of age, becoming increasingly conservative in his views and up against a Treasury determined to spend as little as possible on defence.†

Arthur Wellesley, first duke of Wellington, died peacefully at 1525 hours on 15 September 1852 at Walmer Castle, near Deal in Kent, the official residence of the warden of the Cinque Ports, aged eighty-two and four months. His body lay in state in Walmer, then in London and was finally laid to rest at a state funeral in St Paul's Cathedral – England's greatest general beside Nelson, its greatest sailor.

The legacy of Waterloo and Wellington lived, and lives, on. The First Foot Guards, having supposedly beaten the grenadiers of

---

* He wanted, first, to disestablish the church of Ireland, to whom all had to pay tithes despite the vast majority not belonging to it, and then to license all priests with their salaries paid by government. It was far too radical to be accepted.
† Some things don't change.

the Imperial Guard,* became the Grenadier Guards and all guards regiments adopted a British version of the French imperial bearskin cap. Most infantry regiments bear the battle honour Waterloo on their colours, and schools, railway stations, streets, parks, memorials and statues throughout Britain and the countries of empire abound with the name Waterloo or Wellington – although French tourists visiting England are slightly less grumpy now that Eurostar no longer has its terminal at Waterloo Station.

Militarily, many of the qualities of that 'perfect instrument' commanded by Wellington in the Peninsula and at Waterloo were to evaporate as the victorious army saw no need to change what had been a winning formula. All over the empire officers asked themselves 'What would the great duke do?' when faced with some tactical problem. This was all to the good, for Wellington was a master of the battlefield, but he did not delegate, he rarely consulted and he had no time for discussion, so a whole generation of senior commanders grew up who were not trained to use their initiative and were discouraged from thinking for themselves. Only two years after Wellington's death the British army went to war in the Crimea dressed in very much the same uniforms as they had worn at Waterloo, with a rifle that was still a muzzle-loader, with a commissariat that was corrupt and incompetent, and medical services that hardly existed. That the army won its battles despite Horse Guards, the Treasury and its senior commanders was due to the pluck and resilience of the professional soldiers and the leadership of the regimental

---

* Which they did, but the title may have been bestowed to mark them as elite even among the Guards, as provisional battalions of grenadier companies taken from other battalions had been formed for special operations in the past.

officers. That, at least, was part of the legacy of Waterloo that had not been squandered and which infuses and motivates the British army still.

NOTES

Chapter 1: How It All Began

1　For the full details of the coronation, see Frédéric Masson (tr. Frederic Cobb), *Napoleon and his Coronation*, T. Fisher Unwin, London, 1907.

2　Figures from Lawrence H. Officer and Samuel H. Williamson, *What Was the U.K. GDP Then? Measuring Worth*, 2011, available at www.measuringworth.com/ukgdp; and Phyllis Deane and B. R. Mitchell, *British Historical Statistics*, Cambridge University Press, Cambridge, 1962.

Chapter 2: The Sheep Worrier of Europe is on the Loose

3　Colonel G. Hanger, *To all Sportsmen, Farmers and Gamekeepers*, Richmond Press, Richmond, 1971 (facsimile edition of original 1814 publication). A delightful book full of advice in the care of horses and dogs, with veterinary hints for the cure of all manner of beasts and hints on rat-catching, there is also much good sense about shooting.

4　For full details of musket and rifle, see H. L. Blackmore, *British Military Firearms 1650–1850*, Greenhill Books, London, 1994.

5 For an excellent and detailed examination of the French army of Napoleon, see Philip J. Haythornthwaite, *Napoleon's Military Machine*, Spellmount, Staplehurst, 1988.

6 For a detailed account of the reforms in the Prussian army between 1807 and 1815, and the organization of the Prussian army at Waterloo, see Digby Smith, *The Prussian Army to 1815*, Schiffer Military Books, Atglen PA, USA, 2004.

Chapter 3: The Commanders

7 Quoted by Peter Burroughs, *Oxford Dictionary of National Biography*, Oxford University Press, Oxford, 2004.

8 Jean-Roch Coignet, *Vingt ans de grogne et de gloire avec l'empereur*, Saint-Clair, Paris, 1965 (reprint). His memoirs, written in 1831, long after the event, nevertheless give a fascinating, if somewhat gilded, insight into life as a soldier of the Grande Armée.

9 Figures for purchase and pay rates from Charles James, *The Regimental Companion*, 3 vols, printed for T. Egerton at the Military Library Whitehall, London 1800–15 (annual publication).

10 B. R. Mitchell, *Abstract of British Historical Statistics*, Cambridge University Press, Cambridge, 1962.

11 Alison McBrayne (ed.), *The Letters of Captain John Orrok*, privately published, 2008.

12 *The Gentleman's Magazine*, 1810, quoted in Anthony Bruce, *The Purchase System in the British Army, 1660–1871*, Royal Historical Society, London, 1980.

13 Deputy Adjutant General J. McLeod, *Regulations for the Admission of Gentleman Cadets into the Royal Military Academy Woolwich*, undated but thought to be 1793.

Chapter 5: The Soldiers

14 Michael Crumplin, *Men of Steel: Surgery in the Napoleonic Wars*, Quiller Press, Shrewsbury, 2007.

15 Rifleman Benjamin Harris in his memoirs as told to Henry Curling, first published in 1848 and reprinted many times since, most recently as edited by Christopher Hibbert (Windrush Press, 2000); he tells how one of his first tasks as a trained soldier in 1802 was as a member of a firing squad to shoot a bounty jumper.

16 G. C. Moore-Smith, *The Life of John Colborne, Field Marshal Lord Seaton GCB etc*, John Murray, London, 1903.

17 Ian F. W. Becket, *Britain's Part-Time Soldiers: The Amateur Military Tradition 1558–1945*, Manchester University Press, Manchester, 1991.

18 Alexander Martin, *Records of the 90th Regiment of Perthshire Light Infantry 1795–1880*, originally published 1880, reprinted by Pravana Books, 2008.

19 Sir Charles Oman, *Wellington's Army 1809–1814*, Edward Arnold, London, 1913.

20 All figures from Sir Arthur Lyon Bowley, *Wages in the United Kingdom in the Nineteenth Century*, Cambridge University Press, Cambridge, 1900.

21 All figures from Charles James, *The Regimental Companion*, 3 vols, printed for T. Egerton at the Military Library Whitehall, London 1800–15 (annual publication).

22 The procedure is described in Henry Marshall, *Military Miscellany, Comprehending a History of the Recruiting of the Army, Military Punishments etc. etc.*, John Murray, London, 1846.

23 Roger Parkinson, *The Life of Blücher, Man of Waterloo*, Purnell, London, 1975.

Chapter 6: Battle Joined

24 Lt. Col. John Gurwood, *The Dispatches of Field Marshal the Duke of Wellington*, 12 vols, John Murray, London, 1837.

25 Ibid.

26 Ibid.

Chapter 7: The Crisis Approaches

27 Lt. Col. Willoughby Verner (ed.), *British Rifle Man: The Journals and Correspondence of Major George Simmons, Rifle Brigade, during the Peninsular War and the Campaign of Waterloo*, A. & C. Black, London, 1899.

28 Quoted in David Chandler, *The Campaigns of Napoleon*, Weidenfeld & Nicolson, London, 1966.

29 Captain Sir John Kincaid, *Adventures in the Rifle Brigade* and *Random Shots from a Rifleman*, facsimile edition of 1909 reprint of 1830 and 1835 publications, Richard Drew Publishing, Glasgow, 1991.

30 Captain Charles François (tr. Robert B. Douglas), *From Valmy to Waterloo: The Diary of a Soldier of Napoleon*, Everett & Co., London, 1906.

31 Accurate British strengths at Waterloo can be obtained from Gurwood (op. cit.); Prussian ones from Peter Hofschröer, *The Waterloo Campaign: The German Victory*, Greenhill Books, London, 1999. Exact figures for the French, Dutch and minor allies are more difficult. I have relied mainly on Mark Adkin, *The Waterloo Companion*, Aurum Press, 2001, and Captain W. Siborne, *History of the War in France and Belgium in 1815*, T. & W. Boone, London, 1848.

Chapter 8: The Battle for Europe

32 Howell, John, *Journal of a soldier of the 71st or Glasgow Regiment: Highland Light Infantry from 1806–1815*, William & Charles Tait, Edinburgh, 1819.

33 Kincaid, op. cit.

34 Charles de Gaulle (tr. F. L. Dash), *France and her Army*, Hutchinson & Co., London, 1940.

35 François, op. cit.

Chapter 9: The Decision

36 Captain Gronow, *The Reminiscences and Recollections of Captain Gronow*, 2 vols, John C. Nimmo, London, 1892.

37 Major General Baron von Baring, *Hanoverian Military Journal*, part II, 1831.

38 For the best modern account of medical and surgical procedures during the period, see Michael Crumplin, *Men of Steel: Surgery in the Napoleonic Wars*, Quiller Press, Shrewsbury, 2007.

39 Lt. Col. Willoughby Verner (ed.), *British Rifle Man: The Journals and Correspondence of Major George Simmons, Rifle Brigade, during the Peninsular War and the Campaign of Waterloo*, A. & C. Black, London, 1899.

40 W. S. Moorsom (ed.), *Historical Record of the 52nd Regiment*, Richard Bentley, London, 1860.

Chapter 10: The End

41 Niall Ferguson, *The World's Banker: A History of the House of Rothschild*, Weidenfeld & Nicolson, London, 2000.

42 Lt. Col. John Gurwood, *The Dispatches of Field Marshal the Duke of Wellington*, 12 vols, John Murray, London, 1837.

43 David Cordingly, *The Billy Ruffian: The Biography of a Ship of the Line*, Bloomsbury, London, 2003.

SELECT BIBLIOGRAPHY

While this author has not counted them all, it is a fair estimate to say that to date several thousand books have been published in English alone dealing with the French Revolutionary and Napoleonic Wars and the campaign of Waterloo. Some appeared shortly after the end of the war, written by those who were there, others decades later when participants had had time to recollect what happened, or what they thought had happened, and up to the present day new accounts, revisions, perspectives and occasionally original material lately brought to light continue to appear. To list in this bibliography every book that has contributed to this work would be unhelpful: many are out of print, difficult to obtain or, if they can be traced, very expensive. The more arcane sources, should the reader wish to explore them, are listed as source notes. This bibliography should, therefore, be regarded more as a reading list, of books that are still in print, or have been reprinted from the original, or should be easily obtainable in a good library. I have not, for example, listed Gurwood's *Despatches* (except in the source notes), of which I have a set of the first edition, all twelve volumes and the index, in pristine condition and found by my mother-in-law in a small second-hand bookshop in Suffolk. Very few libraries have a set and there are even fewer in private hands. Similarly there are many excellent books that I have not listed, simply because I aim to give the general reader a broad selection of the available literature, rather than a literary cornucopia that no reader would find the time to empty.

Adkin, Mark, *The Waterloo Companion*, Aurum Press, London, 2001

Barnett, Correlli, *Bonaparte*, George Allen & Unwin, London, 1978

Black, Jeremy, *The Battle of Waterloo*, Icon Books, London, 2010

Blond, Georges, *La Grande Armée*, Robert Laffont, Paris, 1979

Burnham, Robert and McGuigan, Ron, *The British Army against Napoleon*, Frontline Books, London, 2010

Chalfont, Lord (ed.), *Waterloo: Battle of Three Armies*, Sidgwick & Jackson, London, 1979

Chandler, David, *The Campaigns of Napoleon*, Weidenfeld & Nicolson, London, 1966

Chandler, David, *Napoleon's Marshals*, Weidenfeld & Nicolson, London, 1987

Chesney, Colonel Charles, *Waterloo Lectures* (4th edition), Greenhill Books, London, 1997

Corrigan, Gordon, *Wellington: A Military Life*, Hambledon & London, London, 2001

Crumplin, Michael, *Men of Steel: Surgery in the Napoleonic Wars*, Quiller Press, Shrewsbury, 2007

De Chair, Somerset (ed.), *Napoleon on Napoleon*, Cassell, London, 1992

Fletcher, Ian, *Galloping at Everything*, Spellmount, Staplehurst, 1999

Glover, Gareth, *From Corunna to Waterloo*, Greenhill Books, London, 2007

Glover, Gareth (ed.), *The Waterloo Archive*, Frontline Books, Barnsley, 2010

Glover, Richard, *Peninsular Preparation*, Cambridge University Press, Cambridge, 1970

Griffith, Paddy et al, *Wellington Commander*, Anthony Bird, Chichester, 1986

Hibbert, Christopher (ed.), *The Recollections of Rifleman Harris*, Leo Cooper, London, 1970

Hibbert, Christopher (ed.), *A Soldier of the Seventy-First*, The Windrush Press, Moreton-in-Marsh, 1997

Hibbert, Christopher, *Wellington: A Personal History*, Harper Collins, London, 1997

Hofschröer, Peter, *1815 – The Waterloo Campaign: Ligny and Quatre Bras*, Greenhill Books, London, 1998

Hofschröer, Peter, *1815 – The Waterloo Campaign: The German Victory*, Greenhill Books, London, 1999

Liddell Hart, B. H. (ed.), *The Letters of Private Wheeler*, The Windrush Press, Moreton-in-Marsh, 1993

Longford, Elizabeth, *Wellington: The Years of the Sword*, Weidenfeld & Nicolson, London, 1969

McLynn, Frank, *Napoleon: A Biography*, Jonathan Cape, London, 1997

Mercer, General Cavalié, *Journal of the Waterloo Campaign*, Greenhill Books, London, 1985

Roberts, Andrew, *Napoleon and Wellington*, Weidenfeld & Nicolson, London, 2001

Robinson, Mike, *The Battle of Quatre Bras 1815*, The History Press, Stroud, 2009

Siborne, Captain W., *History of the Waterloo Campaign*, Greenhill Books, London, 1990

Siborne, Maj. Gen. H. T., *Waterloo Letters*, Greenhill Books, London, 1993

Smith, Digby, *The Prussian Army to 1815*, Schiffer Military History, Atglen PA, USA, 2004

Summerville, Christopher, *Who was Who at Waterloo*, Pearson, London, 2007

Sweetinburgh, Sheila, *The Role of the Hospital in Medieval England*, Four Courts Press, Dublin, 2004

Thompson, J. M. (tr. and ed.), *Napoleon's Letters*, Prion, London, 1998

Uffindell, Andrew and Corum, Michael, *On the Fields of Glory*, Greenhill Books, London, 1996

INDEX

INDEX

INDEX

INDEX